201 Drills For Coaching Youth Basketball

PLANNING EFFECTIVE PRACTICES

Kevin C. Sivils

KCS Basketball Enterprises, LLC
KATY, TEXAS

Copyright © 2013 by Kevin C. Sivils.

All rights reserved. No part of this publication may be reproduced, distributed or transmitted in any form or by any means, including photocopying, recording, or other electronic or mechanical methods, without the prior written permission of the publisher, except in the case of brief quotations embodied in critical reviews and certain other noncommercial uses permitted by copyright law. For permission requests, write to the publisher, addressed "Attention: Permissions Coordinator," at the address below.

Sivils, Kevin/KCS Basketball Enterprises, LLC
Katy, Texas 77450
www.kcsbasketball.com

Publisher's Note: This is a work of non-fiction.

Book Layout ©2013 BookDesignTemplates.com

Ordering Information:
Quantity sales. Special discounts are available on quantity purchases by corporations, associations, and others. For details, contact the "Special Sales Department" at the address above.

201 Drills for Coaching Youth Basketball/Sivils, Kevin. -- 1st ed.
ISBN-13: 978-1491003244
ISBN-10: 1491003243

Contents

The Spiral of Mastery* 1

Using This Book 3

The Most Important Concept in the Game of Basketball – TEAM 7

You Get What You Emphasize 11

Planning Practice & Selecting Drills* 13

Allotting Time in Practice: Thoughts on Pedagogical Principles of Practice Planning 13

Creating Organized, Efficient, and Productive Practices 16

Improve Your Team by Selecting the Right Drills 24

Defensive Drills 31

Thoughts on Teaching and Practicing Man-to-Man Defense 31

On (the) Ball Defense Drills 33

Closeout Drills 41

Contesting the Shot 48

Drills for Defending Cutters 50

Drills for Defending Screens 53

Drills for Defending the Post 60

Drills for Denial Defense 68

Drills for Early Help Defense 82

Odds and Ends 89

Drills for Defensive Rebounding 99

Drills for TEAM Defense 107

Transition Defense 116

Competitive Rebounding Drills 125

Movement, Passing, Footwork & Essential Fundamentals **137**

Basic Ball Handling Drills for Point Guards and Perimeter Players **163**

Shooting Practice **171**

Develop an Integrated System of Teaching of Skills, Concepts and Tactics 171

Warming Up The Shot: The Shooting Progression 177

Lay-Up Drills..**187**

Free Throws **207**

Developmental Shooting Drills...................................**219**

General Shooting Drills...**245**

Competitive Shooting Drills..**275**

Three-Point Shooting Drills **287**

Shooting Drills for Post Play **305**

Offensive Rebound Shooting...309

Fun Shooting Drills 327
Two-Minute Intensity Drills 335
Fast Break Drills 351
Rebound and Outlet Drills... 408
Pointers for Making the Break Work 426
Primary Break Pointers 427
Pressure Inbounds Game Situations 429
Post Up on the Baseline 430
Set Up for the Lob 434
About the Author 441
To Contact the Author... 443
Drill Index... 445
Other coaching books by Coach Kevin Sivils: 459

The Spiral of Mastery*

In Mastering the Skills you Demonstrate Ability.
Demonstrated Ability breeds Confidence.
Confidence allows you to stay Calm Under Pressure.
Calmness leads to Concentration or the ability to Focus.
Concentration leads to Proper Decision Making.
(Proper Decision Making is defined as accessing the correct skills and strategy learned in practice)
Proper Decision Making leads to
Effective Execution of the Skills.

Effective Execution of the skills leads to Success!

By Jerry Meyer
Collegiate Basketball's All Time Career Assist Leader

*Used with permission

CHAPTER ONE

Using This Book

Basketball by its very nature is a tough sport to master. There are so many skills to learn. Some skills are position specific and others all players need to master. The game itself is constantly evolving and changing in terms of strategy, tactics and rules.

Some things don't change though and that is the need for a systematic, well organized method of teaching skills. Practice planning is both a science and an art. The scheduling of drills for teaching has become a fairly scientific discipline with reasonably clear guidelines for effective use of time.

Selecting the right drills to use is more of an art but is still has reasonable guidelines to follow.

For many coaches, particularly youth coaches, the issue is providing sound instruction for their players involves a fairly steep learning curve. These coaches have to learn the nuances of planning for an entire basketball season as well as quality individual practice sessions.

These issues can be covered reasonably well with a check list that covers the essentials of how to plan for a season and individual practice sessions.

This leaves the challenge of finding drills to use to actually teach skills, strategy and tactics. It can be a daunting task.

I am constantly asked by coaches for my "favorite drill" or a "drill or two" for this or that. I am always hesitant to simply hand over descriptions of my drills to these coaches.

Not because I have some super secret drill that is guaranteed to produce win after win and I want to keep it to myself. Rather the issue is the approach many youth coaches use in selecting drills to use in practice. Here are some of the reasons coaches will select drills:

- Their high school coach used this drill.
- They learned it from a college coach.
- It was their favorite drill to run in middle school.
- Another coach in the league used this drill.
- They saw the drill on a video.

I have been guilty of selecting drills for all of those reasons. Please note I used the word "guilty." When I choose to use those drills for the above listed reasons I failed to meet the most important criterion for selecting a drill for use in practice:

- Will this drill teach and reinforce the system of play I am teaching this particular team?
- Will this drill teach the necessary skills?
- Does this drill reinforce and emphasize the team concept?
- Is this drill appropriate for the abilities and age level of my players?
- Does this drill emphasize the concepts I am teaching?

So, with these questions in mind, allow me to offer some advice on how to use this book. First, it is a collection of drills I have used in my nearly three decades as a varsity coach. The

se drills will work for a range of players though some may need to be adapted for younger youth players.

In fact, my advice is to select drills that will fit your players, your system you are trying to teach and the rules of your league and adapt the drill yourself to make it a perfect fit for your situation.

You will find that many of the best drills you use over time are either drills you created yourself or ones you learned form other coaches and adapted to you team's needs.

The drills in this book are organized by skill or concept. For example, there is a chapter on defensive drills. There is a chapter on shooting drills. Yet you will find that drills for rebounding are included in the defense chapter because these drills emphasize the finishing of the defensive play with a rebound.

Many of the drills in the chapter on movement, footwork, passing and essential fundamentals also involve ball handling. In fact, some of the best drills in this book focus on stringing multiple skills together at one time, just like a player must do in an actual game.

This book is not a "how to" book in the sense it is not a book on shooting methodology or a system of defensive play. It is a book that provides drills that can be easily adapted to teach a specific style of executing a skill or teaching a system of play. By the very nature of both this book and the sport, it is not possible to provide drills for every skill or situation a coach will face.

If you have questions about any of the material in this book, feel free to contact me via e-mail and I will do my best to answer your question. To do this just check the chapter at the end of the book on how to contact me.

Take the time to invest in yourself as a coach. The better prepared you are for conducting great practices, the more skills your players will master, the more success your team will have and the more fun you and your players will have playing this sport well all love.

CHAPTER TWO

The Most Important Concept in the Game of Basketball – TEAM

Early in my coaching career I had the good fortune of attending a coaching clinic where Coach Mike Roller, then the boys varsity coach of Lipscomb High School, was one of the speakers. Little did I know how important what Coach Roller would have to say would be in helping me form my overriding purpose as a coach.

Coach Roller started his talk with a question, "what is the most important thing in the game of basketball?" He patiently let coach after coach respond with suggestions like "rebounding," "defense," "fundamentals" or "offense." Coach Roller gravely responded each time by politely thanking each coach who raised their hand and responded before telling the coach he or she was wrong.

Finally Coach Roller answered his own question by uttering a single word, "TEAM." I am certain there were coaches in the bleachers who disagreed with Coach Roller. But his one word response resonated with me.

As a player I had been a member of teams that were collections of individuals. I had also been a member of TEAMS that were TEAMS! It is no coincidence the seasons I have the best memories of and were the most successful in terms of wins and losses and personal achievement are the seasons I was a member of a TEAM.

We have all seen, or been members of, teams that were a collection of individuals. At some point in the course of the season, this type of team will implode or be rife with strife.

The 2010-2011 Dallas Mavericks were pitted against the so-called "super team" of the Miami Heat in the 2011 NBA Finals. There was no question the Miami Heat had experienced success in terms of wins and losses during the course of the NBA regular season and play-offs.

Yet when it was all over, the Dallas Mavericks were crowned the NBA Champions! In a blog piece, writer E. Chung summed up the less of the 2011 NBA Finals perfectly with this quote, *"One of the biggest lessons learned (and seemingly every year) from the NBA finals is that individuals may win games and awards, but only a true team can win it all. "*

Paraphrasing another portion of Chung's story is equally revealing. In short, Chung credited Maverick Coach Rick Carlisle with forcing the Heat to play 5-on-5 and not 3-on-3, removing from the Heat the advantage of having three of the best individual players in the NBA on the Heat roster. When forced to play 5-on-5 against a TEAM, the Heat struggled and in the end, the TEAM, the Dallas Mavericks prevailed to win the NBA Finals.

Think of a TEAM as a math problem with an unusual answer. If each player is equal to a numerical value, then the team should be mathematically equal to the sum of the numerical value of each player. With a team, a collection of individuals,

This is not only true, but the mathematical answer is often actually lower than the sum of the numerical values of the players.

A real TEAM produces a sum that is greater than the numerical sum of the values of the players! Not only is this true, but TEAMS have more fun, are able to deal with adversity in a more positive manner, accept challenges, are more fun to watch and a significantly more positive experience for each individual who is part of this special group known as a TEAM!

More important than winning games because of the TEAM concept are the lessons truly being part of a TEAM players learn from the experience, as opposed to a being part of a team, a mere collection of individuals.

For the rest of a player's life, long after hanging up the high tops, the player will be part of a TEAM. That TEAM will be the player's family, co-workers, fellow church members and others who live in the community. Life is better when you choose to be part of a TEAM instead of a team.

The most important lesson to be learned from being a member of a TEAM is to look beyond the needs, wants and desires on oneself, to seek to serve others first.

Even in a national culture such as that of the United States that places such a heavy emphasis on individuality, players and coaches can be convinced that putting self aside for the benefit of the group is possible.

Working cooperatively in a group, by choice, for the benefit of all the individuals involved is a critical component for success, particularly in the highly competitive society and culture of the United States. This might seem like a contradictory statement, but the individual who can set aside selfish, or self-centered, goals and ambitions, and utilize his or her skills for

the benefit of the group effort, is almost always positively rewarded.

The concept of selfless thinking so the group can benefit is a key life skill that basketball can teach. It will serve players well later in life when they become spouses with families, business owners or employees at large companies that utilize teams to complete projects.

The ultimate advantage of the TEAM concept is that the unified and combined skills of the individuals are always greater when applied collectively as a team than when the individual players attempt to apply their talents and skills individually.

A simple illustration of this is to take a single twig and measure the effort required to break the twig. Take a dozen twigs of the same size and collect them into a bundle. Measure the effort required to break the bundle, if it is possible to even do so. This simple example is a classic demonstration of why twelve players acting as a team is always better than twelve players acting as individuals.

CHAPTER THREE

You Get What You Emphasize

Players seldom do what their coach teaches. Yet, players always do what their coach emphasizes. Paying lip service to concepts as important as team attitude, mastery and execution of basic fundamentals, work ethic, sound offensive and defensive play will not produce players or teams who demonstrate these traits.

A coach must emphasize the concepts important to the program, the success of the team and the development of the players. Playing a self-centered, selfish player while verbally stressing the team concept teaches players raw ability is more important than demonstrating a team first attitude.

The same is true when if comes to playing defense with passion, intensity and proper execution. Teaching players man-to-man concepts will not produce positive results unless those concepts are emphasized.

Playing time is one of the best ways to emphasize what is important. Sitting down a self-centered, selfish player for lack of team play sends a message to every player on the team. If you want playing time, you must demonstrate a team attitude. Sitting players down for failure to give their best effort on defense also sends a powerful message.

Attaching both positive and negative consequences to concepts taught and practiced in daily practice sessions is another way to emphasize essential concepts of any kind.

Coaches do not need to go overboard setting extreme consequences for the concepts being emphasized. Two push-ups for failure to execute will effectively communicate the desired message. A drink of sports drink instead of water during a hydration break is a simple but effective reward.

Defensive effort must be recognized and rewarded, not just offensive prowess. Make it a point to always praise great individual and team defensive efforts. Give awards for team attitude and defensive performance.

Consistency is essential. Players watch their coach like a child watches their parents. Players, like children, learn almost as much by observing their coach's attitude, actions and choices as they learn from direct instruction from their coach.

Always be aware, players will do what you emphasize, not what you teach!

CHAPTER FOUR

Planning Practice & Selecting Drills*

Allotting Time in Practice: Thoughts on Pedagogical Principles of Practice Planning

How players learn must be taken into consideration when planning a daily practice session and when planning for learning for the entire season. Many coaches jump right into teaching with no consideration of whether or not players have the required prerequisite skills. Coach must also consider the type of skill, strategy, or tactic being taught and if it is simple or complex in nature.

The first thing to be considered is skill progression. As much fun as it is for players and coaches alike to jump right into learning the offense, the season will not be much fun if the offense cannot be executed against quality opponents due to a lack of required fundamentals enabling players to execute the offense correctly and quickly against sound defensive pressure.

What is a skill progression? A great basketball example involves footwork. Players must learn to start, stop, turn (pivot), and change direction (V-cut). These are the skills that should be taught. All other basketball skills, including shooting, start with footwork and the triple threat position. Skills can then be added in a logical sequence, building on what has been learned.

A teaching progression combines skill progression in a logical sequence to build toward teaching an offensive or defensive team concept. For example, a skill progression for basketball offense might include footwork, basic ball handling, passing and receiving, shooting layups, cutting and screening, and introducing the basic offensive framework.

When planning teaching or skill progressions, coaches must select one of two scientific approaches to use for instruction, whole-part-whole or part-part-whole. Whole-part-whole is a teaching method involving introducing the entire concept, then teaching a specific part of the concept and finally the entire concept again.

Whole-part-whole can also be used to practice a concept. For example, the entire fast-break system in basketball can be run in its entirety, players can then work on a position-specific skill for the fast-break system, and then players can run the fast break system again using a different drill to work on the entire system.

Part-part-whole teaches the skills needed to run a given system in a logical sequence, progressing from the most basic skill needed to the most advanced, and then presenting the entire system. In basketball practice part-part-whole starts with basic footwork, moves to passing and catching, then cutting and screening, and then running the basic offense, combining all of the basic skills needed into the offensive system.

Each approach has advantages. Whole-part-whole allows players to see the big picture before working on a skill and then applying it in the big picture. The drawback of the whole-part-whole approach is that many players are not able to grasp the big picture initially early in the teaching phase.

Part-part-whole teaches all the necessary parts and skills in a logical sequence, allowing players to successfully build toward mastering the offensive or defensive system being taught. The disadvantage to part-part-whole is that some players may find the approach boring.

Teaching complex skills requires coaches to use the part-part-whole method. The more complex the skill or concept being taught, the more coaches must reduce the skill or concept to its most basic form and then build by adding one piece at a time until the entire complex skill or concept has been learned or mastered.

Players benefit from using the part-part-whole approach when learning a complex defense, such as a matchup zone. Each of the skills is combined in a logical sequence until the players comprehend the entire defense. When practicing defense, each of the components can be worked on separately before the entire defense is practiced.

Fatigue is a factor in practice and must be planned for. Teaching of new concepts should take place early in practice before fatigue sets in. Rest must be built into the daily practice schedule, allowing players to recover from drills requiring high levels of exertion.

The Four Laws of Learning must be considered as well: explanation, demonstration, imitation, and repetition. A skill or concept is first explained. It is then demonstrated to the players, who are next allowed to imitate the skill or concept and receive constructive corrective feedback. Once the players have imitated the skill or concept, the key to building a quality habit that can be executed under pressure without thinking in a game is repetition.

Creating Organized, Efficient, and Productive Practices

Practice does not make perfect. It makes permanent. Allowing practices to continue while players continue to make the same mistakes simply makes the mistakes permanent. Give corrective feedback and instruction, and insist players act on the feedback.

Also remember that players do what you emphasize, not what you tell them. Fundamentals are critical for success. Paying lip service to fundamentals will lead to a breakdown of key skills at the worst possible time. By practicing fundamentals every practice all season long, you emphasize fundamentals. Whatever concept or skill you want to emphasize, it must be a constant in practice.

Utilize Efficient Practice Groups

Avoid using organizational methods for drills that require a majority of the players to stand and wait. A classic example is the two-line layup drill. Players spend most of their time standing in line talking rather than shooting layups.

A better method would be to pair up players and have one rebound and the other shoot. If six goals are available in the gym, and two pairs are working at each goal, a total of twenty-four players can shoot fifteen to seventeen layups each in three minutes.

This approach accomplishes multiple tasks in a much shorter period of time. Players do not become bored due to standing around, waiting for their turn to execute the skill being practiced. Less overall time is used, allowing other skills or concepts to be practiced. This approach eliminates standing and serves as a game-like source of conditioning.

This does not mean that you must abandon your favorite drills. Drills can be made more efficient by reducing the number of players participating to the absolute minimum, and by having multiple groups.

A drill used to teach motion offense cutting principles might only have four players on the court making basket cuts and filling the perimeter spots to maintain correct spacing. Most coaches would have the other players simply waiting for their turn. This approach might be fine when teaching the concept, but once players have a basic understanding, this is not a productive use of practice time.

A better approach is to utilize all six goals and have groups of four to eight players at each goal. Players execute the cutting, filling, and spacing while also practicing all the key fundamentals involved. The first groups execute the drill at game speed for a period of about thirty to forty-five seconds. A command switches groups, and the drill repeats.

Instead of taking ten or twelve minutes for each player to have an opportunity to perform the drill, the entire team can have multiple repetitions in a matter of three to five minutes. This approach, again, makes better use of time, prevents players from standing idly, and provides game-like conditioning.

Players must also develop their weak hand, meaning right-handed players must work on their left, or weak, hand significantly more than the dominant hand when practicing skills—and vice versa. For example, a left-handed player should shoot three right-handed layups for every one left-handed layup during practice.

Use Small Groupings of Players for Drills

When devising or revising drills, try to create groups of four players or less for drills designed to create repetitions of fundamental skills. Using these small groups, utilize all of the practice space available.

This approach will seem like chaos at first until both the coach and players adapt. The advantage of this approach is the elimination of players standing around. It increases the total number of repetitions and does so in a shorter amount of time. By using this approach, the intensity of practice must increase, and game-like conditioning is a resulting side benefit.

Transition Quickly from One Drill to the Next

One of the biggest time wasters in practice, next to coaches talking too much and players needlessly standing in line waiting, is transitioning from one drill to the next. Once players have been instructed in how to organize and execute both the drill and the skills being practiced, there is no reason to use more than five seconds to transition from one drill to a new drill.

To quickly transition from one drill to the next, simply announce the next drill and begin to count down from five to zero. If the players have not transitioned on their own to the next drill and started executing the drill by the time zero is reached, stop the drill and enforce a standard consequence.

This approach is simple, saves time, and is very game-like. The opponent will not stop to allow your players to organize. Players like this type of practice due to the constant movement, variety, and change. This approach also works as a hidden form of conditioning. Players do not realize they are being conditioned simply by not being allowed to stand in line and rest.

Like anything else, this approach to practice will take instruction on the part of the coach as well as some persistence and patience, but it will pay huge dividends in terms of the quality of practice, creating game-like conditions, and efficient use of time.

Limit the Amount of Time for Each Drill

Players will lose interest if engaged in any one given drill for too long a period of time. As a general rule, players will remain actively engaged if the period of time for each drill is kept as short as possible. A good rule of thumb for individual skills or drills is a three to five minutes. Some drills of this nature, particularly drills with high levels of intensity required, should be limited to thirty seconds to one minute.

For drills that focus on team concepts, a good rule of thumb is to limit a drill to five to eight minutes of practice time.

If a team needs to spend twenty minutes working on team defense, this is not a problem. Simply break the twenty minutes up into three different sessions, and practice other skills or concepts in the intervening time.

The same rule applies to an individual skill, such as shooting. Break up the total allotted time into appropriate segments of time with other drills or skills in the interim time periods.

Always Warm Up before Practicing

Baseball players and softball players would never dream of picking up a ball and throwing it has hard as possible from centerfield to home plate without first warming up their throwing arm. Why, then, do basketball players pick up a basketball and start shooting three-pointers upon entering the gym?

An organized shooting progression that focuses on proper shooting technique and starts the player in close to the goal and slowly works out form the goal to the end of the player's shooting range must be utilized before any and every practice where shooting will be one of the skills practiced.

Make Sure Rest-and-Recovery Time Is Built into Practice

Players do not play the game of basketball all-out for the entire duration of the game. The very nature of the game has stops and breaks in action. Also, regardless of how well the players are conditioned, it is physically not possible for them to maintain maximum effort for an entire game or practice.

It is with this fact in mind that coaches must build in rest breaks in the form of drills that are not physically demanding or actual breaks. This usually takes the form of a water break.

By providing these short breaks, players are able to recover, both mentally and physically, during practice. This allows them to practice and play at a higher level of physical and mental intensity for a greater portion of the time.

Talk Less and Move the Players More

Use as few words as possible when providing directions, instruction, or feedback. Get the players moving and practicing. Players prefer this to listening to a coach talk. It maximizes use of practice time and increases the number of repetitions players perform.

Also, use predetermined verbal cues to provide instruction and feedback. Rather than use long-winded explanations, take the time to create standardized verbal cues that represent entire concepts. Simply stating the concept reminds players of all the information they need to recall.

For example, "think shot, play drive" is a phrase coined by Coach Don Meyer and represents every bit of information a player needs to recall when executing a closeout on the ball. Dick Bennett's "high hands" is another cue about closeout technique and the importance of defending a good shooter properly when closing on the ball.

Try to create phrases with four or less words. If this is not possible, use acronyms. Coach Meyer created the acronym BOPCRO to cover rebounding and out letting the ball. The acronym stands for **B**lock **O**ut, **P**ursue the ball, **C**hin the **R**ebound, and **O**utlet pass. This short acronym contains a large amount of information and can be used as a single-word command for those "in the know."

Practice So Hard Running Sprints Is Not Necessary

Conditioning is a key element of success in the sport of basketball. But does it have to consist only of sprints and other grueling conditioning exercises? There is a place for this type of conditioning, particularly early in the season when the team members need to bond into a solid unit. The shared suffering of each player binds the individuals into a cohesive unit. It is also necessary for the players to reach an acceptable level of conditioning.

Once this level has been reached, it is not a wise use of valuable practice time to only run sprints. Conditioning can be maintained and even improved by having practices with little to no standing time by using drills that keep all the players in a state of constant movement and exertion. Transitioning smoothly from one drill to another will also provide mental and physical conditioning.

The best way to condition, though, is to engage in sport-specific activities that involve large amounts of running at a high rate of speed, such as fast-break drills done under the pressure of meeting a specified time requirement. Practice conditions should be more intense, more demanding, than actual game conditions.

Practice conditions should also be as game-like as possible. If this is the norm for practice, games will seem easier to players, allowing them to play with confidence and poise. Somewhere, at any given time, there is an opponent who is better. In fact, there is an opponent who is the best in the league, the state or the nation. Prepare during each practice to be good enough to defeat that opponent.

This approach is a more effective use of practice time and has the added value of not frustrating the players with the boredom and frustration of having to run sprints at the end of every practice session.

Plan Drills So All Players Are as Safe as Possible

Injuries are a part of sports. Senseless and preventable injuries, however, do not have a place in sports.

As the coach responsible for planning and conducting practice, you should take every possible precaution to insure a physically safe practice area. This involves planning for efficient use of available space with the intent of both teaching and practicing skills but also with an eye toward player safety.

Often overlooked when planning for safety is the location of players who are waiting for a chance to engage in performing a skill or engaging in a scrimmage. Make sure these players are positioned in such a way that they cannot be injured and are aware they must pay attention to avoid a possible collision.

Move Players from One Area to Another

Basketball is a full-court game, yet I've seen coaches stay at one end of the court to practice a particular drill or concept. If the space is available, the concept of "change" should be introduced: simply yell, "Change," without warning, and your players have three to five seconds to change ends of the court and immediately resume the skill or concept being practiced.

This simple concept makes practice more game-like mentally for the players and requires them to think, communicate, and organize on the move just as they must during a game.

Use Handouts: Players Can Read

Coaches can be long-winded. What was meant to be a three-minute talk can turn into a fifteen-minute talk, consuming twelve minutes of valuable practice time. There are times when talks like this are both necessary and productive. Most of the time, though, that is not the case.

Players can read. In fact, most players like to get handouts about their sport or team and not only read the material once, but over and over. Some even save the handouts for years. Take advantage of this typical, and normal, behavior. A great deal of important information can be successfully transmitted by the use of handouts instead of longwinded speeches.

A three-minute talk combined with a handout is a more effective use of time than a rambling fifteen-minute talk. Players want to practice, not listen to their coach talk.

If you decide to use handouts to convey information, be sure to hold players accountable for reading the material. Accountability methods can be as simple as asking a player a question about the content of the handout while passing in the school hallways, before practice or after practice. If there is a need to really drive home the information in the handout, a written test is a great way to communicate importance.

Handouts can be used to provide players with motivational material, scheduling information, or methods and procedures about certain upcoming activities. The information that can be conveyed using this method is extensive.

E-mail, Texts, and Tweets

Just as handouts can be used to share information with players and avoid using practice time, so can the various new communication technologies. E-mail, texting, and the Internet are the means of communication most of today's players use to exchange information with one another. We as coaches can effectively utilize this new method of communicating as well. It bears saying, only send appropriate communications to players and always have a way to verify and track the messages you send using these formats.

Improve Your Team by Selecting the Right Drills

Picking the right drills is essential in order to teach fundamentals, build confidence, and create the right habits for excellent performance in actual games. Drills are how we as coaches build the foundation for the strategy and tactics we will use to compete. Drills are part of how our athletes learn to compete and challenge themselves. If planning practice in detail is part of the process of building a winning team, picking the right drills for practice is another essential part of the process!

As a result, I have some favorite drills that I no longer use. Ever. These drills simply serve no purpose in the system I teach. I wish I could say I was the one who figured this out, but it was actually one of my players. Fortunately, it was early in my career as a head coach when this young man pointed out after practice that we spent a lot of time on two particular drills, getting the execution just right, and never used a single skill in either of the drills in a game.

He was right. That was wasted practice time. I started thinking more about the drills I used and how and if they taught or practiced skills and concepts integral to our system of play.

Are the Drills You Use Part of the Problem with Your Team's Play?

So many teams seem poorly prepared, and yet the players and coaches have worked very hard in practice. The problem is not the system or the effort, but rather the drills used to prepare.

Coaches often ask me for drills that teach this skill or that concept, and I am always a bit hesitant to do so. Not because I want to keep my "secret" drills to myself, but because the way I use the drill or what the drill teaches fits my system of play. It might not work for the coach asking for the favorite drill. Think of it as taking a piece from one puzzle and trying to make it fit in another puzzle. It simply won't work.

Some of the best drills I have I just dreamed up. They fit exactly what I am trying to teach within the system of play for that season with that team. Other successful drills are ones I learned from other coaches and then modified to fit my situation.

When choosing drills, don't just assemble a collection of drills you like, for whatever reason, from other coaches and use them as "your drills" in practice. Only use drills that fit your system. Here are some principles to use in planning which drills to use in practice:

- What are the essential fundamentals required for my system of play to succeed?
- What drills teach these fundamentals?
- How can the drills be structured to simulate the system while teaching the essential fundamentals?
- What are the concepts to the strategy and tactics utilized by my system of play?
- What drills teach these concepts and reinforce them?
- How can these drills be structured to simulate the system while teaching the concepts?
- How can I create a logical progression for teaching and building a foundation with these drills?
- How can drills be combined to teach both fundamentals and strategy?

Once you have invested time in answering the above questions, go back through your list of drills. Some you might be able to use as they are, others can be used after modification, and others will simply have to go by the wayside. Design or find drills that will fill out your needs in terms of teaching and refining your system of play.

Over the twenty-plus years in the coaching game, I have arrived at a checklist of twelve items to use when selecting drills. Here is the list:

1) Create a master list of drills to use prior to the start of each season and stick to the drills on the list. The exception is if

you need to create a *new* drill to teach something unforeseen during the off-season planning process. You can then create this "custom" drill and add it to the list.

2) The first question to ask when creating the master drill list is "does the drill fit the system?" If the drill does not teach a key fundamental or concept essential to the system, it does not make the list. If there are better drills to teach the same things, the drill does not make the list. Be ruthless when creating the master drill list.

3) Is everything covered? In addition to the master drill list, I create a master list of skills, concepts, strategy, tactics, and special situations. The drills have to teach all of this *and* fit all of the above requirements to make the master drill list. *Begin with the end in mind!*

4) How many fundamental skills are taught in the drill? Some drills only teach one simple skill. If possible, and it probably is, drop this drill from the master skill list, and try to select drills that string, or combine, multiple skills. I have a list of favorite drills that I use early in practice sessions for both warm-ups and skill repetitions. These drills are a progression of rapid and intense movement, footwork, cutting, passing, catching, communication, pivots, live ball moves, dribbling, and conditioning. In five minutes the players have gotten a lot of fundamental work in, broken a sweat, built some intensity for the day's practice, and warmed up. This set of drills replaced drills that typically took about twenty to twenty-five minutes to accomplish the same amount of fundamental work.

A word of a caution: when designing drills with this approach, each drill must have a stated, designated primary purpose. A three-point shooting drill might include passing, dribbling, and footwork, but the primary emphasis must be on shooting three-point shots with good shooting technique. A drill may include a defensive component and an offensive component, but players must understand the drill is primarily a defensive drill (or an offensive drill).

5) While I prefer to use drills that string together concepts and multiple skills, some skills are complex and must be learned in isolation from other skills until players have mastered it enough to begin combining it with other skills. In this case, there is a need for what I refer to as an "isolation" drill. The more complex the skill, concept, strategy, or tactic, the more its component parts must be broken down into individual components, mastered one at a time, and then reassembled into the entire whole again. This is the part-part-whole concept taken to an extreme.

Other specific isolation drills may be needed to isolate the complex skill as a whole to practice it as a complete skill. Strategy may need to be applied to a variety of possible counters used by the opponent, but in an isolated situation so the single strategy can be mastered against variable responses.

6) When a drill can be adapted to be competitive, it becomes more challenging. This can make the drill more fun for the athletes, teach them how to compete, or teach them how to use strategy and tactics in order to win. When the drill does all three, it is a keeper!

Any drill that has a standard to work against, even if it is not athlete versus athlete or squad versus squad, will introduce competition and focus. Completing a skill successfully while under the pressure of time, achieving a specific number of successful repetitions, or preventing an opponent from being successful a specific number of times teaches a variety of skills and thinking abilities, and builds confidence when successful.

7) Competitive drills produce teachable moments. Players hate to lose. When they are tired of losing, they are willing to take instruction they had previously resisted in order to change the outcome—losing—they wish to avoid. When done appropriately, attaching consequences, both positive and negative, can hasten the creation of teachable moments.

8) Space and equipment are a consideration. Some drills are not feasible due to space constraints. If you have to share your facility with other teams or sports, drills that require the use of the entire facility will rarely be usable.

As a basketball coach, I think the device known as the Shoot-A-Way is a great tool! But if my program does not have one, it makes no sense to include drills on the master drill list that require the use of one. If I only have six balls, it does not make sense to have drills that require more than six balls.

9) Building intensity is essential but can be hard to develop. Short bouts of extremely hard, focused effort build intensity. As players develop intensity in these short sessions or drills, they can be transferred to regular drills that last longer. Include a series of drills on the master drill list that are one minute or less in duration and focus on a single task requiring great effort.

10) Personnel impacts drill selection. If your team this season will largely be novice players, simpler drills to teach basics are required. A more experienced and skilled team will need to

be challenged and offered opportunities to apply their skills against competition.

11) The amount of time available for the average practice can impact drills. As much as I like to break things into their individual parts and reassemble them, time often will not allow this. Drills that can in time incorporate more skills and concepts in one session of practice time, replacing a larger number of drills, make better use of the time available.

12) Progressive drills should make the list. Some of the drills I use as a basketball coach in every practice are the shooting progression, the footwork progression, and the feed the post progression. By using progressive drills, more fundamentals are practiced, with some specificity of skill, in less time; and the progressions are often designed to practice the skills in a way that combines the offensive and defensive systems I teach.

Make sure the drills you use are the correct ones for the players and the style of play you teach. It might mean sacrificing some of your favorite drills, but it will be worth it!

*The information in this chapter was excerpted from the author's book **Designing Effective Team Practices**.

CHAPTER FIVE

Defensive Drills

Thoughts on Teaching and Practicing Man-to-Man Defense

To really get a team to play intense, fundamentally sound man-to-man defense as a team unit takes a lot of effort on the part of the coaching staff. Many teams play at playing man-to-man defense but few truly play the defense well. Those that do possess a well deserved reputation for being hardnosed defensively.

Defense is hard work and does not have the intrinsic fun built in that shooting a basketball and making a shot does. Yet few things can bring as much pride in a successful group effort as a well played defensive game.

Just as shooting a ball is more fun to learn for players, the creative aspects of coaching offense are more fun for coaches. Coaching defense is hard work, particularly coaching and most of all teaching man-to-man defense.

The key to any endeavor is often not the big picture but rather in the details. Most coaches understand basic man-to-man concepts such as denying the ball one pass away or help side triangle positioning. But how many coaches take the time and effort to learn about the best way to closeout on the ball, the nuances of post defense or contesting a shot?

Learning the details to teach players is only half the battle. Planning and carrying out practices designed to teach and emphasize sound defensive principles and details take effort and forethought as well.

Building a great defense also takes teaching and practice time. Some seasons it may take almost as much as half of the practice time available. Other seasons, particularly with experienced teams, less time is required. Sound practice planning can combine offensive and defensive work periods together to use valuable practice time efficiently.

The concepts presented in the first half of this book will make a difference if added to a sound existing defensive system, man-to-man or zone.

The drills included in the second half of this book were the drills I used to teach my teams man-to-man defense. Some of these drills were used on a daily basis and some were used at different times of the season depending on the concept being taught.

Many of the drills, out of necessity, are designed to focus on one single defensive skill. Others combine several skills and a few of the drills require the players to use all of their defensive skills and knowledge to achieve success.

Do not feel married to these drills. Those included are meant to serve as a starting point. Adapt the drills to your team and your system.

On (the) Ball Defense Drills

Number 1
Mass Defense

This drill is designed to teach basic defensive stances, footwork and build stamina in staying in a defensive stance. The basic structure of the drill is shown in **Diagram 1-A**.

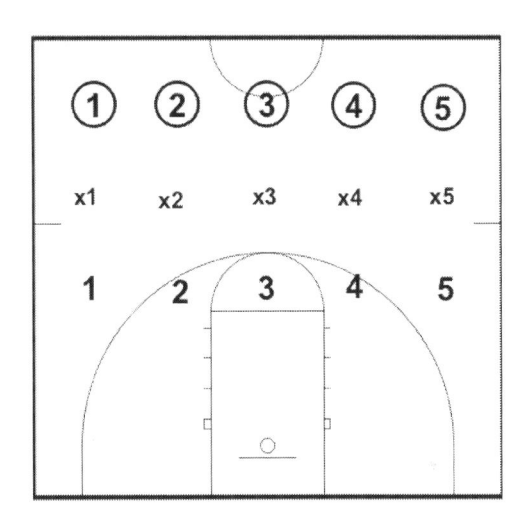

Diagram 1-A

The basic commands for this drill are "ready" and "down" followed by the command to perform the specific skill to be worked on.

To build endurance and teach perfect stances, start with short bouts of simply having the players quickly drop into a basic defensive stance. Begin with work periods as short as 15 seconds and build up to the desired time period. In addition to the basic stance used for on the ball defense, the help stance and denial stance can be taught using this drill.

Mass defense is a great drill to the push step, swing step and sprint two steps and introduce the closeout footwork. It can also be used to introduce the contesting the shot and blocking out the shooter.

Introducing any of these skills is simple. Provide clear and detailed instruction for the players, have the players slowly walk through the movement skill in the correct stance. Once the players have demonstrated an understanding of the basic movement, progress to having the players execute the movement or stance on command.

Early in the season this drill should be used daily to teach technique and build endurance. Insist on perfect execution and master of technique at this stage of teaching. Time invested at this stage of the season will pay large dividends as the season progresses.

Sound defense begins with players who can play in a proper defensive stance and have the stamina to do so an entire game.

Number 2
Zig-Zag Drill

This drill is the drill where players actually learn to play on the ball defense, move their feet, execute a swing step and sprint two steps and master the concept of head on the ball. The drill can be done without an offensive player to introduce the skills and a defensive player added shortly afterwards.

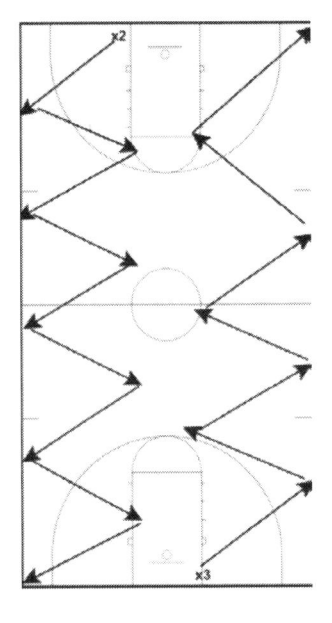

Diagram 2-A 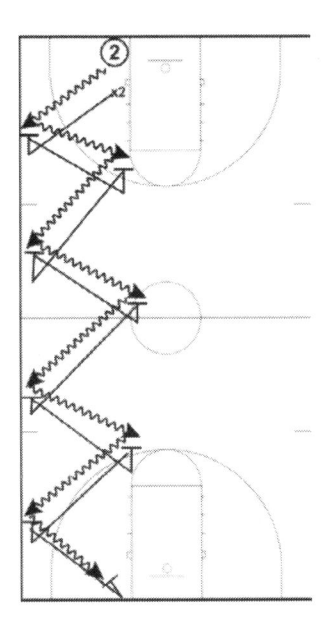   Diagram 2-B

Diagram 2-A depicts the zigzag drill being executed with only a defensive player. Technique and not speed should be the initial goal in teaching with this stage of the drill. As players become more proficient, speed can be increased.

When the players have progressed enough an offensive player can be introduced to the drill. The offensive players must be given strict instructions in how to drive up the court initially.

The ball handler must go from sideline to the lane line extended, allowing the defensive player to maintain a head on the ball position, cut the defender off at the line, execute a swing step and sprint two steps to regain head on the ball position. Note, emphasis should be placed on the defender keeping his or her head below that of the ball handler.

As the defenders improve, the offensive players may be allowed to speed up. When the defenders have progressed to live play, the defender should be required to cut off and turn the offensive player. Eventually the drill can go live and the two players play full court one-on-one.

Number 3
Steer Drill

Once the ball has been pushed to the outside it is highly desirable to keep the ball on one side of the court. This can be accomplished by eliminating ball reversal and steering the ball handler.

To develop the ability to contain and steer a ball handler the Steer Drill is a great drill to teach this skill. The defender points both sets of toes at the sideline and impedes the path of the ball handler as the ball handler attempts to drive to the middle of the court. The defender must cut the offensive player and turn the ball handler

(**Diagram 3-A**). Multiple pairs can work throughout the court at the same time. The drill begins with the defender passing the ball to the offensive player and closing out on the ball.

Diagram 3-A

Number 4
4/4/4 Drill

This drill is for both offense and defense and is great to build intensity for the defense and confidence in handling the ball under pressure for the offense.

The drill starts when the coach starts counting in a loud voice. The coach must count to four three times. The first four seconds the offensive player pivots and makes pass or shot fakes while the defensive player applies maximum pressure while maintaining a perfect defensive stance with head on the ball and head below the that of the offensive player.

The second four seconds the offensive player must dribble with a purpose and attempt to cover as much ground as possible. On the count of four the offensive player must pick up the dribble. The on the ball defender gives the dead call, crowds the pivot leg of the offensive player, practices hand discipline, keeps bend in the knees and maintains an appropriate defensive stance and position.

The final four seconds the offense must pivot and maintain balance and control of the ball while the on the ball defender maintains maximum ball pressure.

This is an excellent drill for the offense to learn to handle extreme pressure as well as to learn to be closely guarded for the maximum legal 12 seconds.

Number 5
Mirror Drill

The mirror drill is used to build intensity, create on the ball defense habits such as hand discipline, tracing the ball and reacting to the sweep move or the ball being brought over the offensive player's head.

Player's pair up with a partner and a ball and partners can be spread all over the court making maximum use of space. One the coach's command the drill starts. The offensive player pass fakes, shot fakes, sweeps the ball or brings it over his or her head. After ten or twelve seconds the coach ends the session and the player's switch offense and defense.

The defensive player stays in a stance and is head on the ball at all times. The defender must trace the ball with both hands while staying in a stance.

If the ball is dropped for a sweep the defender takes a step back to absorb the drive. If the ball is brought above the head of the offensive player the defender steps in and crowds without fouling while at all times maintaining a proper defensive stance.

Number 6
Continuous 1-on-1

Continuous 1-on-1 will be a favorite of players in practice. It is not a drill that can be done for long due to the effort required. Schedule no more than five minutes a day for this drill.

It is a great drill due to its combination of multiple defensive skills, physical and mental conditioning and the competitive component of the drill, making it a player favorite.

Players are organized in groups of three with a ball. Four players can be placed in a group if necessary. Games are for 1.5 minutes or a designated score. Note, 1.5 minutes is about the limit in terms of endurance for the players.

Two players play one-on-one. The third player serves as the official and passer for both players. All regular rules apply to the games with the additional modification, there is a two-dribble limit. If an offensive player cannot get a shot with two dribbles and takes a third, it is a turnover. If two dribbles are used, the offensive player can pass the ball back to the passer and must move to get open for a pass back.

If the defense obtains a rebound or steals the ball, it must be passed to the passer and the defensive player is now on offense.

Other possible modifications may include a limit on the number of passes, scoring modifications, rewarding points for offensive rebounds and drawing a charge.

This drill can be used to have a team one-on-one tournament with either a round robin format or a bracket tournament with one round being played each day during practice. It is also a great off-season drill and off-season one-on-one tournaments are a great motivator for the players. The winner has legitimate bragging rights!

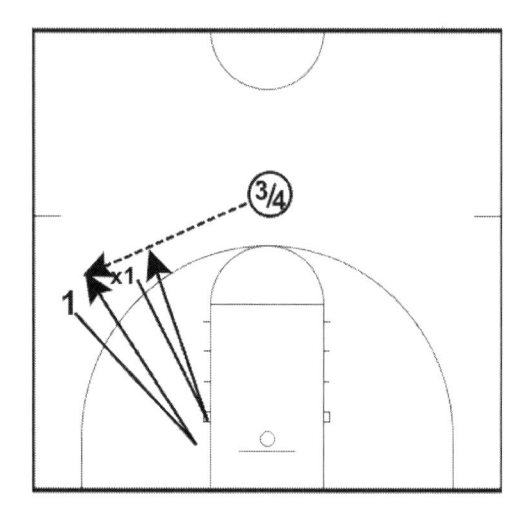

Diagram 6-A

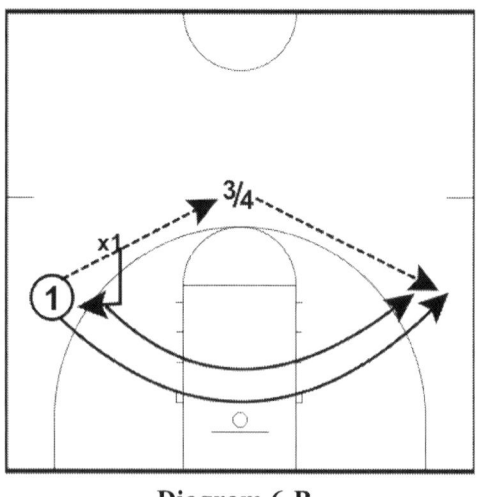

Diagram 6-B

Diagram 6-A depicts the cutter #1 getting open using a v-cut against the defensive player X1. ¾ is the passer for both players for the duration of the game.

Diagram 6-B shows a pass has been made to #1. X1 has executed an L-cut and closed out on the ball. #1 decides there is no clear driving lane and passes back to ¾ and executes a long cut to the other side of the court. X1 denies the initial portion of the cut, opens up while crossing the lane and resumes denying on the other side of the court after leaving the lane area. ¾ is again able to successfully make an entry pass to #1 and play continues.

Closeout Drills

Number 7
3-on-0 Mass Closeouts

Early in the season it is essential to make maximum use of the available practice time and focus on teaching and mastering fundamental skills. Having the largest number of players involved in performing skill repetitions maximizes time.

3-on-0 Mass Closeouts utilizes this principle (**Diagram 7-A**). Three players line up in help side position and stances. On command from the coach the players closeout in unison beyond the three-point line. After closing out the three players execute baseline cut-off moves defensively.

As soon as the first group is done, another group of three defenders immediately moves up into position and the cycle repeats itself. While **Diagram 7-A** only shows three players ready to execute the drill, six players can perform the drill by placing three players on each side of the court by line up in a mirror image of the alignment shown.

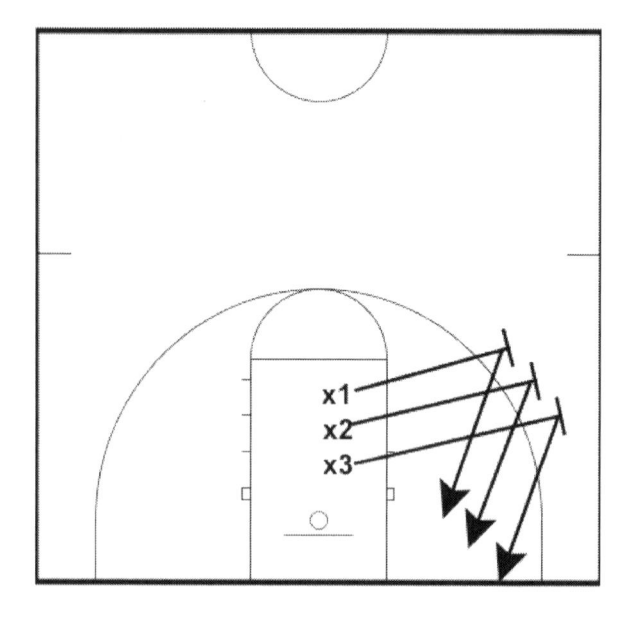

Diagram 7-A

Number 8
Full Court Closeouts

Full court closeouts allow a high volume of closeouts to be executed in a very short period of time. Players line up as shown in **Diagram 8-A**. On the first whistle by the coach, the players begin executing 1-on-0 closeouts down the court. Once the first group has passed the foul line extended the next group can commence executing closeouts.

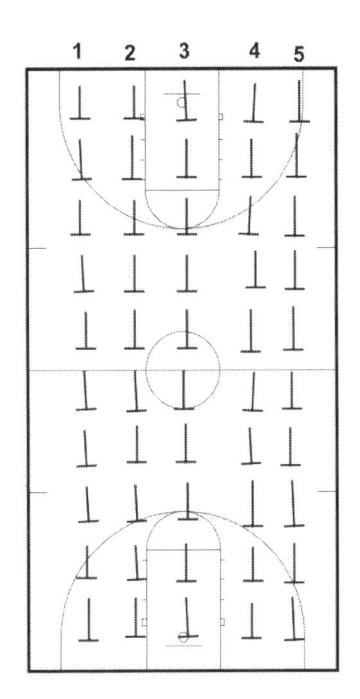

Diagram 8-A

Number 9
1-on-1 Closeouts

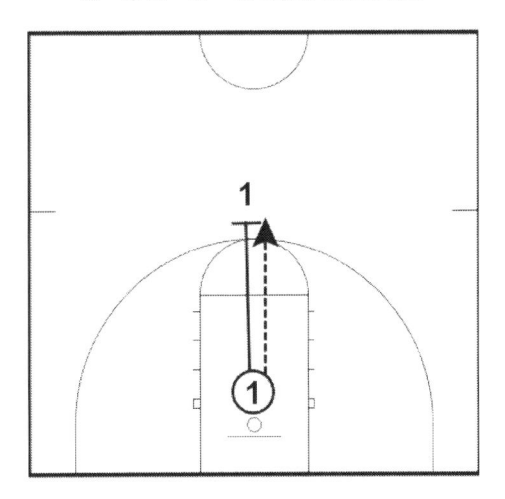

Diagram 9-A

One-on-one closeouts introduces an offensive player to the equation. The defensive player starts out in the middle of the lane in front of the goal with the ball. The defensive player passes the ball to his or her offensive partner and executes a closeout (**Diagram 9-A**).

The offensive player allows the defensive player to execute a closeout, shot fakes or pass fakes and then dribbles twice, forcing the defensive player to explode in the direction of the ball. When the offensive player picks up the dribble the defender gives a "Dead" call and crowds the offensive player's pivot foot (**Diagram 9-B**).

The drill can be varied by moving the location of the offensive player, having the offensive player shoot the ball requiring the defender to BOPCRO and work on the contesting the shot.

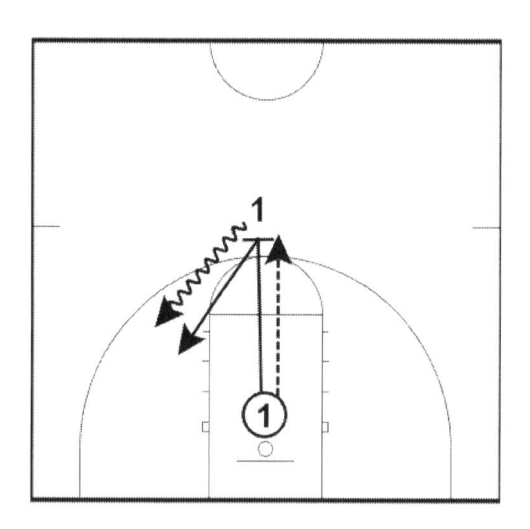

Diagram 9-B

Number 10
2-on-2 Closeouts

Two-on-two closeouts introduces both help side defense or denial defense and moves towards teaching team defense. The drill starts with two defenders under the goal with possession of the ball (**Diagram 10-A**).

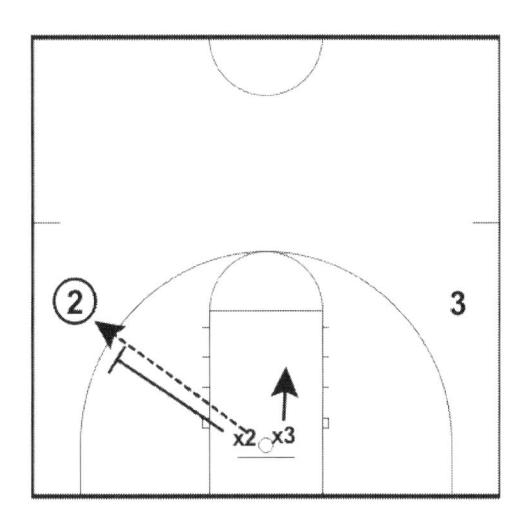

Diagram 10-A

The defensive player with the ball passes to the offensive player he or she is paired with and closes out on the ball. The other defensive player moves to an appropriate help side or denial position (**Diagram 10-A**).

Once the defensive players are in proper position the players may play two-on-two until the offense scores or the defense obtains possession of the ball.

The defense goes on offense and the offense goes to the end of the line. If there are multiple groups working at several goals the offense and defense may simply exchange places as quickly as possible.

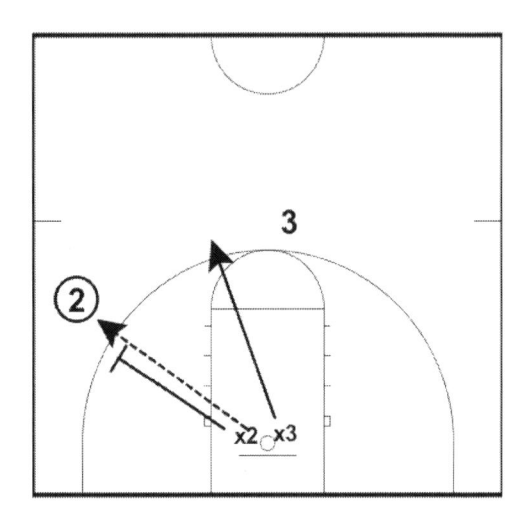

Diagram 10-B

Number 11
3-on-3 Closeouts

Three-on-three closeouts should be a daily drill. It allows for multiple individual defensive fundamental skills to be practiced while combining team defensive concepts of denial, early help and defending screens.

This drill also presents a constant disadvantage situation as the defense is never able to obtain a numerical advantage by pushing the ball to one side of the court.

The drill exposes defensive weaknesses and forces players to learn the need to master both technique and team concepts. It also places a premium on effort and heart.

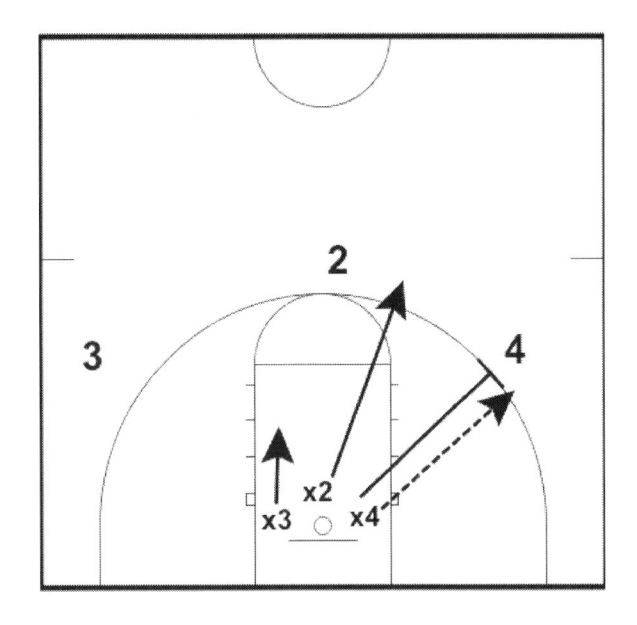

Diagram 11-A

Diagram 11-A shows the initial alignment for the drill. The defense may choose whom they want to pass the ball to start the drill. The defenders closeout to the correct position and then play begins. As players progress in mastering skills and concepts the drill goes live as soon as the ball is passed (**Diagram 11-B**).

Play continues until the defense is able to obtain possession of the ball or the offense scores. The offense then hustles off and the defense assumes the offensive positions on the court. The next defensive group then initiates the drill with a pass out to the offensive player of choice. The drill can be made competitive by keeping the score.

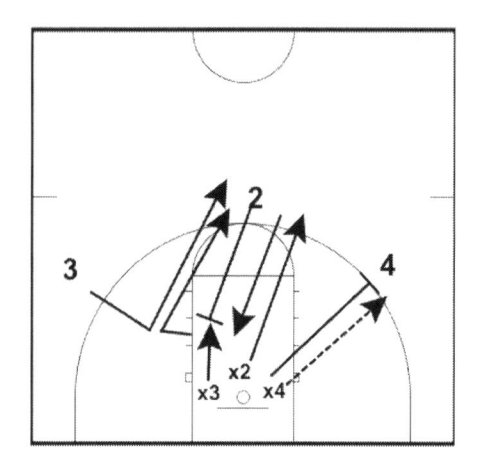

Diagram 11-B

Contesting the Shot

Number 12
Mass Contesting the Shot

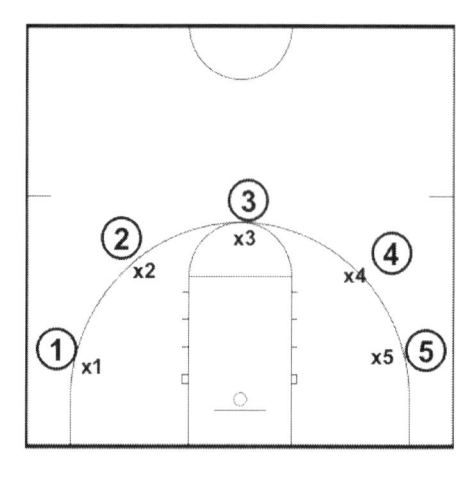

Diagram 12-A

Mass one-on-one contest the shot is an excellent drill to both introduce the skill of contesting a shot and obtaining a large number of repetitions in a short period of time. **Diagram 12-A** shows the initial alignment of the drill.

The drill begins when the coach gives the command for the defense to assume an on the ball defensive stance. The next command is to shoot. The offensive players shadow shoot and the defensive players contest the shot. After several repetitions the players change from offense to defense.

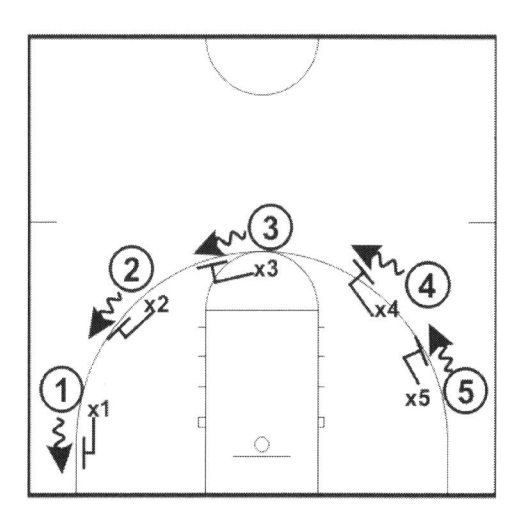

Diagram 12-B

Once the basic skill has been mastered the offensive players can be given basketballs. Adding balls allows the offense to dribble and then shoot the ball just over the defense players who contest the shot, block out, pursue the ball and outlet pass it back to their partner. The same commands are used. No more than two dribbles should be allowed (**Diagram 12-B**).

Drills for Defending Cutters

Number 13
2-on-1 Flash Cutter

Cutting an offensive player to the ball is an excellent offensive tactic and can be difficult to defend. Two-on-one flash cutter drill teaches players to defend a flash cutter from a help side position (**Diagram 13-A**).

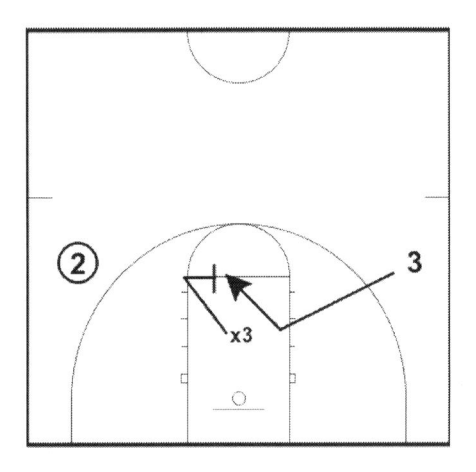

Diagram 13-A

The initial alignment for the drill starts with two wings and a defender in help side position. (**Diagram 13-A**). The cutter, #3, flashes to the ball side forcing X3 to beat the cutter to the spot and chest the cutter to obtain denial position.

An alternative start to the drill is for #2 to skip pass the ball to #3 (**Diagram 13-B**), forcing a closeout by X3. #3 can then skip pass the ball back to #2, forcing X3 to sprint to help side position before #3 flash cuts to the ball side.

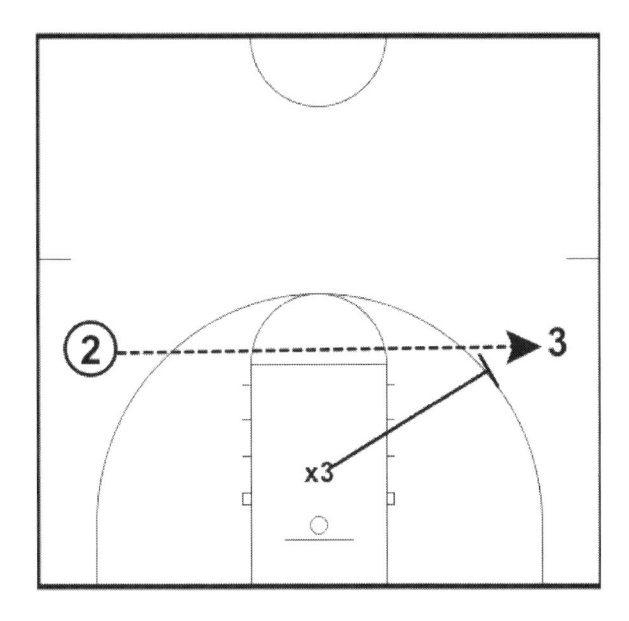

Diagram 13-B

Number 14
2-on-1 Ball Side Cutting

One of the most difficult offensive cuts to defend is the ball side cut (**Diagram 14-A**). The drill begins with #3 passing to the wing #2 who has made a cut to get open. X3 sprints to denial position, fronts and chests the cutter #3, forcing #3 to go behind and then X3 denies #3 the ball.

201 DRILLS FOR COACHING YOUTH BASKETBALL| 52

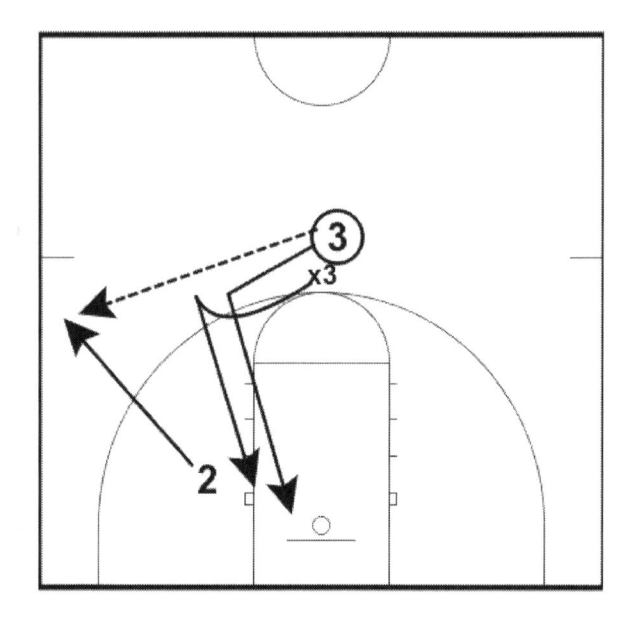

Diagram 14-A

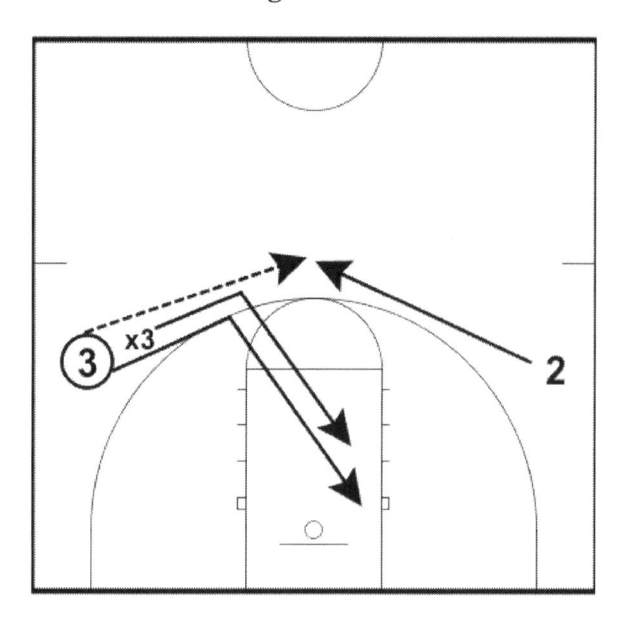

Diagram 14-B

A variation of the drill has #2 cutting from a help side wing to the top of the three-point arc to receive a pass from #3. X3 must again sprint to denial position, front and chest the cutter and deny a return pass as #3 cuts through the lane (**Diagram 14-B**).

Drills for Defending Screens

Number 15
2-on-2 Ball Screens

Two-on-two ball screens is the most basic drill for teaching and perfecting defending on the ball screens. The initial formation can be situated for any of the possible ways a ball screen can be set (**Diagram 15-A**).

Key techniques to focus on are the initial recognition of the ball screen by the defender of the screener, X4, who gives the verbal for a ball screen and indicates the direction it is coming from.

X4 gets wide early and turns to form a square or right angle with the on the ball defender. This must be executed "early" and before the screener can arrive to set the screen. This action will force the ball handler to "go wide" and makes the screening action ineffective. It is also the angle required to trap a ball screen.

The on the ball defender, X2, upon hearing the verbal for a ball screen immediately gets into the ball handler and prepares to step over the screen as soon as it is set, skinnies up and fights through the screen.

X4 must be certain to provide space for X2 to slip by and stay with the ball handler. Immediately after giving early help X4 must recover to position (**Diagram 15-B**). In this instance, a denial position to prevent a quick pass back from #2.

Diagram 15-A

Number 16
3-on-3 Ball Screens

Three-on-three ball screens introduces a third defensive player. The initial alignment for the drill is shown in **Diagram 16-A**.

The screening action and the method of defending the screen is the same as described in two-on-two ball screens. The added defensive action is X5 must sprint to help side and be ready to cover a "slip" cut by the screener or any other tactic used by the offense (**Diagram 16-B**).

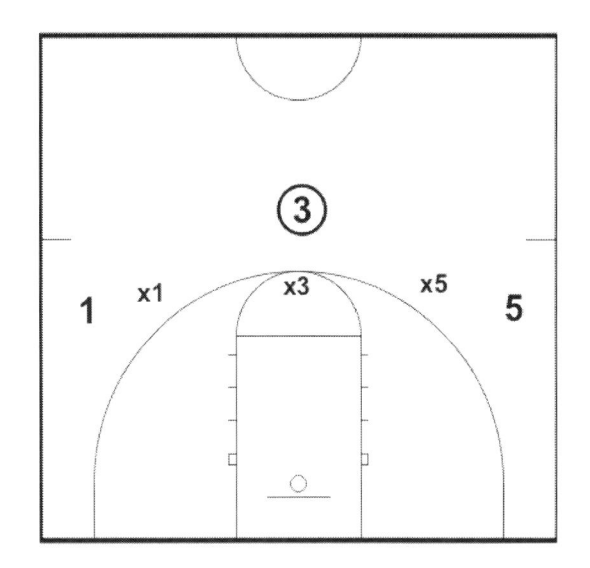

Diagram 16-A

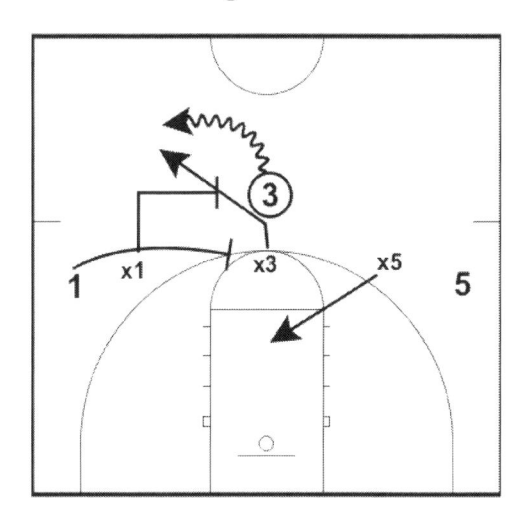

Diagram 16-B

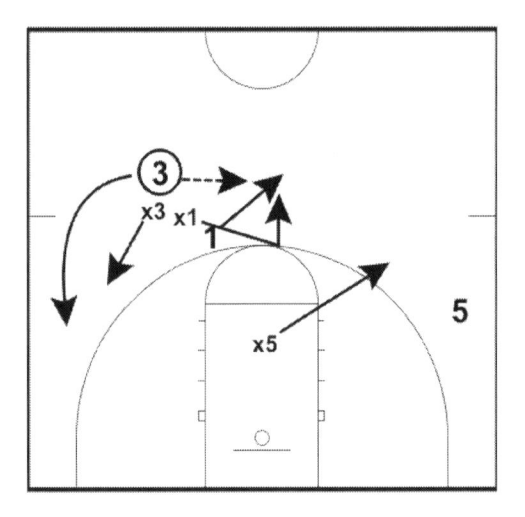

Diagram 16-C

When the ball is passed back to the middle to reset the drill, X1 must execute an L-cut and closeout, X5 must sprint to denial position and X3 must sprint to denial position (**Diagram 16-C**). The drill can then continue with another ball screen.

Number 17
3-on-2 Screening Series

Diagram 17-A shows the initial alignment for this drill as well as the initial screening action, a down screen. #2 passes and executes a proper down screen. X2 denies #2, calls the screen verbal and opens up to protect the rim at the level of the screen.

X4 gets into the cutter #4 and denies #4 as #4 cuts to the ball. After the screen and cuts have been defended the offensive player balance the floor and the defenders adjust position accordingly so the next screen in the sequence can be executed.

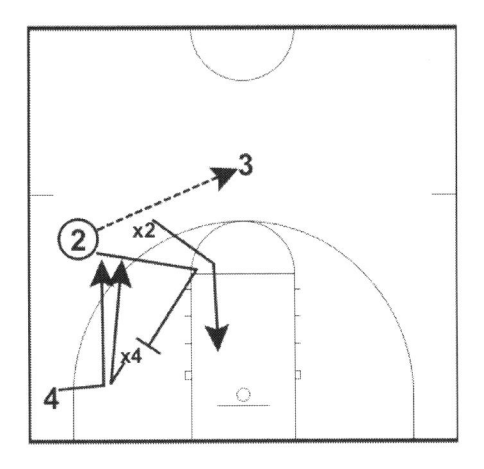

Diagram 17-A

Diagram 17-B shows the action for a flare screen, the next screen in the sequence.

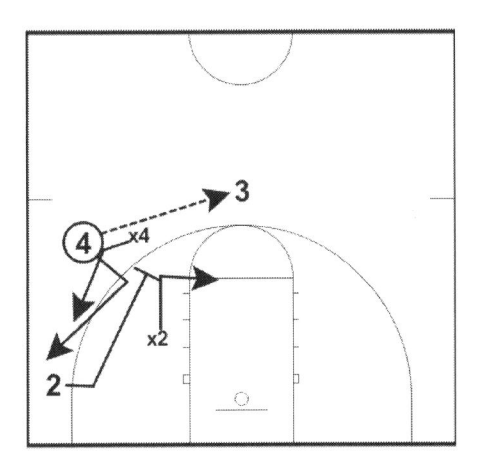

Diagram 17-B

201 DRILLS FOR COACHING YOUTH BASKETBALL | 58

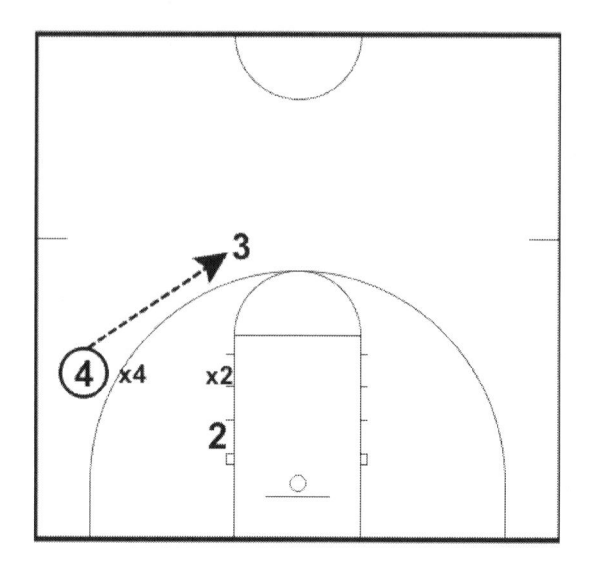

Diagram 17-C

Diagram 17-C shows the initial alignment the offense moves into for the third screen in the sequence. In this sequence the screen being set is a pin screen or down screen.

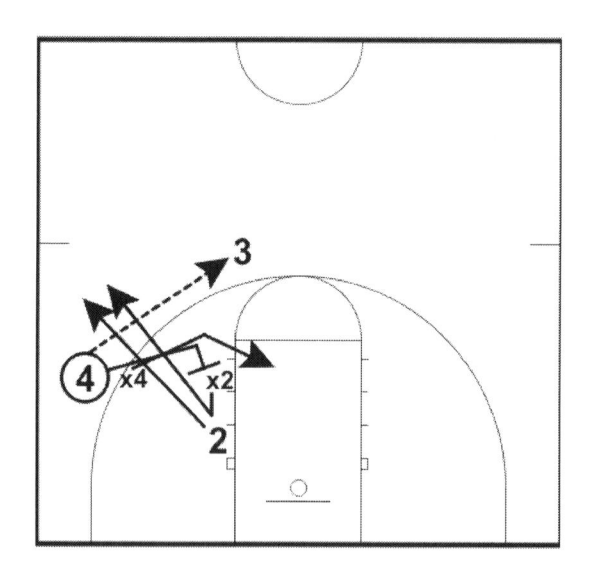

Diagram 17-D

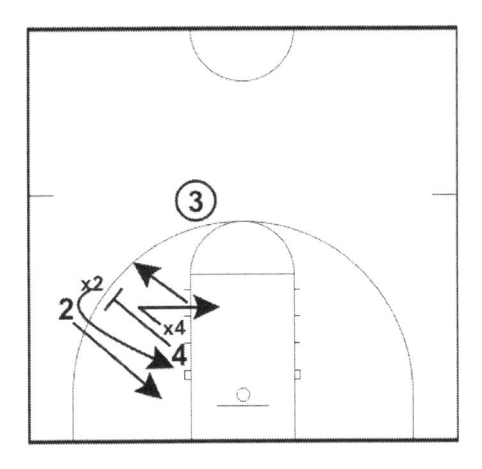

Diagram 17-E

Diagram 17-E shows the final screen in the sequence, a back screen from the low post. In all of the screens the same techniques and rules apply. The exact starting positions can and should be varied on a day-to-day basis.

Number 18
5-on-4 Screening Series

The five-on-four screening series starts out in the alignment as shown in **Diagram 18-A**. The defenders must utilize all the appropriate techniques, tactics and positioning for both defending screens and team positioning.

The sequence of screens follows the same order as in the three-on-two screening series. Either three-on-two or five-on-four screening series should be done daily in practice.

201 DRILLS FOR COACHING YOUTH BASKETBALL| 60

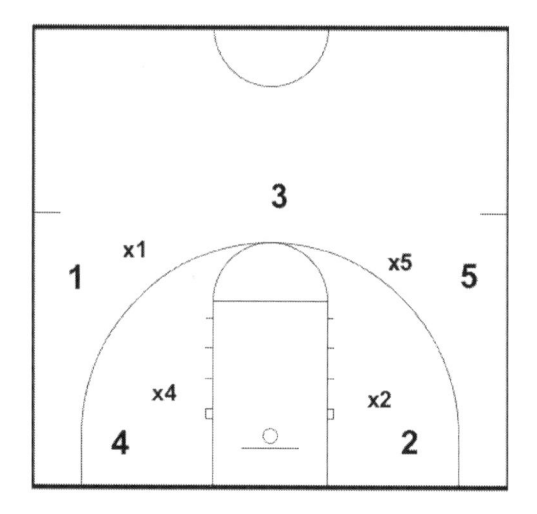

Diagram 18-A

Drills for Defending the Post

Number 19
Post Denial

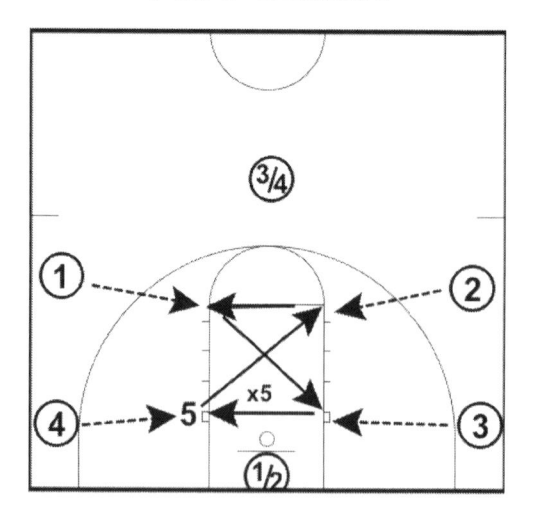

Diagram 19-A

Post denial is an excellent drill for teams that play either man-to-man defense or zone defense.

The drill starts with one offensive post player, #5, and one post defender, X5, four passers each with a basketball and two players to chase down deflected passes that go astray (**Diagram 19-A**).

The offensive post #5 starts as shown from the left hand low post and flashes to the right hand side high post. #2 pass the ball to #5 and the defender, X5 (not shown in the drill other than initial position for clarity) must deny and deflect the pass away without fouling. If the offensive player catches the pass the ball is passed back to the offensive player who made the pass.

#5 then flashes across the high post to receive a pass from #1. Note, X5 MUST stay beneath #5 at all times. Should X5 go above #5 and #5 catches the ball, it will be impossible for X5 to obtain ball-you-basket position on the ball. X5 denies and deflects the pass from #1.

#5 then flashes from the high post to the low post to receive a pass from #3. X5 beats #5 to the spot and again denies and deflects the pass. The final cut is directly across the lane towards #4 and X5 again denies and deflects the pass to #5.

Players rotate and the drill continues. Insist on perfect positioning. As players improve on defending post flash cutters the offensive post player can be allowed to catch the ball and score if the defender does not deny and deflect the pass.

Number 20
Low Post Denial (Dead Front)

Low post denial drill, also called Dead Front drill, is essential to teach low post defense and should be done for several minutes each day in practice. Every player on the team must master this skill, as teams will post up any defender who might be unable to defend the offensive low post.

The basic alignment is shown in **Diagram 20-A**. The ball starts above the free throw line extended and is passed to the offensive player in the corner. The low post defender steps across with the foot closest to the baseline and quickly steps in front of the offensive low post player with both hands raised above the defender's head.

The ball is passed back above the free throw line extended. The low post defender executes a rear pivot and jumps towards the ball and into a denial position (**Diagram 20-B**).

If the defensive scheme calls for the low post to be dead fronted, it is important the low post defender never allow the offensive post player to make physical contact, allowing the offensive post player to seal the low post defender.

If a more traditional denial form of low post defense is to be utilized, the drill should be modified to have the post defender deny the ball on the high side or low side depending on the ball location and the defensive scheme.

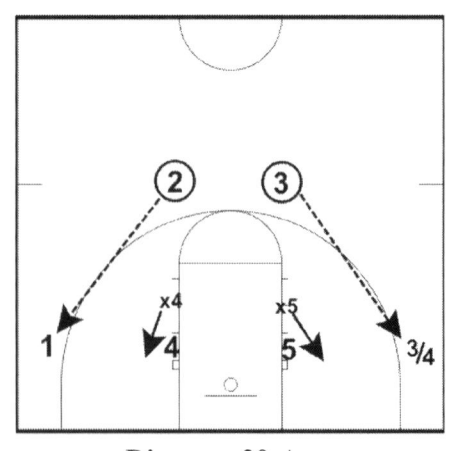

Diagram 20-A

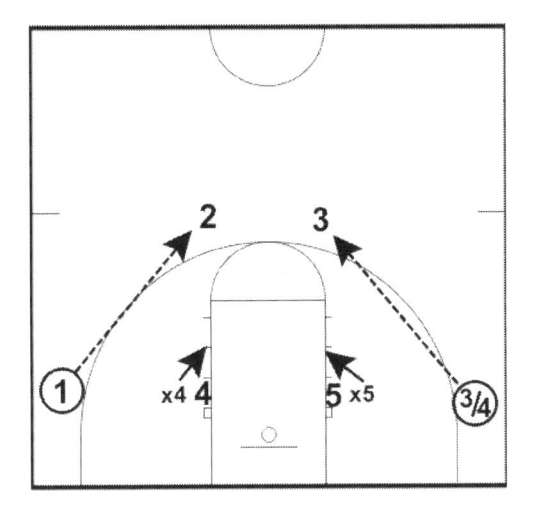

Diagram 20-B

Number 21
3-on-3 Low Post Cover Down

Cover down defense should also have several minutes allocated to this tactic on a daily basis. Depending on the concept that needs the most work or the upcoming opponent, either low post cover down or high post cover down should be practiced.

Diagram 21-A shows three-on-three low post cover down. In this example the offensive player #2 has the ball to start the drill. X5 plays behind deliberately to allow the ball to enter the low post.

The instant the ball leaves #2's hands X5 and every defender who sees the pass verbalizes "cover down." X2 executes a rear pivot on the foot away from the baseline and sprints to the high side of the low post defender and forms a trap with X5. It is the responsibility of X2 and X5 to not allow the offensive low post to make a post move to the middle of the lane.

X3 executes a rear pivot on the foot closest to the baseline and sprints to form a trap with X5 on the low post offensive player. It is the responsibility of X3 and X5 to prevent a post move by the offensive low post to the baseline side.

X5 must be in a ball-you-basket position the instant the offensive low post player catches the basketball.

All three defensive players are in an on the ball stance, with no space between to allow the offensive player any space to operate and the defender's hands are raised above their heads. Hand discipline must maintained as well as bend retained in the knees.

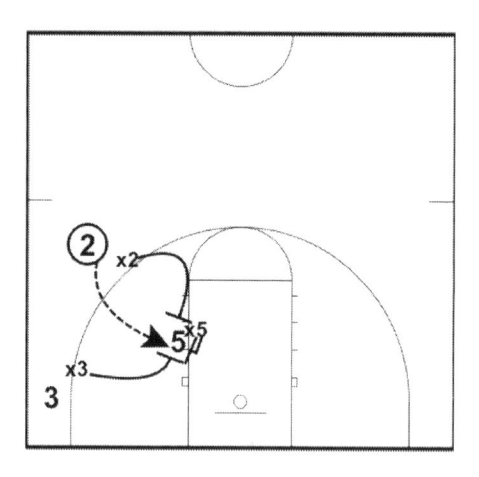

Diagram 21-A

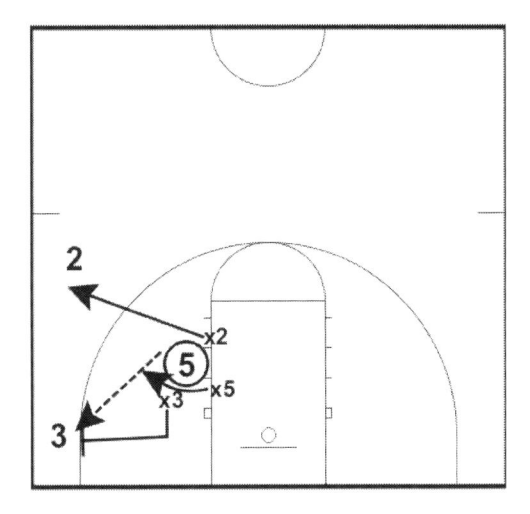

Diagram 21-B

The offensive low post passes the ball out to one of the perimeter offensive players (**Diagram 21-B**). In this example the pass is to #3 requiring X3 to execute an L-cut to have proper ball-you-man position after closing out on the ball. X3 must arrive at the same time the ball does. X2 sprints to proper denial position and arrives in denial stance when the ball does. X5 assumes proper low post defensive position, arriving when the ball does and then moves back behind the offensive low post to allow another entry pass.

This drill must be done with great intensity to create proper habits. Offensive post players operate quickly and in a rhythm. The defenders who are providing help by covering down must arrive before the post player can "feel" the rhythm and execute a post move for a score.

Number 22
High Post Cover Down

Three-on-three high post cover down follows the same sequence but starts as depicted in **Diagram 22-A**. The only other significant difference is the two defenders who will be covering down will execute rear turns, or pivots, on their foot closest to the sideline.

As players improve in both of these drills the offense can be given freedom to attempt to score on either the cover down phase or the pass out and recovery phase (**Diagram 22-B**).

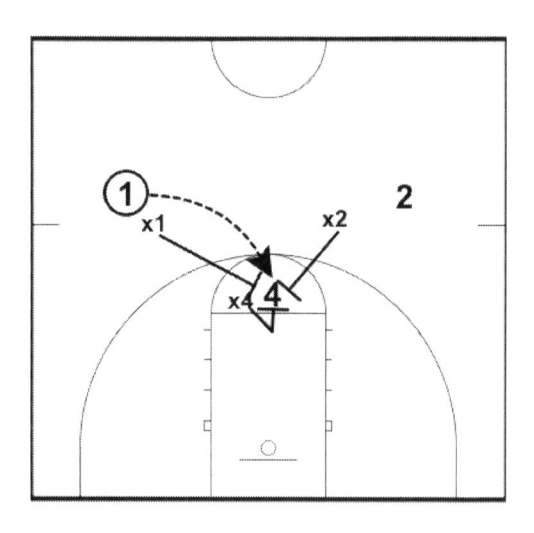

Diagram 22-A

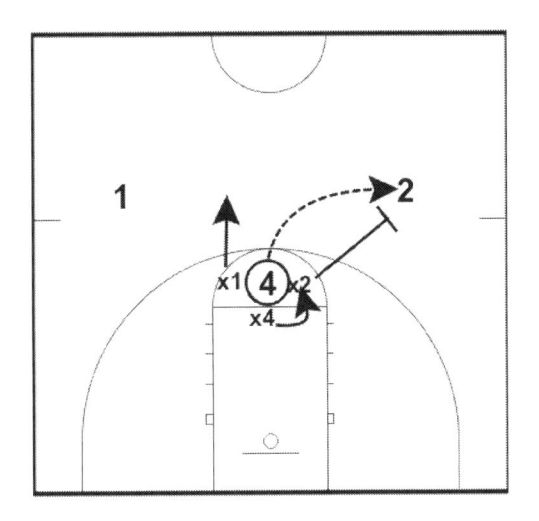

Diagram 22-B

Number 23
3-on-4 Low Post Defense With Help Side

If the decision is made to front the low post and use the low post defender as part of the help rotation, it is essential to practice having the next help side defender rotate and front the post on early help when the low post defender provides early help.

Diagram 23-A depicts the alignment and baseline early help action with the low post defender X4 providing early help to stop the ball and help side defender X5 momentarily fronting the low post. The instant the ball is stopped X4 and X5 recover to their normal defensive positions.

X2 works to eliminate ball reversal with a pass out if #3 kills the dribble.

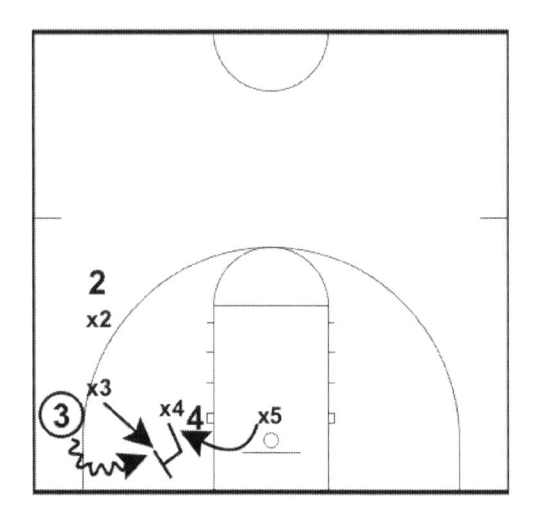

Diagram 23-A

Drills for Denial Defense

Number 24
3-on-0 Mass Denial

Three-on-zero mass denial allows for a high number of repetitions early in the season when techniques and fundamentals are being introduced.

Diagram 24-A shows the initial alignment. The coach gives the command down and the three defenders assume a correct denial stance with the toe of their outside foot pointing in the direction the players will be moving.

The coach gives the command to deny and the players take three hard and quick denial steps advancing outside the three-point line. Once the command to deny has been given the players continue the drill on their own.

The players will deny out and back three times. After the third time to deny the players will open up in the lane and "cover" their imaginary offensive player across the lane (**Diagram**

24-B) and repeat the denial process three times on the other side of the court.

As soon as the first group of defenders has opened up and crossed the lane the next group of three defenders hustle out and the coach starts the next group.

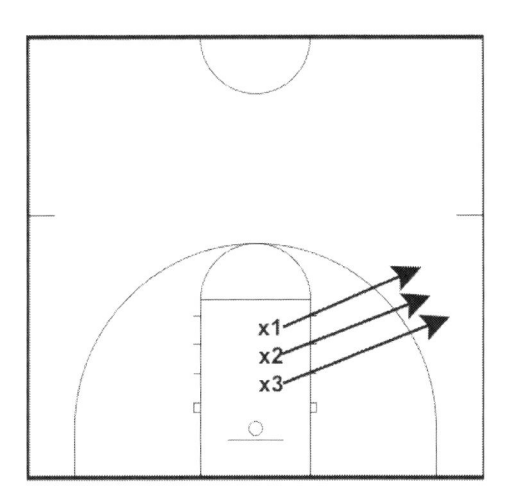

Diagram 24-A

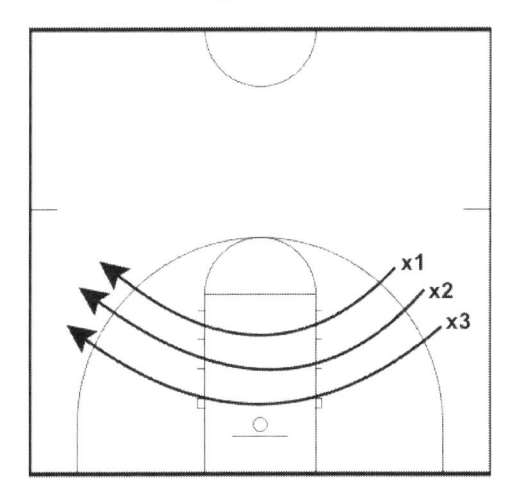

Diagram 24-B

Number 25
1-on-1 Denial

One-on-one denial places the individual defender in a game like situation. There is no possibility for help from other defenders.

The drill starts as shown in **Diagram 25-A**. X2 denies the ball to #2 who may cut from one side of the court to the other. The individual player should defend from 15 to 30 seconds maximum before the players rotate positions.

Groups of three can be working at a basket through out the gym, allowing for a large number of repetitions in a short period of time.

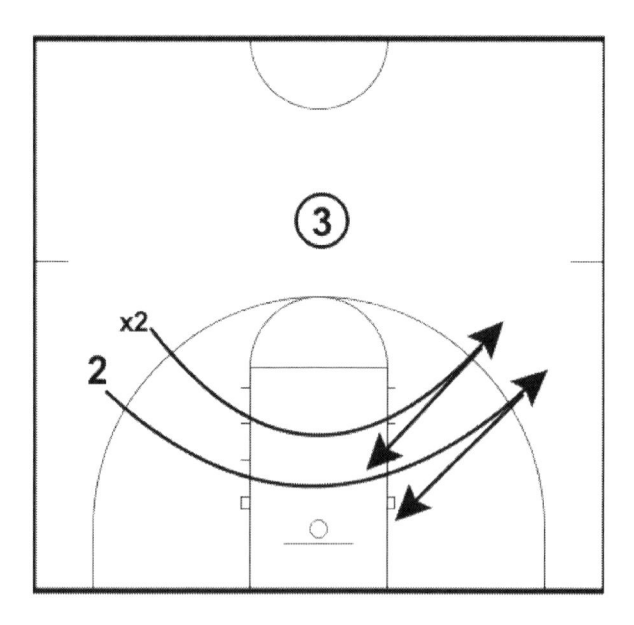

Diagram 25-A

Number 26
L-Cut Denial

Executing an L-cut is not a natural, instinctive tactic for defensive players. It is a habit requiring considerable repetition to build and emphasis from the coaching staff.

The starts using the same alignment as one-on-one denial. The offensive player executes a hard v-cut to get open with X1 denying. X1 allows #1 to catch the pass (**Diagram 26-A**).

X1 then executes an L-cut and closes out on the ball. The two players may either play one-on-one or the ball is passed back to the passer and the sequence repeats (**Diagram 26-B**).

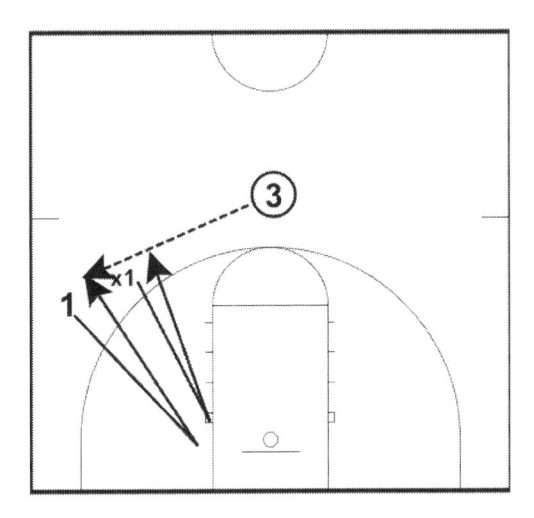

Diagram 26-A

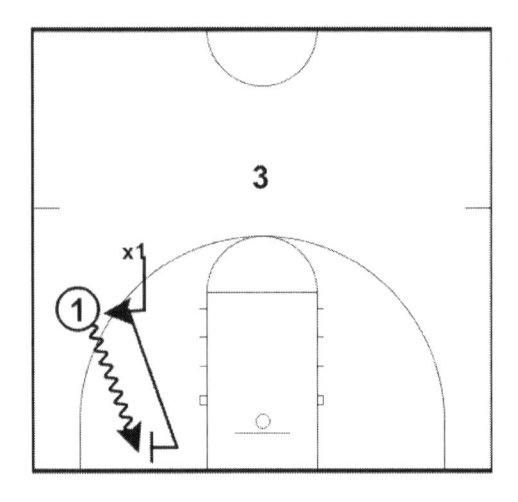

Diagram 26-B

Number 27
3-on-2 Denial

Three-on-two denial builds on one-on-one and L-cut denial by adding help side defense to the drill (**Diagram 27-A**)

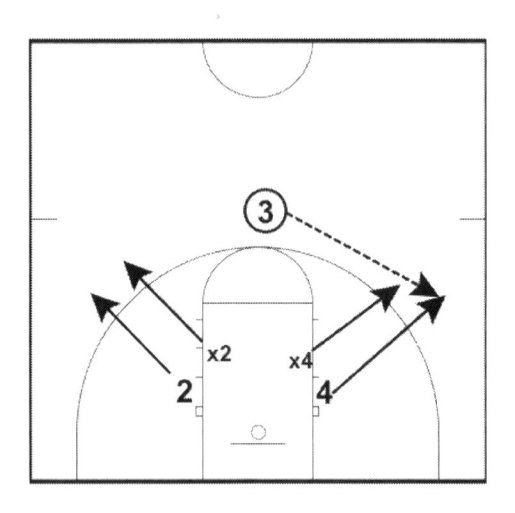

Diagram 27-A

The two offensive wings move to get open. The defense denies as hard as possible. The cutters may go back door and change sides (**Diagram 27-A**). Do not allow screens early in the learning phase of the season.

The passer passes to an open cutter and the defender of the cutter executes an L-cut (**Diagram 27-B**). The other defender sprints to help side position.

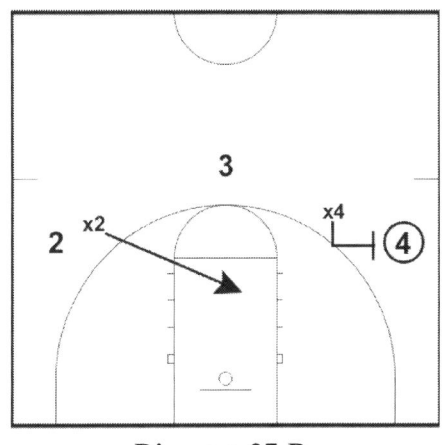

Diagram 27-B

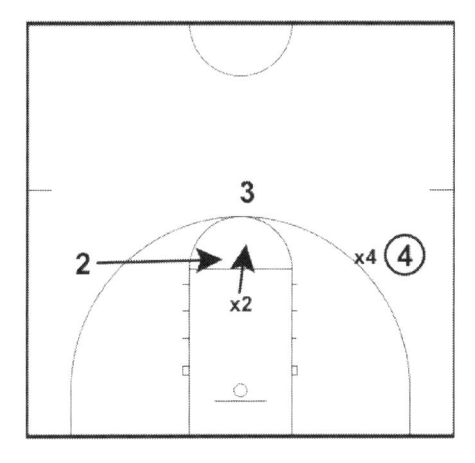

Diagram 27-C

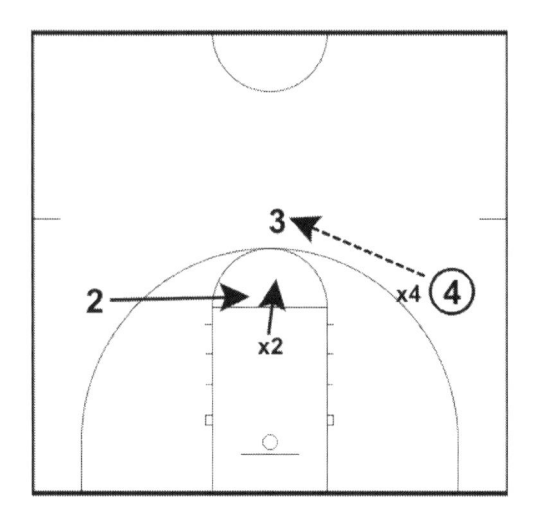

Diagram 27-D

Other skills and tactics can be introduced to the drill. In **Diagram 27-C** X2 must defend against a flash cut into the high post. In **Diagram 27-D** the ball is passed back to the passer and the defenders must sprint back to appropriate denial position and stances.

Number 28
3-on-2 Eliminate Ball Reversal

Eliminating ball reversal is an important element of any defensive system, particularly man-to-man defense. It allows the defense to maintain a numerical advantage with help side positioning and makes creating open space for the offense to flash a cutter into in the lane area difficult.

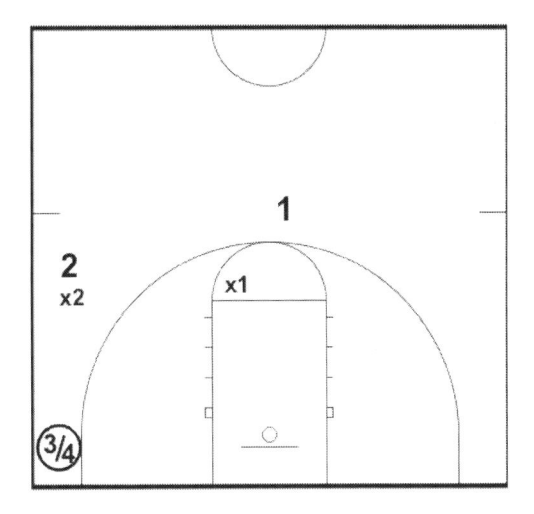

Diagram 28-A

Diagram 28-A shows the initial alignment. X2 works extremely hard to prevent the pass out of the corner (**Diagram 28-B**). If the pass is successfully made X1 moves from a help position into denial and exerts extreme effort to deny the wing to point pass (**Diagram 28-C**).

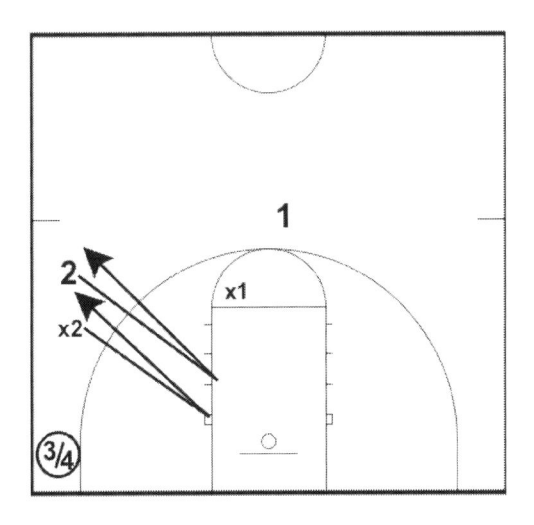

Diagram 28-B

201 DRILLS FOR COACHING YOUTH BASKETBALL| 76

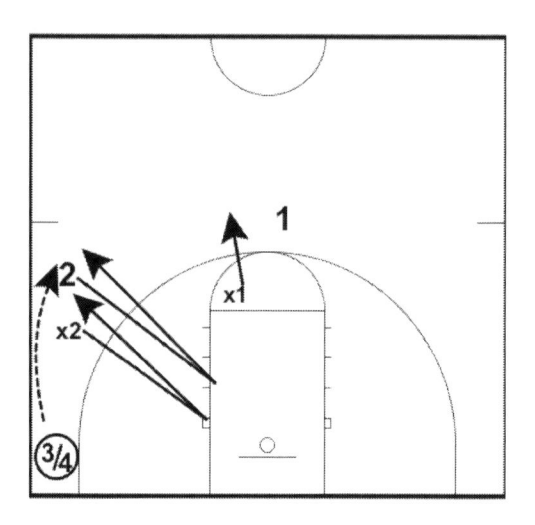

Diagram 28-C

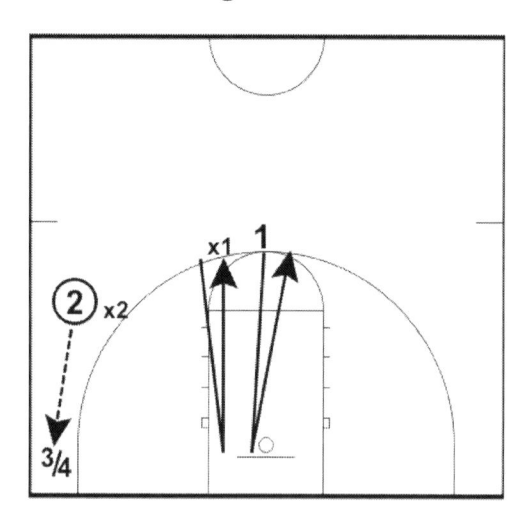

Diagram 28-D

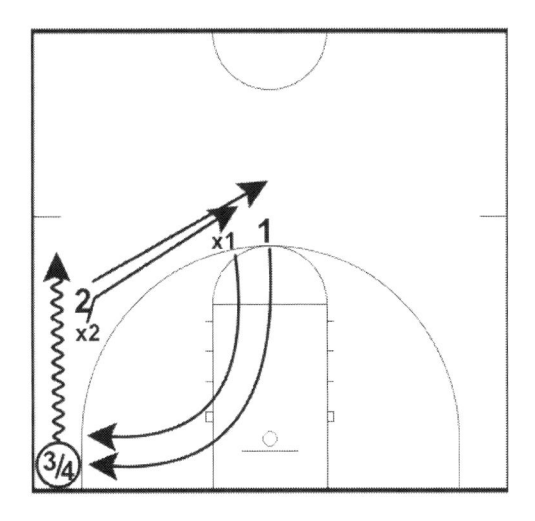

Diagram 28-E

Diagrams 28-D and **28-E** show variations of cuts to create game like conditions for the defense. In Diagram 28-D #1 has cut hard to the basket on a pass from #2 to ¾ forcing X1 to deny a basket cut.

In **Diagram 28-E** the undefended ball handler dribbles out of the corner forcing cutting action on the part of the offense requiring the defenders to adjust and deny accordingly.

Number 29
Double Denial

Double denial combines denial positioning and technique with defending flash cutters and help side defense. The alignment to start the drill is shown in **Diagram 29-A**.

For the purpose of allowing the defense to work on denial in a manageable when learning the offensive cutters are required to cut directly to the wing and back (**Diagram 29-B**). Once the defenders have improved the offense can be given a little more latitude in how cuts are made to get open on the wings.

Diagrams 29-B through **29-F** show the various cuts for the defense to defend. After cutting the offensive players should move to the original alignment for teaching purposes.

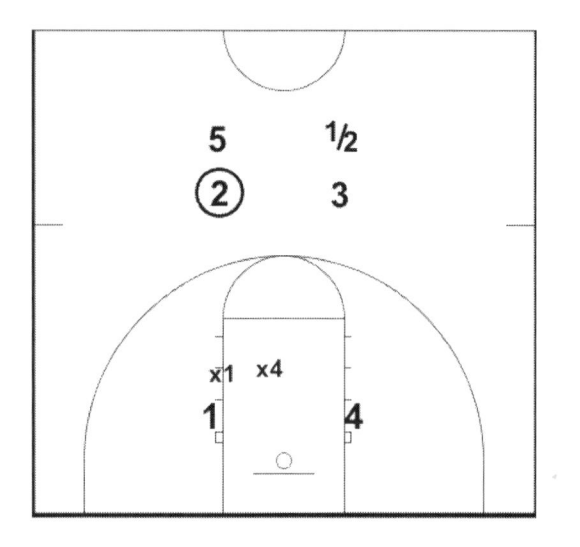

Diagram 29-A

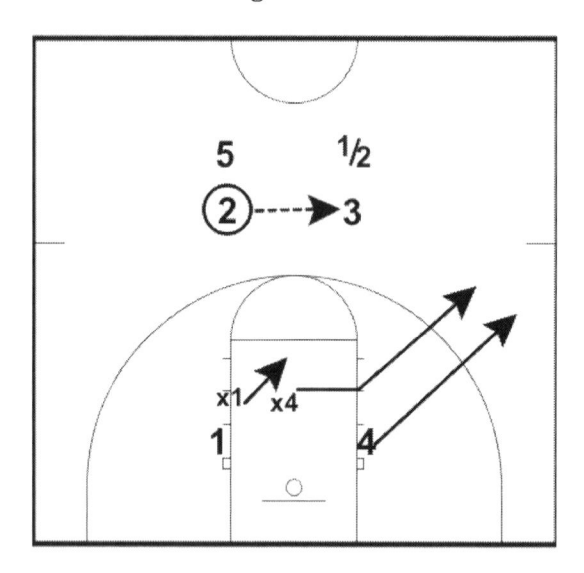

Diagram 29-B

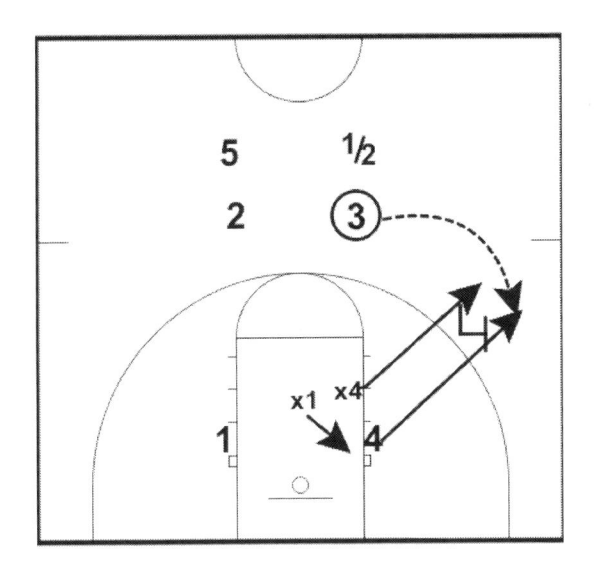

Diagram 29-C

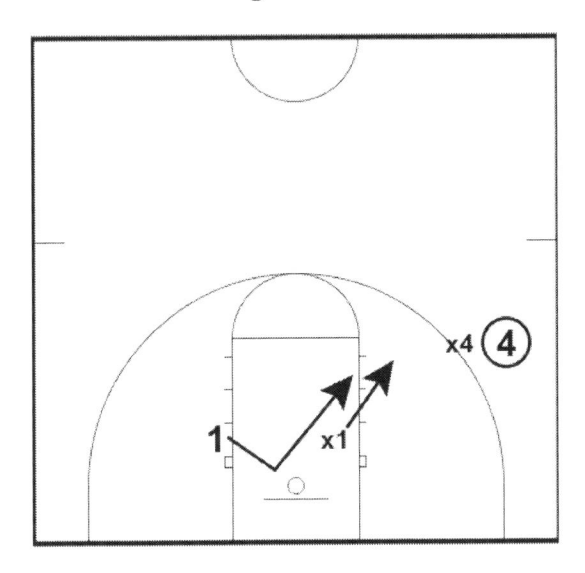

Diagram 29-D

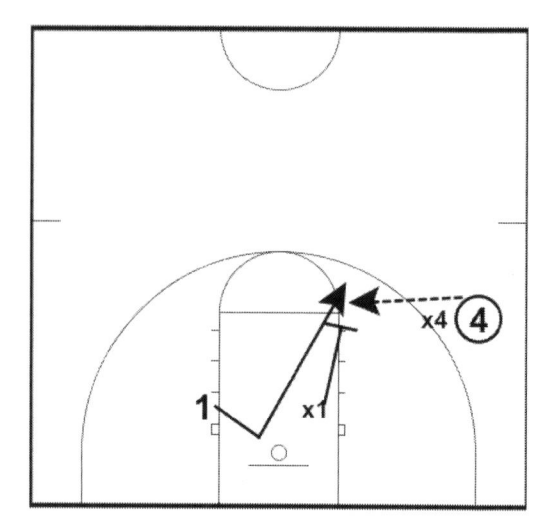

Diagram 29-E

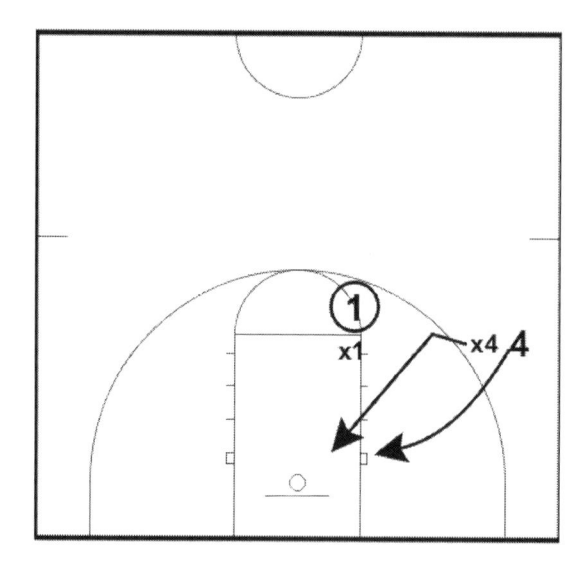

Diagram 29-F

Number 30
5-on-1 Denial

Five-on-one denial is meant to be an extreme disadvantage drill for the lone denial defender. **Diagram 30-A** shows one possible alignment to start the drill. The players who are not participating should offer considerable verbal encouragement to the lone defender working to deny the cutter.

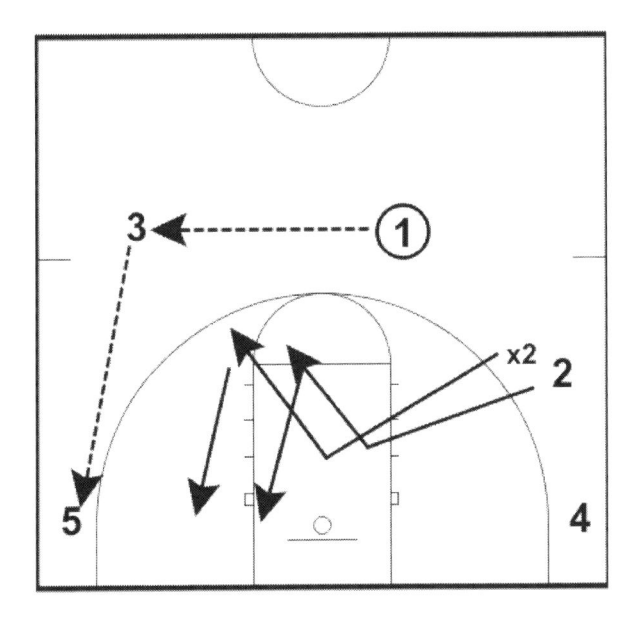

Diagram 30-A

Drills for Early Help Defense

Number 31
2-on-2 Early Help

Early help, and with it early recovery, is the key to making any man-to-man defensive system (or zone defense for that matter) work after the all important ball pressure.

Diagrams 31-A through **31-D** show basic two-on-two early help situations for perimeter defense and early help from the low post defense.

Diagram 31-C depicts defending a basket cut as the drill transitions from guard to wing early help to wing to low post early help.

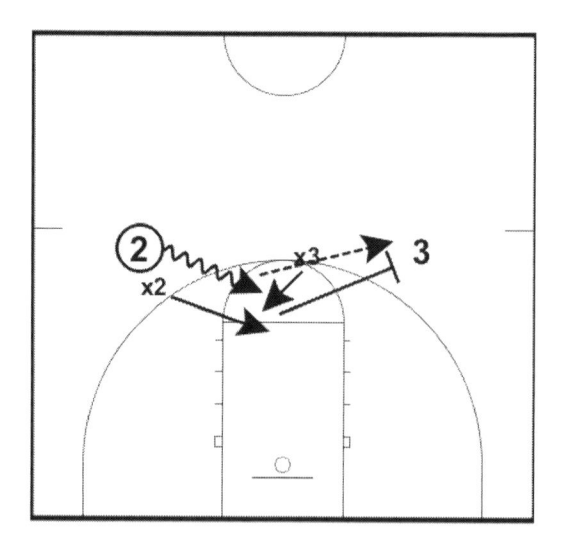

Diagram 31-A

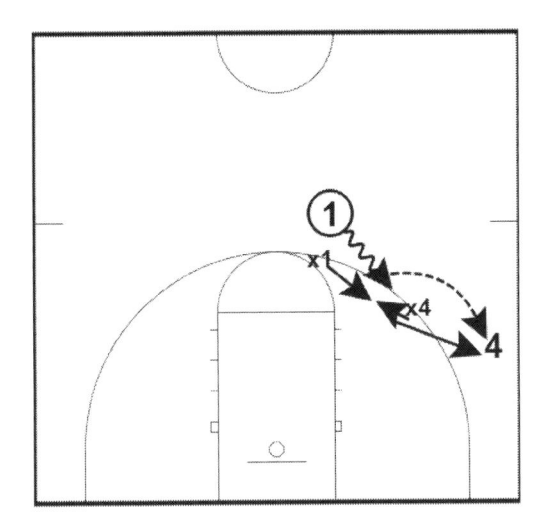

Diagram 31-B

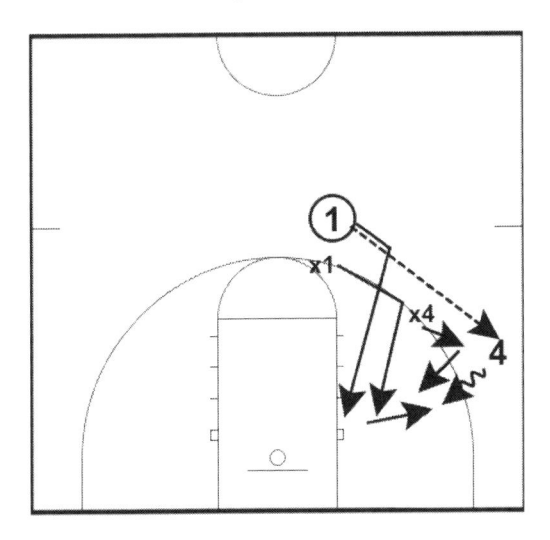

Diagram 31-C

Diagram 31-D

Number 32
3-on-3 Early Help

Diagram 32-A depicts the initial alignment for three-on-three early help. This drill combines early help with denial defense, help side positioning, defending ball side and help side cutters and closing out.

Diagrams 32-B and **32-C** depict an early help situation combined with pass and recovery. Also depicted is help side positioning, denial of a basket cut and denial of a flash cutter and eliminating ball reversal to the top of the three-point line. For the purposes of the drill the offense may make a variety of cuts, and later screens, but must always return to the initial alignment.

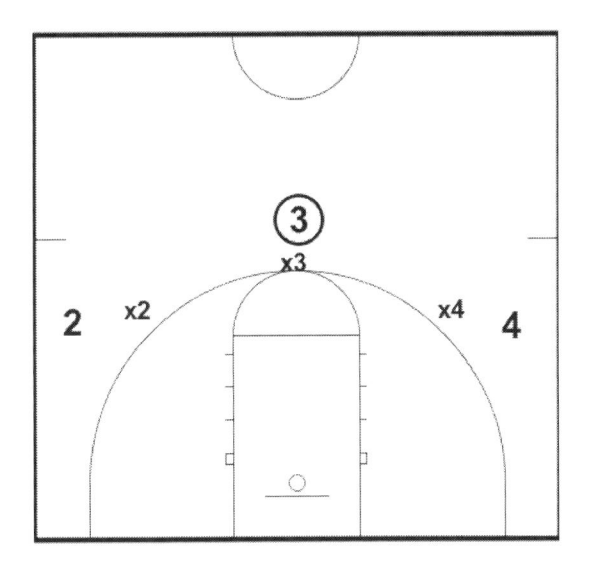

Diagram 32-A

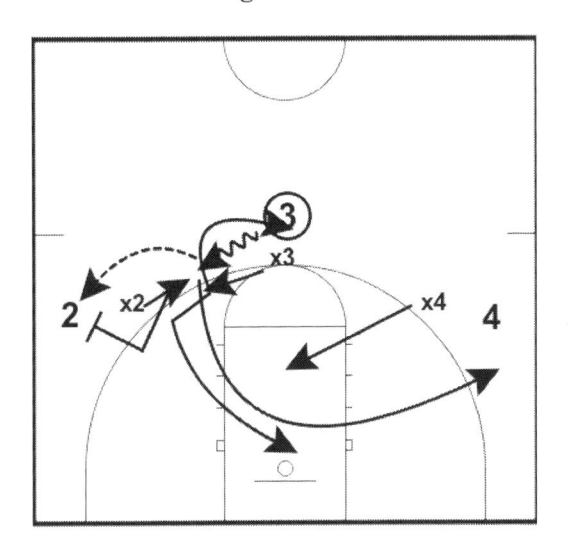

Diagram 32-B

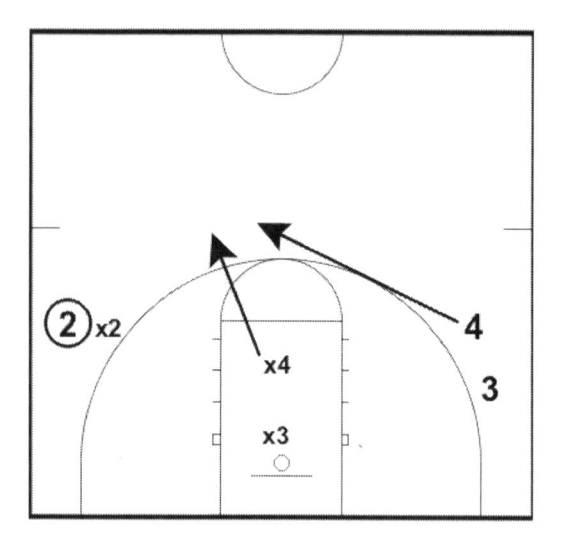

Diagram 32-C

Number 33
4-on-4 Early Help

Four-on-four early help adds either a offensive post player or utilizes four perimeter players, depending on the alignment chosen by the coach to work on defending (**Diagrams 33-A and 33-B**)

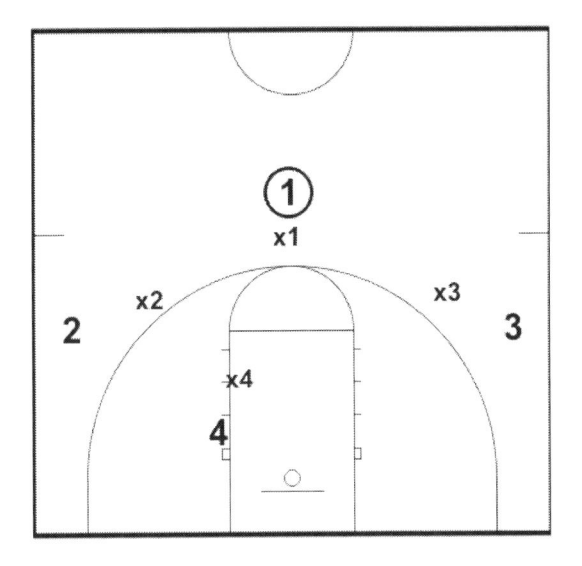

Diagram 33-A

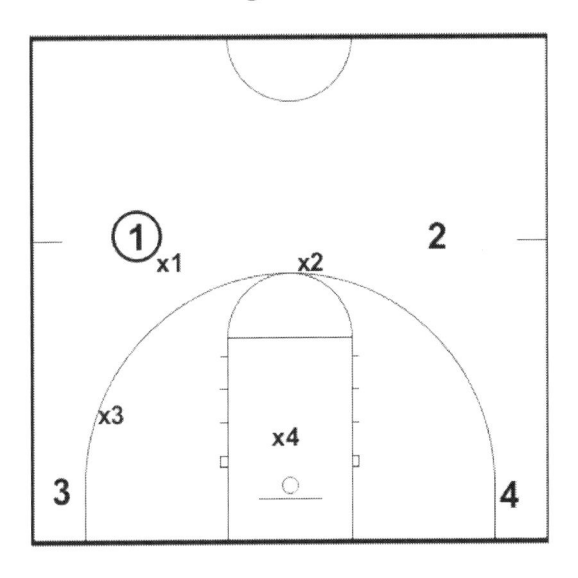

Diagram 33-B

All perimeter and low post early help situations can be practiced in the two alignments shown. Baseline early help with fill and sink (**Diagram 33-C**) can be practiced as well.

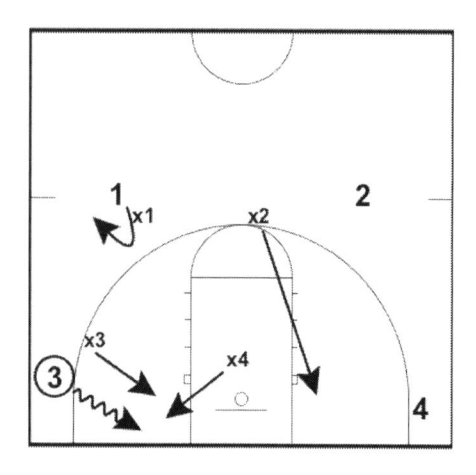

Diagram 33-C

Number 34
5-on-5 Low Post With Early Help Rotation

Five-on-five early help allows every possible early help situation to be practiced. Using the alignment shown in **Diagram 34** allows for low post early help with rotation to be practiced. Moving the low post to the high post changes the baseline early help rotation.

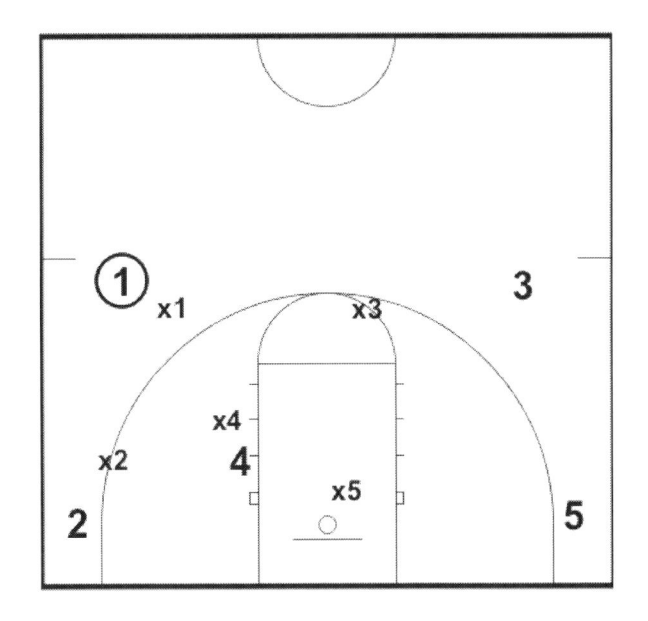

Diagram 34-A

Odds and Ends

Number 35
2-on-1 Cutter/Closeout//Help Side

Two-on-one cutter/closeout/help side combines all of these defensive skills and tactics into one drill. **Diagram 35-A** shows the drill's initial alignment. #2 makes a skip pass and X3 closes out on the ball from a help position.

#3 makes a skip pass back and X3 must return to help side position. #3 can flash cut to the ball side, forcing X3 to defend a flash cut.

Early help or taking a charge can be worked into the drill as well by having #2 drive baseline or middle, forcing X3 to give early help and possibly draw a charge.

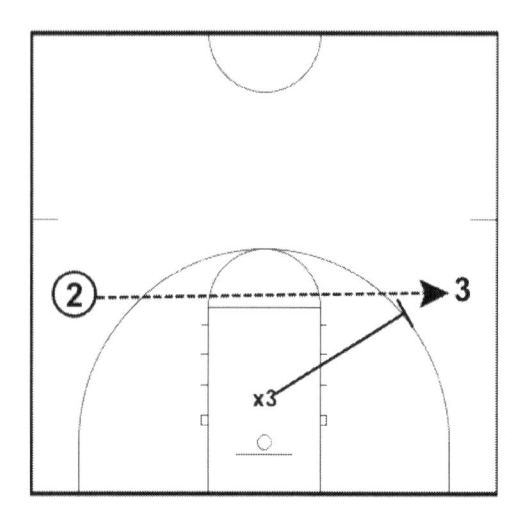

Diagram 35-A

Number 36
Continuous 2-on-2

Continuous two-on-two is a competitive defensive drill. Two teams of two compete with a passer available for both teams. Score is kept and the teams compete to be the first to reach a pre-determined score or until time elapses.

Intensity is important in this drill so the length of time the teams play must be kept short to insure maximum effort.

The offense retains the ball if it scores. If the defense obtains the ball via a turnover or defensive rebound the defense must outlet the ball to the designated passer.

Any offensive tactic can be employed by the offense. If a specific defensive tactic needs extra work the offense can be required to start its possession with the specific tactic. The offense is starting its attack with a down screen as depicted in **Diagram 36-A.**

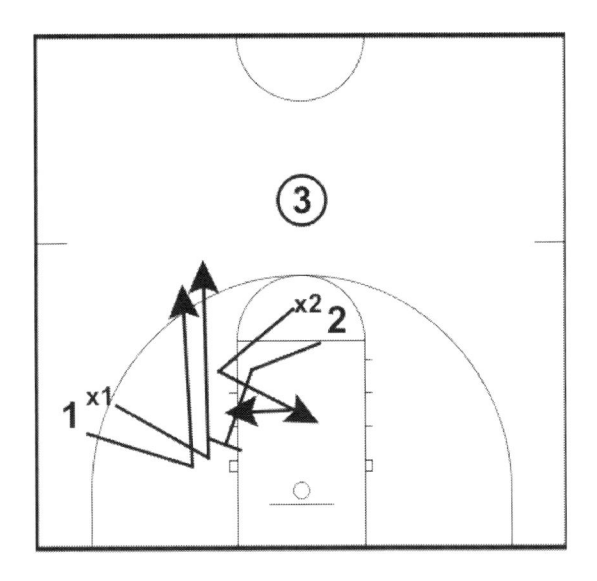

Diagram 36-A

Number 37
1-on-1 Charge Drill

One-on-one charge drill is simple. Diagram 37-A depicts the basic alignment. X2 passes the ball to #3 from a help position. #3 drives to the basket and X2 moves to cut #3 off. X2 positions properly and takes the charge using proper technique. The players then switch places and the drill continues.

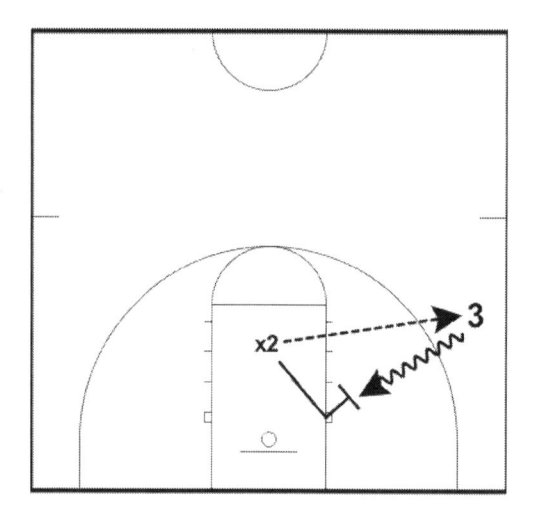

Diagram 37-A

Number 38
2-on-1 Charge Drill

Two-on-one charge drill adds other elements of defense and makes the drawing a charge more challenging (**Diagram 38-B**).

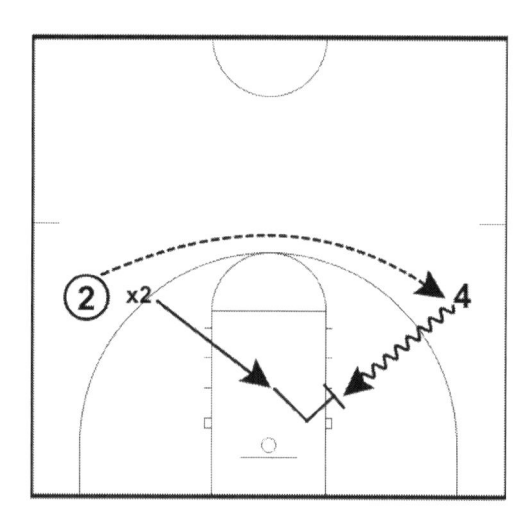

Diagram 38-A

As shown in **Diagram 38-A** the drill starts with X2 defending the ball. #2 makes a skip pass to #4 who drives to the goal. X2 must sprint to a correct help side position while the ball is in the air and arrive when the ball does. X2 must then #4 off and with proper technique and position draw a charge from #4.

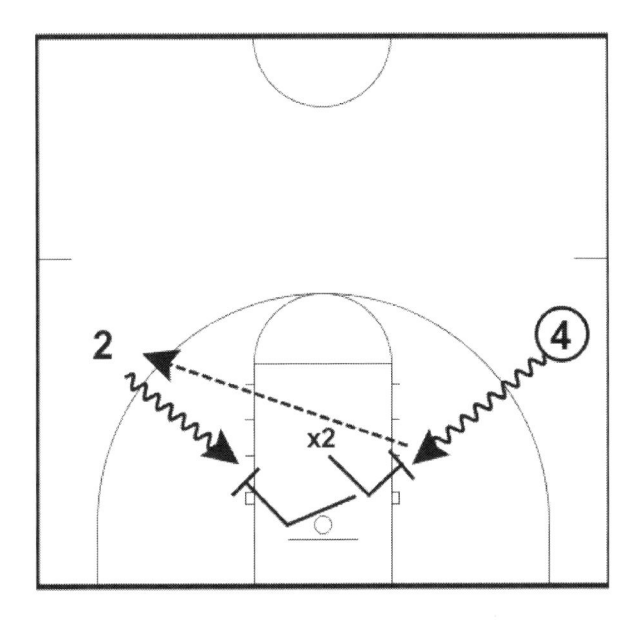

Diagram 38-B

The drill can be made even more challenging and game like by having #4 execute a penetrate and skip pass to #2. This forces X2 to provide early help on #4's baseline drive and then recover in time to take a either closeout and defend #2 or position correctly to take a charge with proper technique form #2 (**Diagram 38-B**).

Number 39
Loose Ball Drill

Fans love it when a player dives on the court for a loose ball! But that is only half of a great hustle play. The other half is a teammate recognizing the need to get open for a pass from the player on the court.

Loose ball drill requires players to pair up and obtain a ball. The pairs spread out throughout the court (**Diagram 39-A**).

The player with the ball rolls it on the court and dives for the ball. The partner makes a v-cut and travels at least 15-17 feet to get open and calls for the ball. The player on the court passes the ball without rolling or moving to the cutter. The cutter turns and faces his or her basket on the other end of the court.

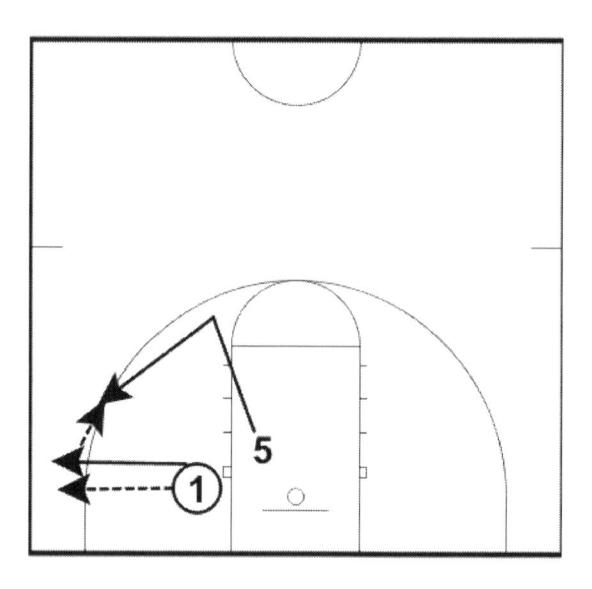

Diagram 39-A

Number 40
Save the Ball Drill

Saving the ball from going out of bounds, like diving on the court for a loose ball is a fan favorite. Like saving a loose ball, the player who obtains the ball has made only half of the play. A teammate must recognize the situation and move to receive a pass from the player saving the ball.

Players pair up with a ball and a partner and line up on the sidelines of the court (It is not wise to do this drill on the baseline. Saving the ball on the baseline is not a good habit to develop as it often goes to the opponent under the opponent's basket, leading to an easy score).

The player with the ball bounces it hard and jumps, catches the ball and turns to find the partner who has moved to get open for the ball (**Diagram 40-A**). The partner moves behind the player who has saved the ball and calls for the ball.

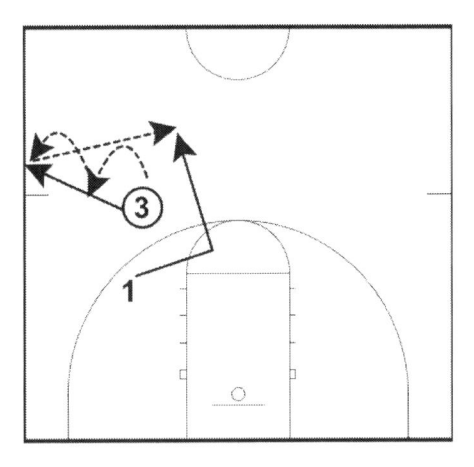

Diagram 40-A

Number 41
2-on-1 Trap and Fast Break Drill

This drill teaches players how to trap and transition from the trap into a fast break quickly and effectively while a player who has committed a turnover learns to defend against a two-on-one fast break attack. **Diagram 41-A** shows the initial alignment and how multiple groups can go at the same time.

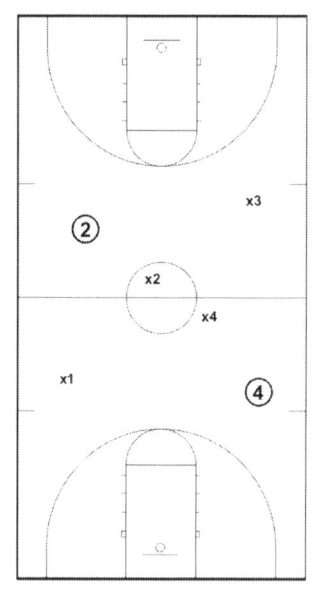

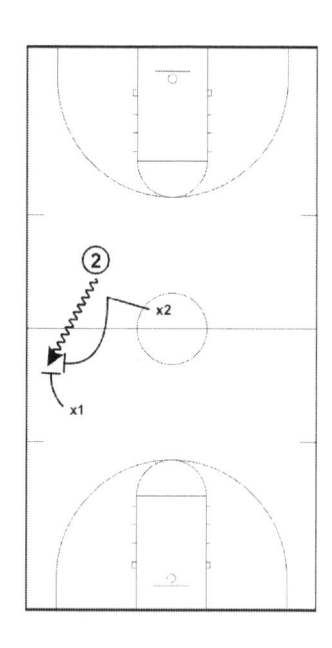

Diagram 41-A   **Diagram 41-B**

In **Diagram 41-B** #2 dribbles into the trap. X1 and X2 properly execute a trap and exercise hand discipline and pressure the ball. #2 deliberately turns the ball over. X1 and X2 transition into a fast break while #2 sprints back to defend the rim and defend a two-on-one fast break.

X2 and X1 get wide first and attack at proper fast break angles, forcing #2 to choose which attacker to defend (**Diagram 41-C**).

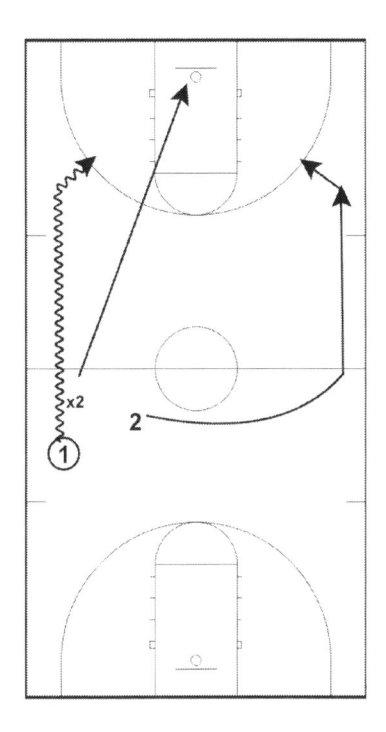

Diagram 41-C

Number 42
Wolf Drill

The "Wolf Drill" teaches players to hustle back and play defense after committing a turnover. In this instance, the defense attempts to steal the ball back without committing a foul. The drill starts with the defense one step behind the offensive player and on the opposite side of the hand the offensive player will be dribbling with (**Diagram 42-A**).

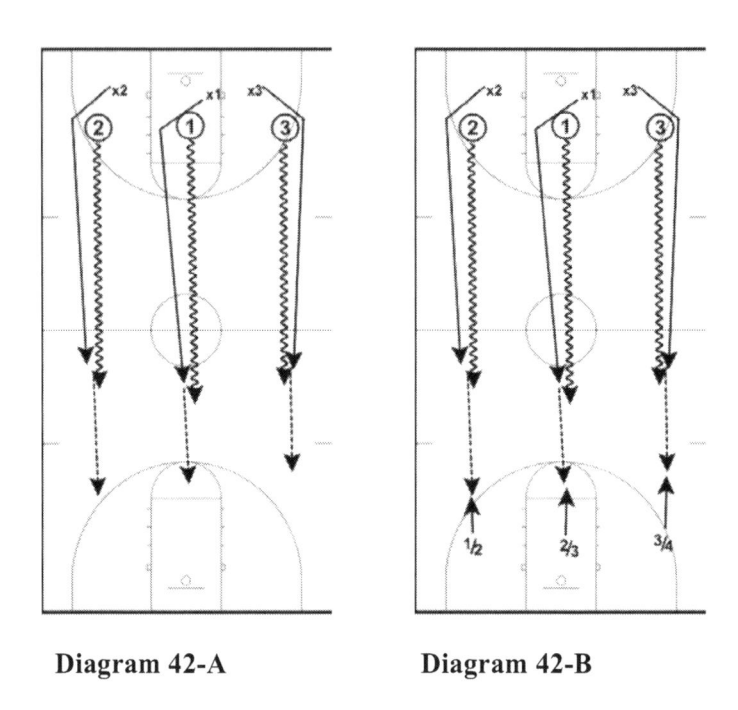

Diagram 42-A

Diagram 42-B

The defensive player must not only sprint to catch up with the offense, but must change sides of the court so the defensive player is on the same side as the hand the offensive player is dribbling with. If the offensive player is dribbling with the right hand, the defensive player must be on the right hand side of the offensive player.

The defensive player reaches with his or her left hand, if on the right side, and tips the ball forward, if possible to a teammate down the court (**Diagram 42-B**). This technique prevents obvious fouls but the defense must be certain to tip the ball and not make contact with the offensive player.

The drill can be made continuous by having the offensive player sprint past the teammate the ball was tipped to, touch the baseline and pursue the new offensive player who begins dribbling after the old offensive player touches the baseline and turns around. The old defensive player becomes the player waiting for a back tip.

Drills for Defensive Rebounding

Number 43
Finish Every Drill With BOPCRO

Coach Rick Majerus did not use rebounding specific drills and his teams always were among the leaders in the nation in rebounding. Coach Majerus assigned an assistant coach to stop practice if one player did not block out and then a consequence would be administered. This is a great concept as it emphasizes the importance of always blocking out. For those who skipped ahead in the book, BOPCRO stands for **B**lock **O**ut **P**ursue **C**hin the **R**ebound and **O**utlet pass.

Number 44
NBA Drill

NBA stands for "no babies allowed." (**Warning:** *Use common sense with this drill. It is an aggression drill and as such is not appropriate for all ages of youth basketball players. Suggested earliest use is with middle school aged players. Use at your own risk.*) This simple drill has few rules. The head and pushing with the hands from behind are prohibited. The first player to score three points wins with goals counting as one point apiece.

Players waiting to take their turn spread out in a semi-circle to catch long balls and pass them to the coach who shoots.

The three players who are participating treat every shot, make or miss, as a rebound and attempt to score. Fouling is permissible and players may travel and double dribble with the ball. If a player scores the made basket is treated like a rebound. The same is true of shots made by the coach.

If a rebound travels too far the coach simply shoots another shot and the long rebound is run down by the players waiting for their turn (**Diagram 44-A**).

Players must be supervised closely in this drill. While it is a player favorite, tempers can flare and play can become rough quickly.

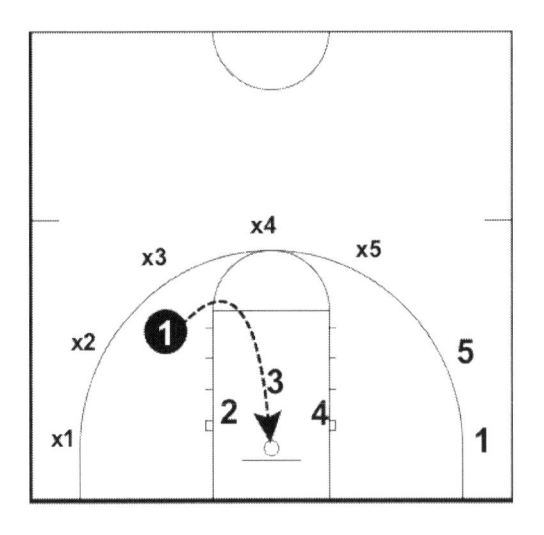

Diagram 44-A

Number 45
Circle Block Out

Circle block out drill provides a high number of repetitions while players are mastering basic block out skills. **Diagram 45-A** shows the basic alignment of players who have been partnered.

Initially the drill starts with the coach giving the command ready to alert the players to assume a defensive stance and triple threat position. The coach then gives the verbal command of shoot and the offensive players shoot an imaginary ball. The defensive players contest the shot and then block the offensive player out.

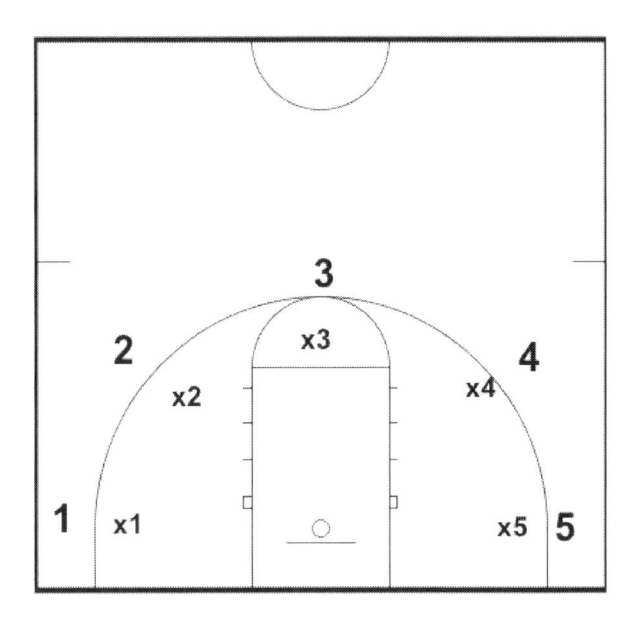

Diagram 45-A

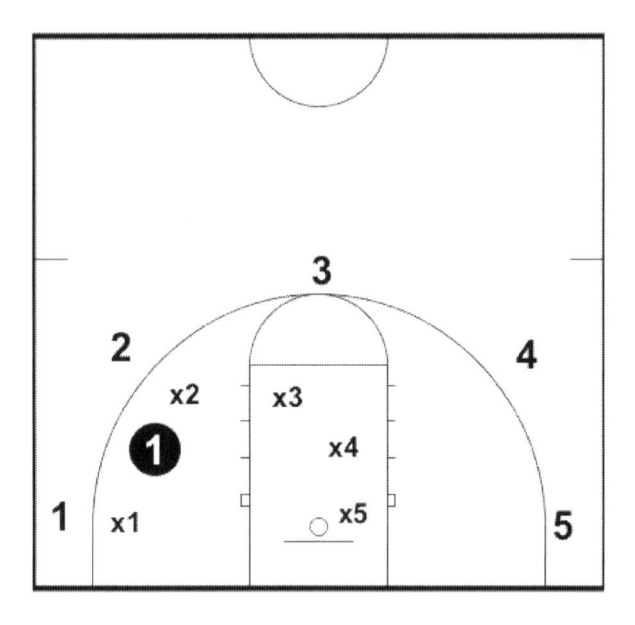

Diagram 45-B

Diagram 45-B shows the alignment when the shooter has been added to the drill. The defensive players must position themselves in correct denial or help position. The coach shoots the ball and the defensive players block out. Initially the offensive players allow the defensive players block them out. As the defensive players skills improve, the offensive players can go live and pursue the rebound for an offensive rebound. The shot taken by the coach should be treated as a miss regardless of whether or not the shot is made or missed.

Number 46
3-on-0 Mass Block Out

Three-on-zero mass block out is used to introduce block out technique and provide a large number of repetitions in a short period of time. Players are divided into groups of six with three defensive players on either side of the three-point line.

The coach shoots the ball and the players execute a block out and then pursue the rebound. After securing the rebound the player who obtains the rebound chins the ball and makes an outlet pass to the coach.

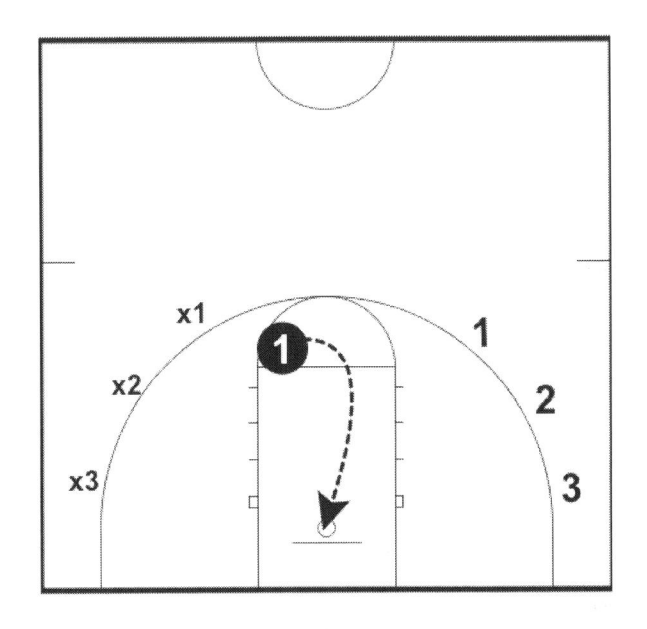

Diagram 46-A

Number 47
1-on-0 Block Out and Outlet

One-on-zero block out and outlet is to be used early in the season to teach technique and build habits. Either a teammate or a coach shoots the ball and the defender blocks out an imaginary offensive player, secures the rebound and makes an outlet pass to the shooter.

The drill continues for the allotted time for the rebounder. This drill can be used at each basket of the gym to gain maximum repetitions in the shortest amount of time (**Diagram 47-A**).

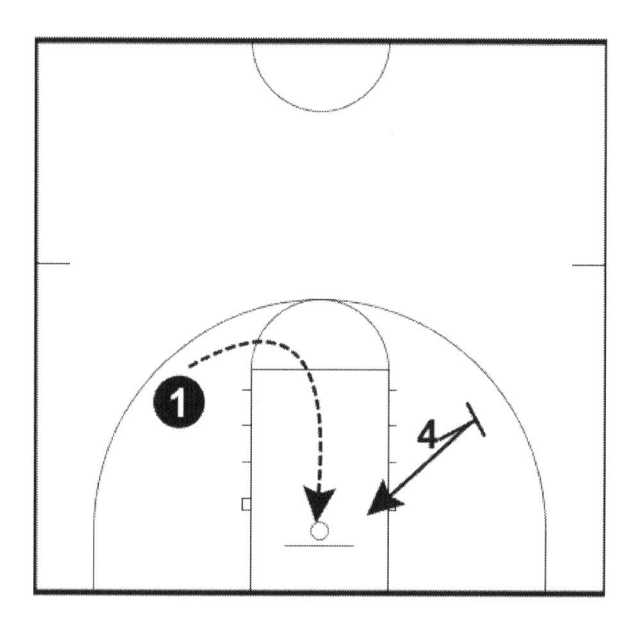

Diagram 47-A

Number 48
1-on-1 Rebound and Outlet

One-on-one rebound and outlet adds an offensive player to the drill. The coach or teammate shoots the ball and the defensive player executes a block out, obtains the rebound and outlet passes it back to the shooter.

Initially the offensive player should make a token effort to obtain the rebound, allowing the defender to block him or her out. As the defender's block skills progress the offensive players are allowed to go live and attempt to obtain the rebound (**Diagram 48-A**).

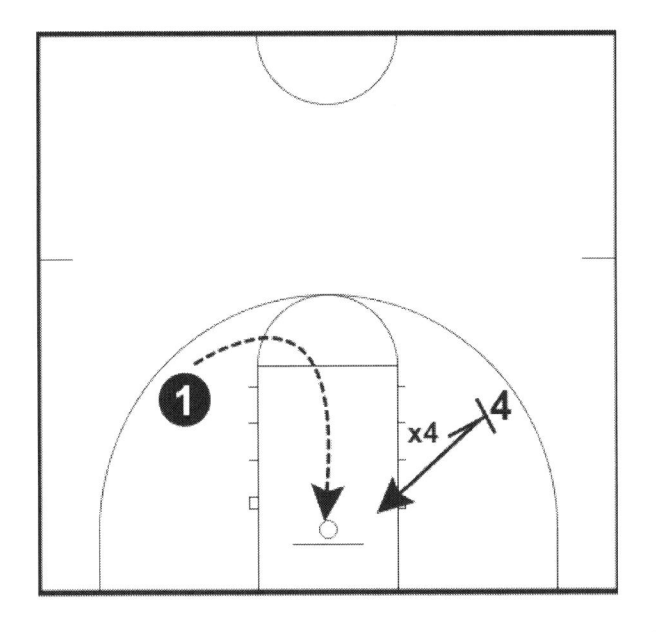

Diagram 48-A

Number 49
Competitive Rebounding

Competitive rebounding is a player favorite! Divide the players into two groups and put five minutes on the clock. From the perspective of the players the goal of the "game" is to be in the group on the baseline. Each group is divided into two groups.

The baseline group simply forms two lines, one on each side of the lane and plays defense. The other group can have it's two lines placed anywhere by the coach in order to work on different defensive positions and rebound angles (**Diagram 49-A**).

The drill starts with a pass out from underneath the goal to one of the lines away from the goal. The defense closes out on the ball and sprints to help or denial position as needed. The offense counts to one after catching the pass and then shoots.

The defense attempts to block out and the offense attempts to obtain the offensive rebound. If the defense obtains the rebound the two defenders stay in the baseline group on the baseline and the two offensive players must stay in the offense lines away from the goal.

If the offense obtains an offensive rebound they may either score it immediately or play offense for a scoring opportunity. If the offense is able to score, the offense goes to the end of the defense lines on the baseline and the defenders must join the offensive and go to the end of the line. When time expires, the players in the defense lines are the winners.

The normal duration of time for this drill is five minutes. Setting a consequence for the loser and a reward for the winner increases the intensity level of play in the drill.

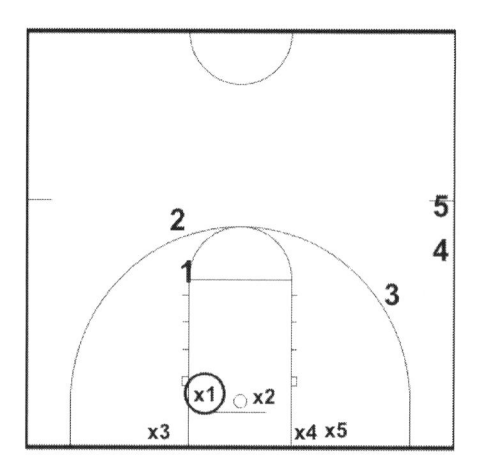

Diagram 49-A

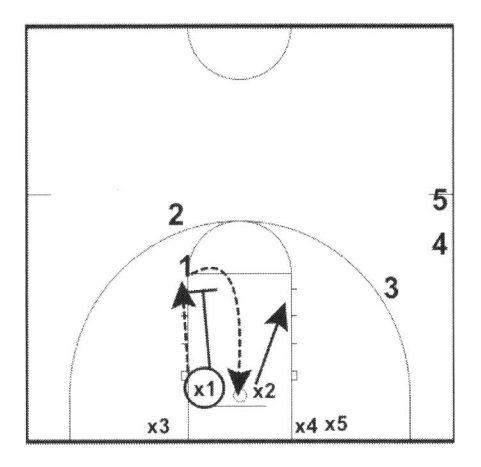

Diagram 49-B

Drills for TEAM Defense

Number 50
2-on-2 On a Side

Two-on-two on a side forces the defense to play ball side defense without the advantages of help side defense. The offense is limited to attacking only on the ball side of the court and is allowed to use any offensive tactic that can be executed on one side of the court. **Diagrams 50-A** and **50-B** show some initial movements that can be utilized.

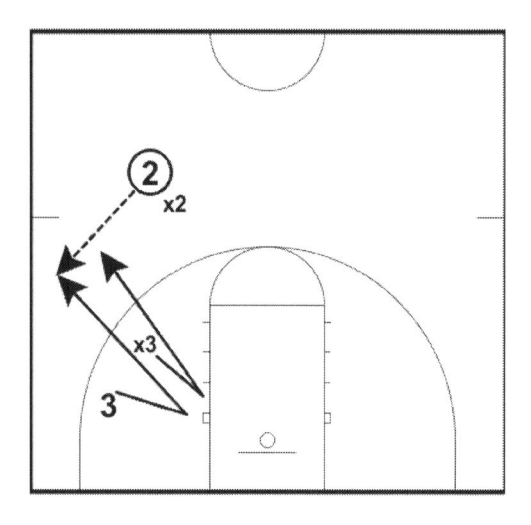

Diagram 50-A

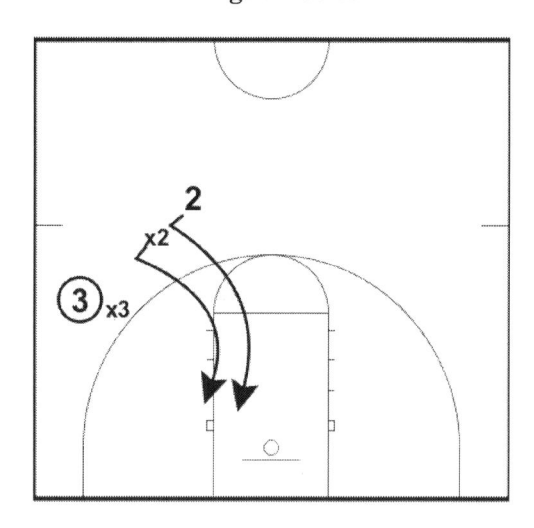

Diagram 50-B

Number 51
3-on-3 On a Side

Three-on-three on a side forces the defense to practice ball side defense with out the advantage of additional help side defenders once the ball has been pushed to one side of the court.

Diagrams 51-A and 51-B show two possible alignments the drill can be started from. The offense is required to stay on the ball side of the court. Any offensive tactic ranging from cutting to screening may be used to attack the defense.

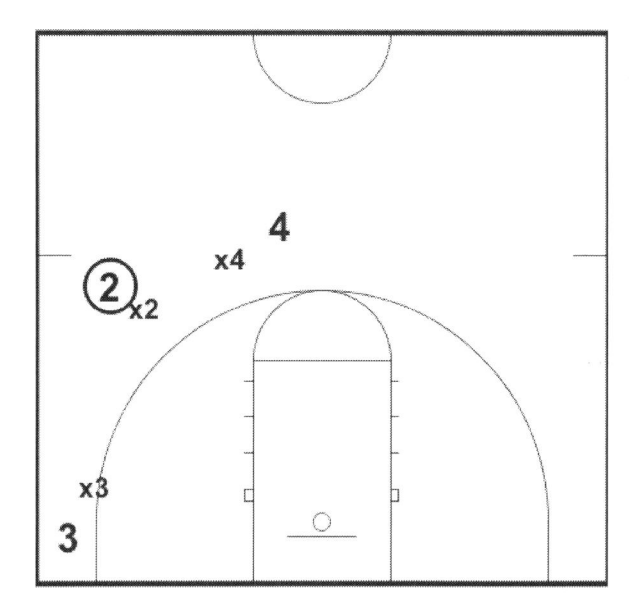

Diagram 51-A

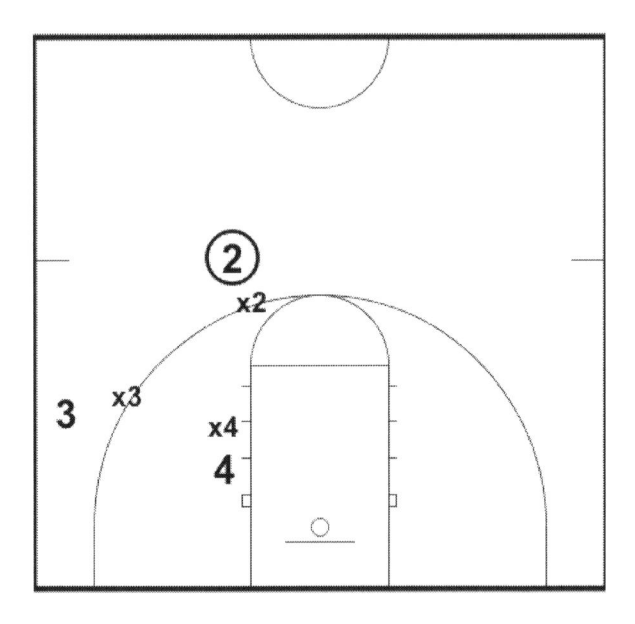

Diagram 51-B

Number 52
Shell Drill

The shell drill is perhaps the best drill for teaching basic positioning and introducing and mastering team defensive concepts. Individual fundamentals are combined with team concepts as well.

Defense against moving offensive players while maintaining proper position can be taught as well. Finally, transition to shell drill can be added to combine transition defense with half court position defense. **Diagrams 52-A** through **52-E** show alignments to start the drill with.

SIVILS | 111

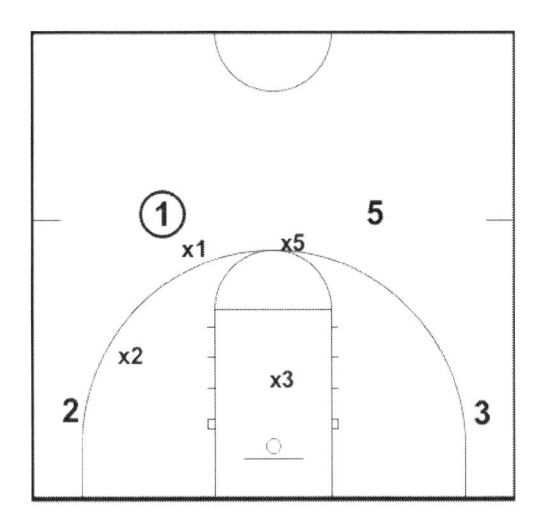

Diagram 52-A

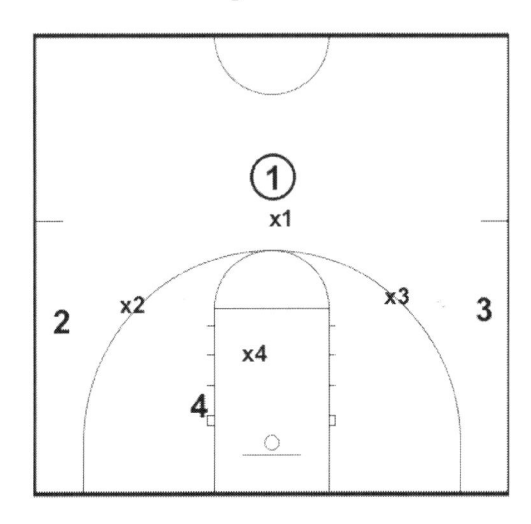

Diagram 52-B

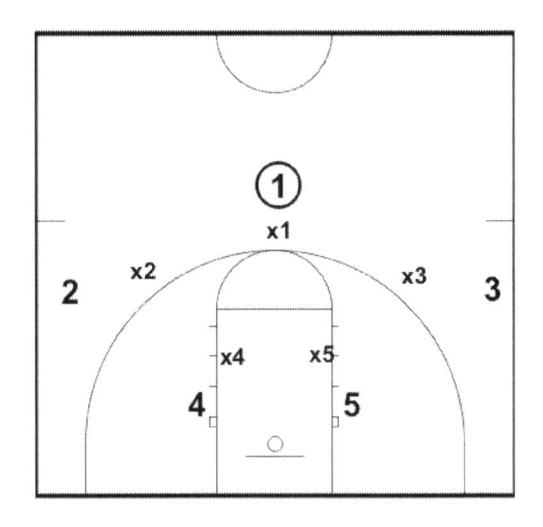

Diagram 52-C

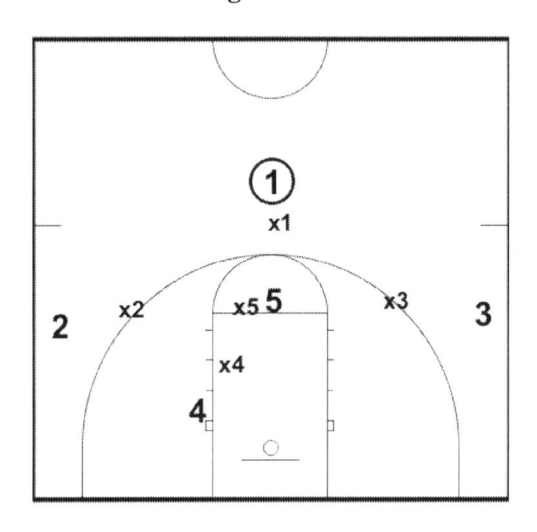

Diagram 52-D

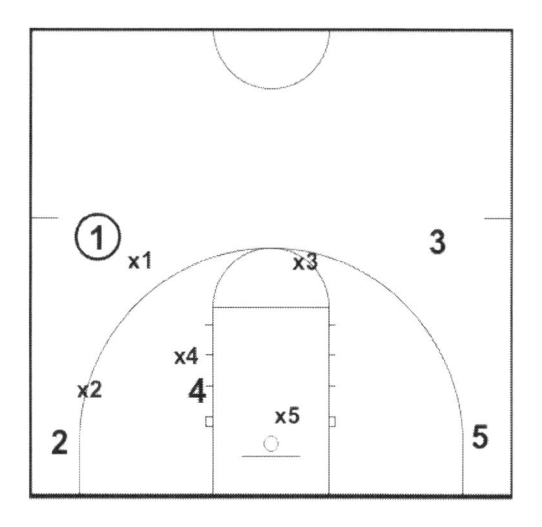

Diagram 52-E

Number 53
Defensive Cutthroat

Defensive cutthroat is a variation of the tradition competitive game cutthroat. Instead of scoring points on offense, points are scored by defense. Points are awarded for obtaining a defensive rebound, forcing a turnover or drawing a charge. The offense can score points by obtaining an offensive rebound.

Diagram 53-A shows the initial alignment for the drill. The team is divided into groups of four. When the defense scores it stays on the court. The old offense rotates off and the new offense must outlet pass the ball to a coach near mid-court. The old offense hustles off.

If an offensive group scores the defense rotates off and the offense becomes the defense. The next group rotates on as offense. Each team is responsible for saying its score aloud as it scores.

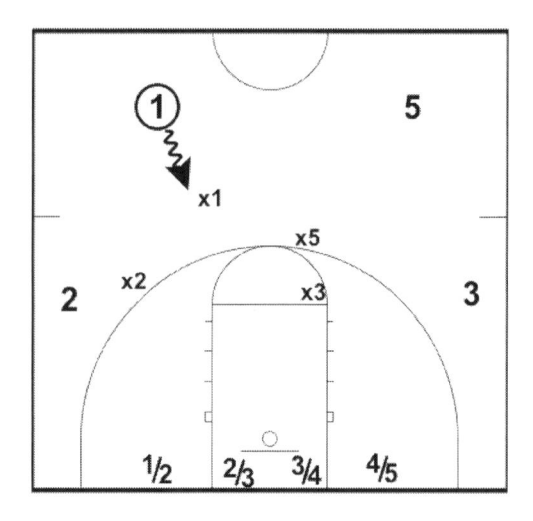

Diagram 53-A

Number 54
5-on-4 Disadvantage Drill

The essential purpose for all disadvantage drills is to teach the defense to embrace adversity and learn to persevere and stop the offense from scoring.

Five-on-four disadvantage places the defense at a disadvantage by allowing the offense a one player advantage, regardless of how the defense plays the offense.

Diagram 54-A shows a possible initial alignment. Note #1 is undefended. The defense does not defend the offensive player furthest from the ball.

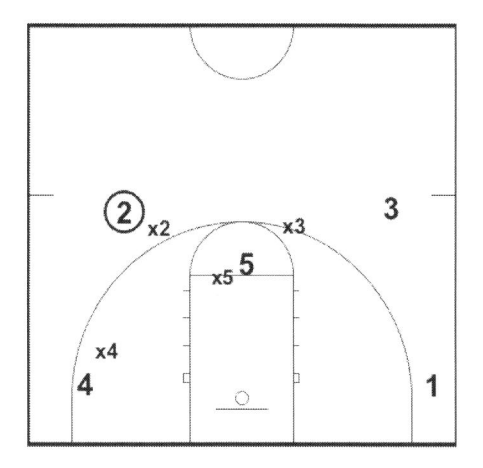

Diagram 54-A

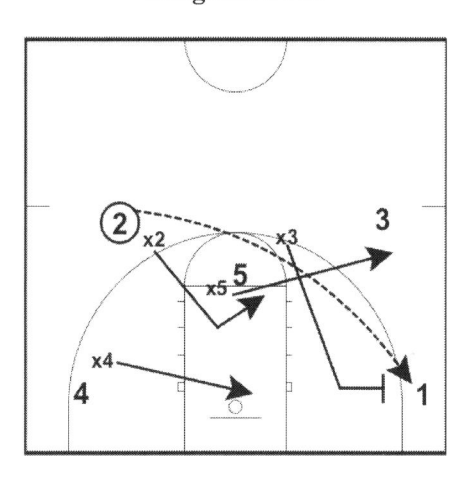

Diagram 54-B

Diagram 54-B shows how the defense reacts on a skip pass from #2 to #1. The closest defender in this example is X3. X3 executes an L-cut and closes out on the ball. Each defender takes the next closest defensive assignment. X5 denies #3. X2 denies the offensive high post #5. X4 takes the help side defensive position.

Initially the offense should be required to maintain a stationary position. After several passes the offense should be allowed to begin cutting and finally the offense should be allowed to screen defenders.

The drill can be made competitive in a variety of ways such as points scored for the number of passes successfully forced by the defense before the offense scores.

Initially the drill should be kept short in duration for each defensive group in order to build intensity and provide a sense of success so the defense will not give up.

Transition Defense

Number 55
Transition Sprints

Learning to execute defensive transition sprints is the core of all defensive transition. This drill is both simple and a great conditioning drill (**Diagram 55-A**).

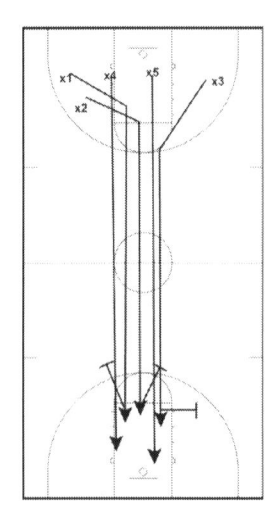

Diagram 55-A

Players are divided into groups of five and spread out in the offensive area. The other groups wait out of bounds on the baseline. The coach gives a command to go and the players execute a defensive transition sprint.

Once players have mastered the basic skill the coach can start the drill by shooting the ball off the glass to another coach who then makes a pitch-a-head pass up the court to a student assistant or a third coach.

The defenders must beat the pass up the court making the speed required game like. The next group must immediately move on to the court to be ready to execute.

Number 56
1-on-1 Full Court "Stop Ball" Drill

One-on-one full court stop ball drill is a grueling one-on-one drill requiring maximum effort on the part of the defender. It is an excellent disadvantage drill and requires the coaching staff to be very positive and up beat with the defensive players who will experience certain failure when the drill is introduced.

To combat this, use restrictions on the offense to give the defender a realistic chance. As the skill and effort of the defender improves, remove restrictions on the offensive player.

The drill begins with the defender slightly behind the offensive player who initiates the drill by taking off at maximum (or less if this is a necessary restriction) speed dribbling down the court. The defensive player must pressure the ball handler out of the center of the court and to one side and if at all possible either contain the ball handler or better yet, force the ball handler to pick up his or her dribble (**Diagram 56-A**).

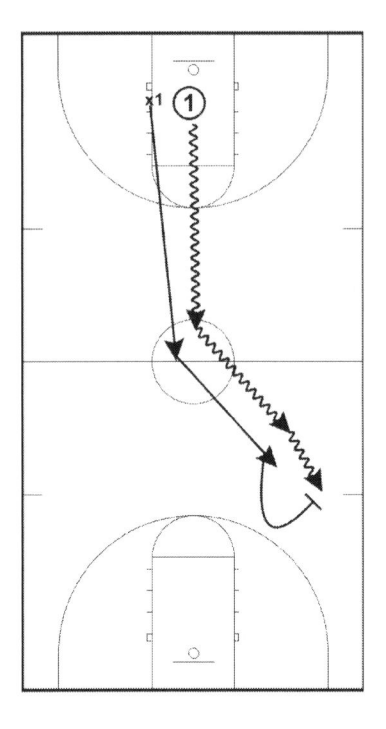

Diagram 56-A

Number 57
2-on-2 Full Court "Stop Ball" Drill

Two-on-two full court stop ball drill introduces a second defensive player. Diagram 57-A shows the initial phase of the drill. X2 slows the ball handler and turns him or her. X3 is in a help position and can either trap or provide early help and recovery.

If the ball handler kills the dribble, for the purpose of the drill after the dead call is given the ball handler can resume dribbling. The defense must stop the ball as many times as possible.

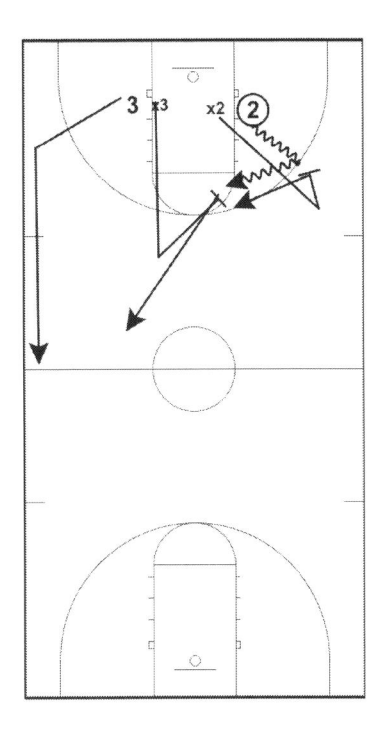

Diagram 57-A

Number 58
3-on-3 Conversion

Three-on-there conversion combines every element of man-to-man defense except for the ability to establish a numerical advantage by establishing help side defense, with defensive transition. In addition the drill can be made competitive.

The team is divided into two equal groups. The drill starts as shown in **Diagram 58-A**. Each group always attacks and defends the same end of the court.

Diagram 58-A **Diagram 58-B**

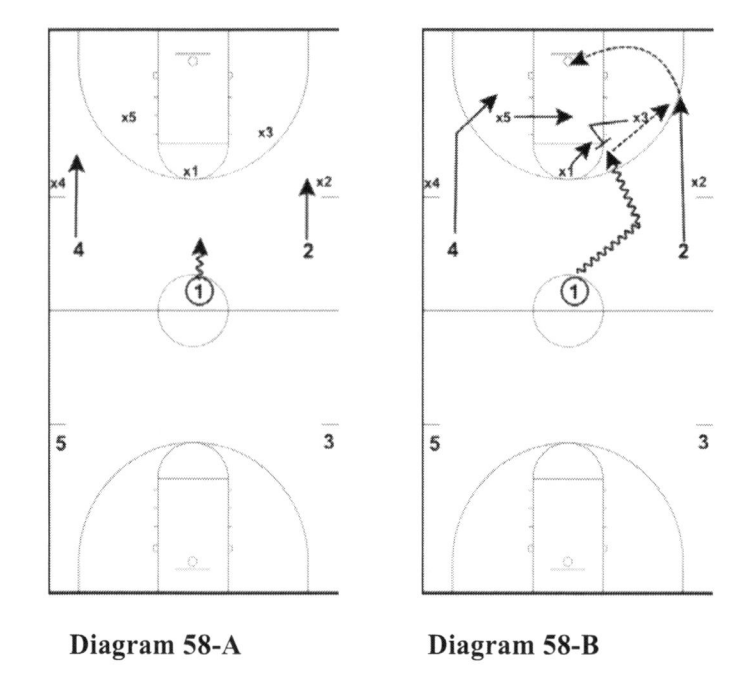

In **Diagram 58-C** X5 has obtained the rebound and makes an outlet pass to X4 who drives the ball in the middle. X1 fills behind X4 and X2 fills the other fast break lane. X5 moves out of bounds to wait until the next opportunity to play.

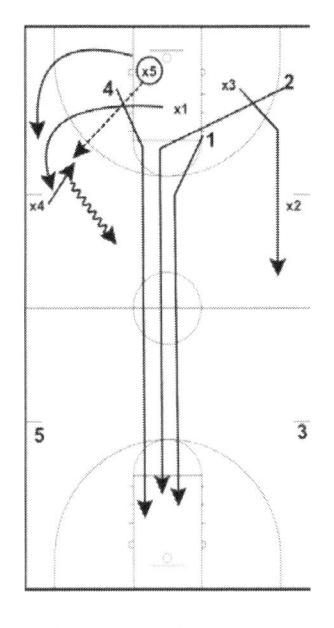

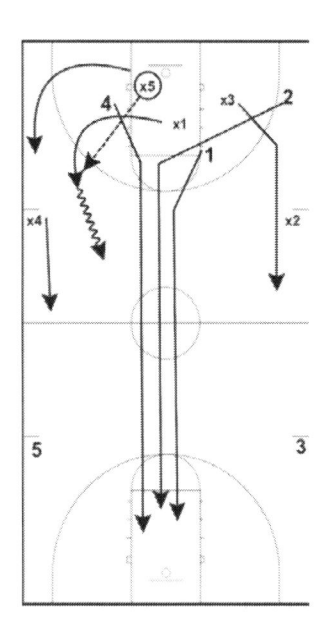

Diagram 58-C   Diagram 58-D

Note, the defender who inbounds the ball or obtains the rebound always rotates off. If the defense steals the ball or forces a turnover the offense immediately goes on defensive transition and the defense fast breaks.

Diagram 58-D shows the drill after a made basket. X5 inbounds the ball to X1 and the fast break starts. X5 moves off the court and X4 takes X5's place filling a fast brake lane.

Number 59
4-on-4-on-4 Transition Defense

Any drill resembling game action is a player favorite. Four-on-four-on-four transition defense is one such drill. It combines working on defensive transition with offensive player and four-on-four defense. It can also be used to introduce full court pressing and press offense. Once the players have mastered the workings of the drill and improved enough in the area of fundamental skills and understanding of tactics and strategy a running score can be kept to make the drill competitive.

A minimum of twelve players are needed for the drill. Players are divided into three squads of four and lined up as shown in **Diagram 59-A**. The first offensive unit attacks and the waiting defensive players closeout to correct position.

When a change of possession takes place wither by an offensive score, drawing a charge, obtaining a rebound or forcing a turnover, the former offensive unit rotates to the baseline to await its turn to play defense. The defensive unit outlets the basketball and fast breaks up the court.

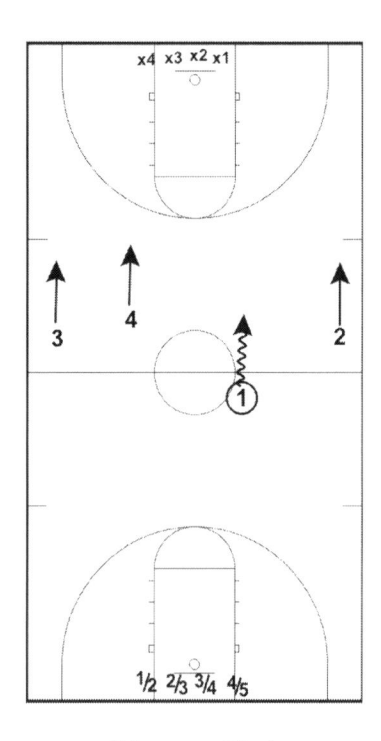

Diagram 59-A

If working on press defense and offense is desired, simply have the offense press until the ball crosses half court. If the pressing defense is able to steal the ball, it transitions over to offense and the former offensive unit must play defense after turning the ball over.

Number 60
5-on-5 Head Start Transition Drill

Five-on-five head start transition drill combines transition defense with live shell drill work and an immediate disadvantage. This is an excellent drill to teach persistence and rapid defensive transition.

The offense lines up in a straight line across the court just beneath the foul line extended. The defense lines up just behind the offense (**Diagram 60-A**). The drill starts when the coach shoots and makes a shot. The offense runs its fast break as shown in **Diagram 60-B** (the defense has been omitted for clarity).

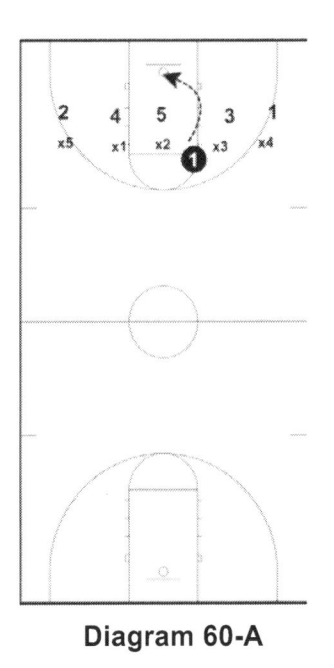

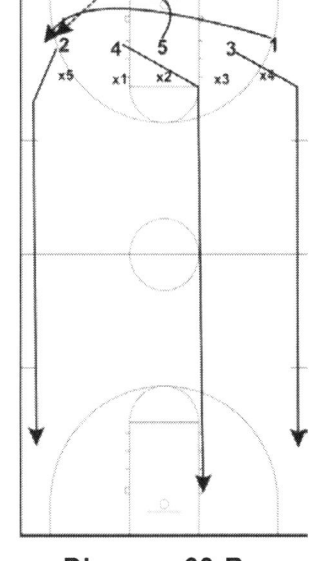

Diagram 60-A   Diagram 60-B

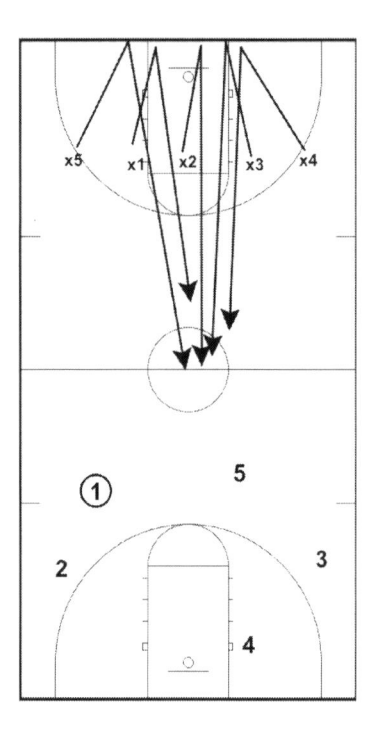

Diagram 60-C

As soon as the shot is made the defensive unit sprints to the baseline and touches it. The defense then makes a defensive transition sprint in the middle of the court. The defense must prevent the offense from scoring and then establish a five-on-five defense.

CHAPTER SIX

Competitive Rebounding Drills

Number 61
1-on-1 Competitive Offensive Rebounding Back Roll or Swim Drill

Diagram One

This drill is all about offensive rebounding. The defense is given the complete upper hand before the start of the drill by allowing the defender to block out the offensive player as shown.

The coach shoots the ball and the offensive player must either "back roll" or "swim technique" the defensive rebounder and pursue possession of the ball. The defensive rebounder attempts to prevent the offensive rebounder from doing so.

This can be a single elimination competition or a best of series.

Number 62
1-on-3 Competitive Closeout and Contest Rebounding

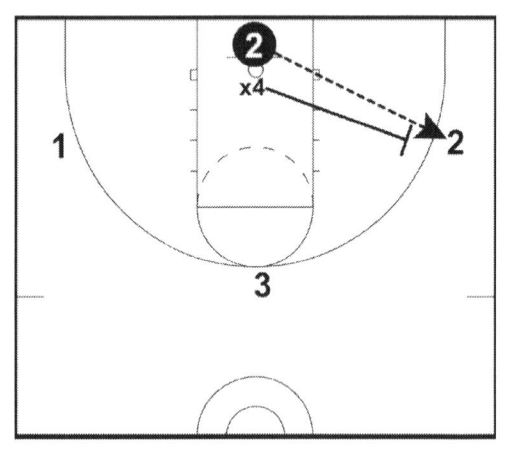

Diagram One

Three offensive players and one defensive player are positioned as shown. The coach passes the ball to an offensive player. The defender closes out on the shooter.

For the purpose of the drill, early in the season the shooter should give the defender enough time to close out before shooting. The defender contests the shot and blocks the shooter out.

Both players pursue the rebound, regardless of whether the shot is made or missed. The player who obtains the rebound immediately goes on offense and tries to score.

The player who scores and ends the possession fills one of the three offensive spots. The lose plays defense.

Creativity can be used in scoring. For example if the defensive player obtains the rebound and scores to win, the defender is awarded an extra point. Because of the advantage of the extra point, the winner could go on defense instead of offense.

Number 63
1 versus 5 Competitive Block Out Drill

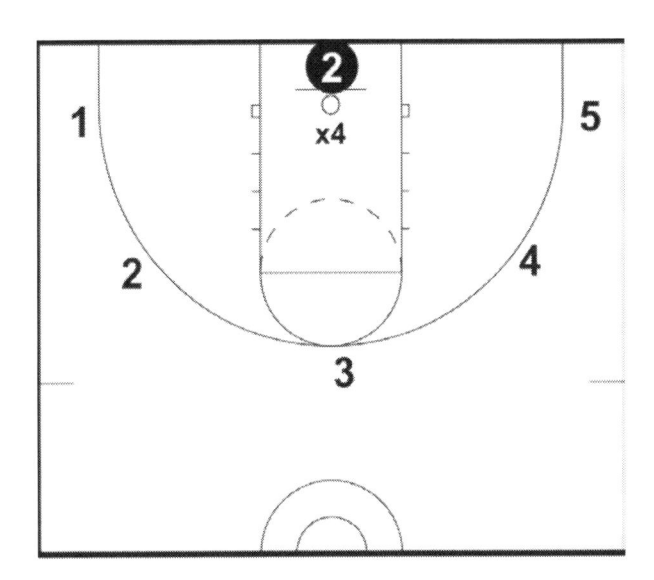

The players are deployed as depicted in the diagram and numbered. The coach passes the ball to a player on the periemter who shoots the ball.

While the pass is in the air the coach calls the number of the player to be blocked out. The defender must reach quickly and block out the offensive player whose number has been called.

The possession ends when the defender obtains the initial rebound, made or missed, or the offensive player scores off the rebound.

The winner moves off, or stays if that is the chosen reward. The loser occupies stays, or again moves off it that is the negative consequence selected.

Number 64
2 versus 5 Competitive Block Out Drill

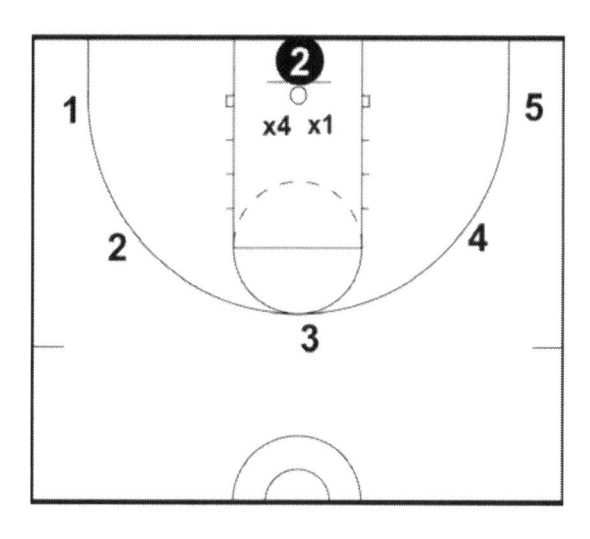

Diagram One

This drill pits two players against a possbile five. The players are deployed as shown in the diagram and the offensive players are numbered. The coach passes the ball to a player on offense and calls two numbers the instant the ball is passed.

The player shoots the ball upon receiving it. The two defensive players must block out the two offensive players whose numbers were called.

The possession continues until the defensive players have obtained possessionof the ball. If the offensive players obtain possession the competitors play 2-on-2. So long as the two offensive players continue to obtain possession, make or miss, the game continues. It does not end until the two defensive players obtain possession. This places an emphasis on rebounding makes for quick inbounds passes.

Number 65
2-on-2 Competitive Reaction Block Out

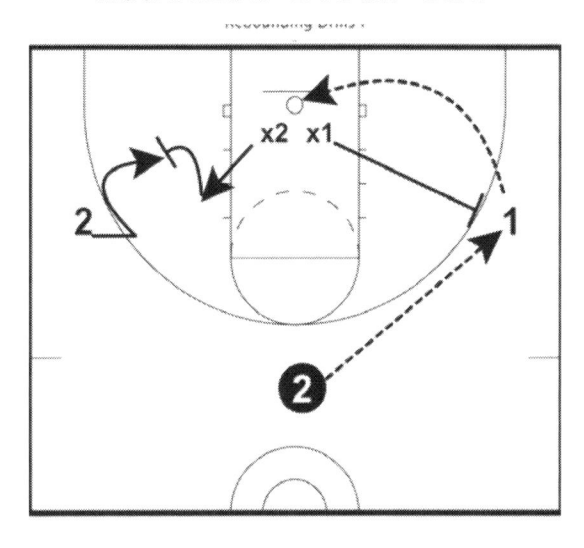

Diagram One

The players are deployed as shown. The drill starts with the coach passing to one of the offensive players on the wing.

In this example, X1 closes out and contests the shot. X2 must block out #2 for the offense.

If the offense obtains the rebound the possession continues until there is an outcome.

If the defense obtains the rebound, make or miss, the ball must be successfully outleted to the defender's teammate.

Number 66
3-on-3 Competitive Block Out Drill

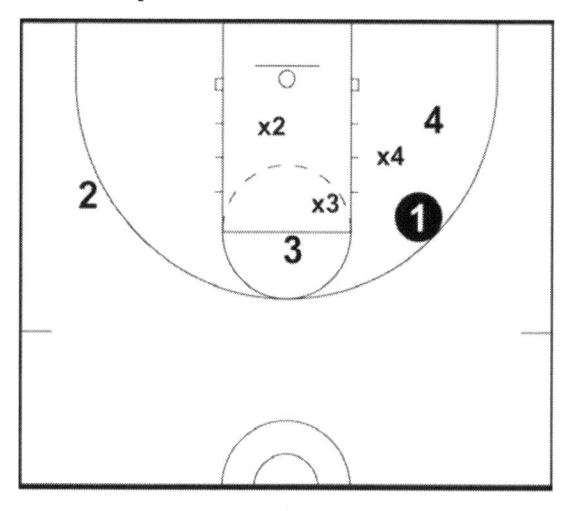

Diagram One

Players work in 3-on-3 shell type situations. The drill starts with players correctly deployed in defensive position based on the style of defense the team runs.

The coach shoots the ball, or passes it to an offensive player who shoots the ball, and the players attack. The defenders attempt to block out and the offensive players attempt to obtain the rebound.

Some variations of this drill include:

- Allowing the defense to fast break if they obtain the ball – make or miss
- Playing until one side scores – half court or full court
- Playing a best of series with the team who obtains the rebound scoring a point

Number 67
Competitive Cross Block Out Drill

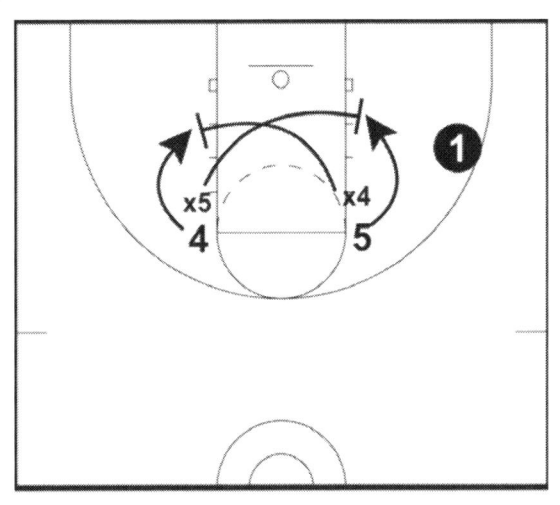

Diagram One

This drill is great for working on free throw situations, zone defense and blocking out a man no defender is assigned to or who has "escaped" the defender assigned to block that player out.

The players deploy as shown. The coach or student assistant shoots. The offensive players cut as shown and the defenders cut across the lane to block out.

Players pursue the ball and obtain possession. If the defense obtains the ball they must make an outlet pass in 1.5 seconds or less.

If the offensive players obtain possession of the ball the players play until the offense scores or the defense is able to obtain possesion of the ball.

This drill can be made competive by having the winner stay on and the loser go off or by playing the best of 3, 5 or 7 rebound opportunities.

This is a drill that can be done at multiple goals to maximize the time allotted.

Number 68
Competitive Rebounding

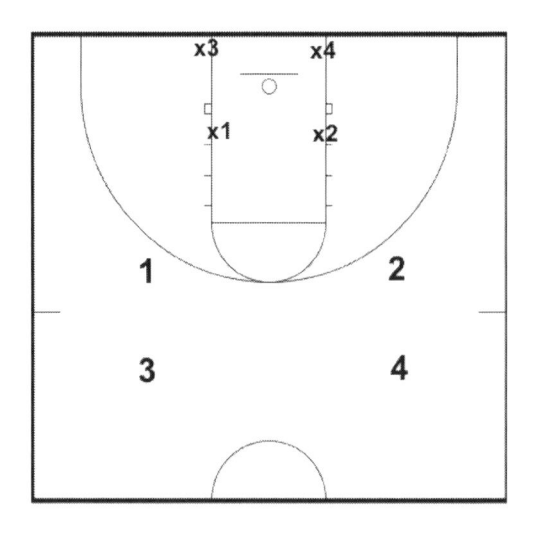

Diagram One

Competitive rebounding will be a team favorite as the season progresses and has the added benefit of emphasizing both offensive and defensive rebounding. Players are divided into two teams. The drill runs for five minutes. The objective is to finish the five minutes and be one of the players on the baseline team. To make the drill even more competitive have the losing team run. **Diagram One** depicts the basic alignment prior to the start of the drill.

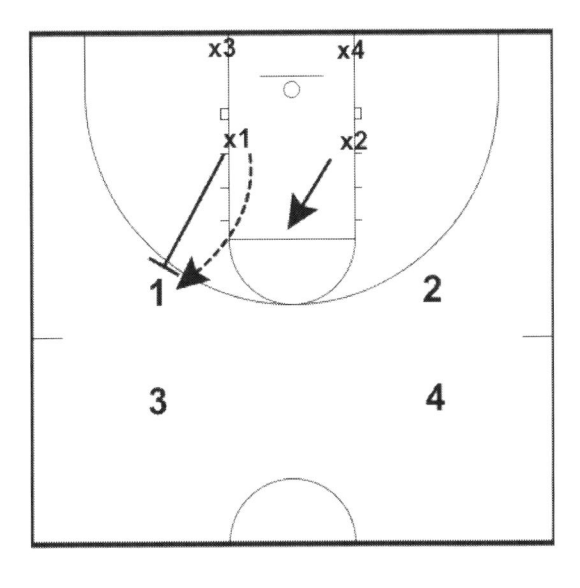

Diagram Two

Diagram Two depicts the start of the drill with X1 pass to #1 and closing out on the ball. X2 moves to an appropriate help defense position. Early in the season do not allow #1 to shoot the ball until the defense has finished positioning.

X1 and X2 block out on the shot attempt and all four players attempt to secure the rebound as shown in **Diagram Three**. If X1 and X2 obtain the rebound, they pass the ball to the next player at the front of the baseline team and go to the end of the lines for that team. #1 and #1 return to the end of the lines of the shooting team.

If either #1 or #2 obtain an offensive rebound, the two play offense and attempt to score. If #1 or #2 score, they move to the end of the lines on the baseline team and X1 and X2 move to the end of the lines of the offensive team. Note, regardless of whether the initial shot attempt is made or missed by #1 (or #2) it is treated as a missed shot.

Diagram Four presents an alternative the offensive team can use to increase their advantage in possibly obtaining an offensive rebound.

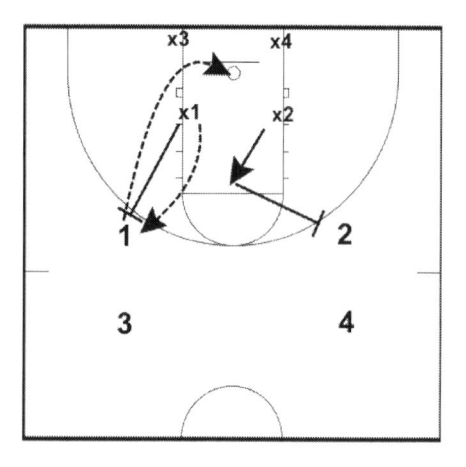

Diagram Three

Following the initial pass from X1 to #1, instead of shooting the ball, #1 passes the ball to #2, forcing the defenders X1 and X2 to adjust their position. #2 may shoot the ball upon catching it. The shifting of the defense may present offensive rebounding opportunities that otherwise might not have been available.

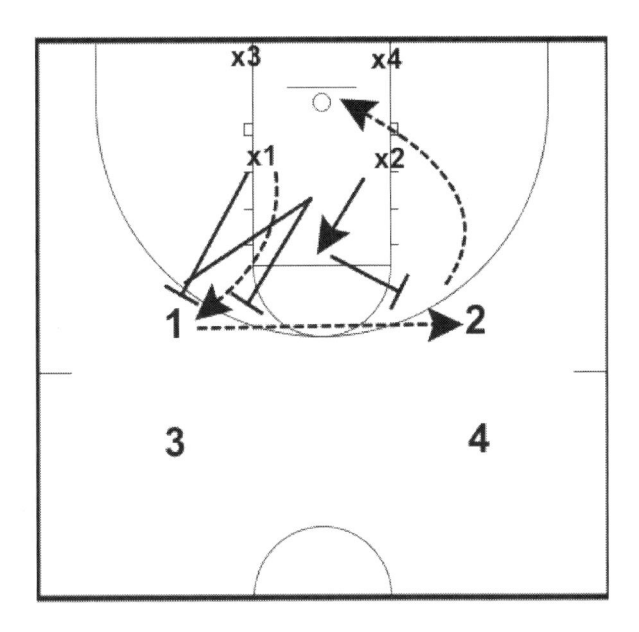

Diagram Four

CHAPTER SEVEN

Movement, Passing, Footwork & Essential Fundamentals

The drills listed in this chapter cover a wide range of essential skills that are often overlooked to the detriment of the both the individual player and the team. While most of these drills are not "ball handling" or "dribbling drills" per se, they incorporate basic ball handling and combine it with the overlooked skills of cutting, turning and moving. By adding passing to the mix you have created a total fundamentals drill.

Players struggle with these drills initially exactly because of the combination of so many basic skills into a single, intense, string of skills. While skills do need to be mastered individually and often in an isolated setting, basketball is a game of movement and skills must be executed while in motion. The skills covered in the drills in this chapter need to be included in every practice in some shape or fashion.

Number 69
Fundamental Lines: Easy Running

Ideal Duration: 30 seconds to one minute total.

Grouping: Groups of three or four with one ball.

Frequency of Usage: Daily during preseason practice and one or two times a week as the season progresses..

This drill teaches:

1) change of pace.
2) v-cutting.
3) flick passing.
4) handoff or dribble exchanges if so desired.
5) meeting (shortening) the pass.
6) rear turns (pivots).

Fundamental lines is a series of drills designed to practice essential fundamentals, provide a high number of repetitions in a short period of time, build intensity and force players to concentrate on execution.

The drills shown in this section can be run from the baseline, the ideal location, or the sideline if space and numbers dictate. Players ideally are in groups of three with a ball but groups of four or five are acceptable.

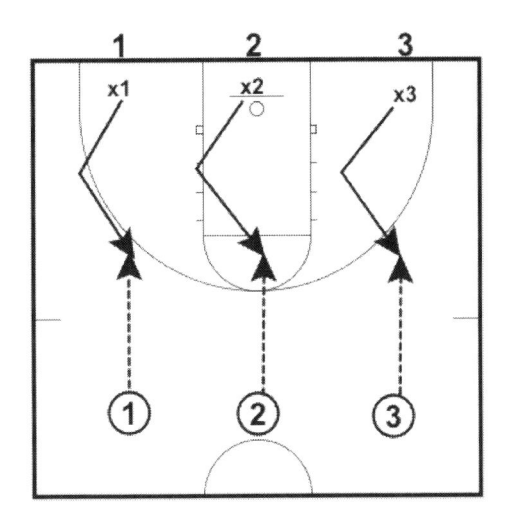

Diagram A

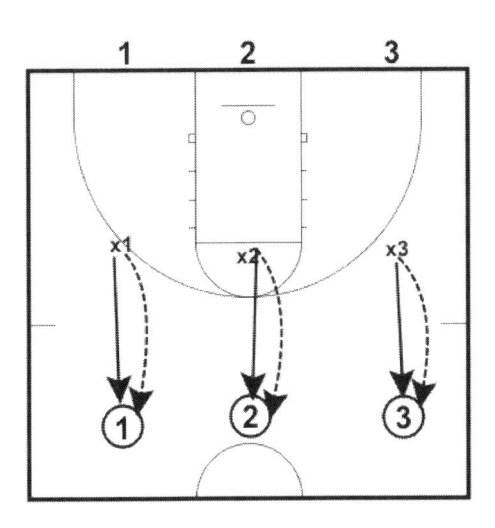

Diagram B

Diagrams A and B depict the drill sequence known as "easy running." This is drill is not meant to be performed at a high rate of speed and is a good warm-up for the more intense drills in this sequence. The first half of the sequence is shown in **Diagram A** as the players on the baseline execute v-cuts. The passers are located near half court and pass to the cutter using their weak hand. Upon catching the pass, the cutter lands in triple threat and executes a weak hand pass back to the passer.

The cutter follows the pass to the passer and executes a jump stop into triple threat and takes an exchange from the passer, who is in triple threat with the ball, by pulling the ball from the grasp of the passer and then executing a rear turn. The passer moves out of bounds and hustles to the end of the cutter line on the baseline (**Diagram B**).

Number 70
Fundamental Lines – Live Ball

Ideal Duration: 30 seconds to one minute total with players rotating after each repetition.

Grouping: Groups of three or four with one ball.

Frequency of Usage: Daily during preseason practice and one or two times a week as the season progresses.

This drill teaches:

1) live ball dribble moves such as direct drive or crossover.
2) long, low, start steps.
3) the concept of "going somewhere with your dribble" due to the two dribble limit.
4) rear turns (pivots).
5) flick passing.
6) moving to meet (shortening) the pass.
7) jump catching into triple threat position.
8) use of the shot fake.
9) closeouts.

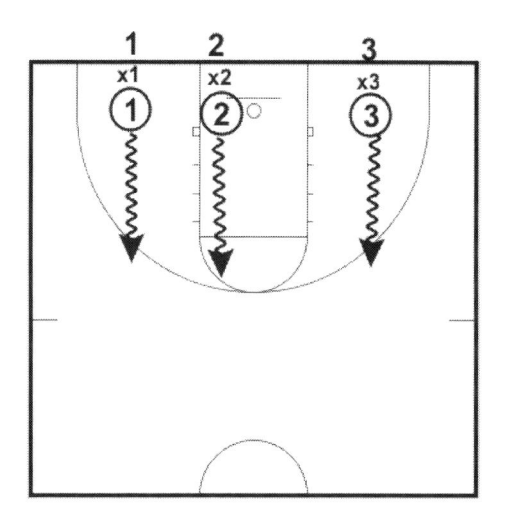

Diagram A

The next sequence in fundamental lines is "live ball." Transition to this second sequence by verbally calling "live ball." The player with the ball in each group, at that time, passes the ball to the first player in line, follows the pass and closes-out on the ball.

Diagrams A and B depict how the live ball series works. The first player in line executes a two-inch up fake or pass fake and then executes a long, low, straight start step, either a direct drive or a crossover. The player is to travel as far as possible with two dribbles, jump stop and execute a rear turn (pivot) in triple threat position. The player then passes the ball to the next player in line using a weak hand pass.

The player receiving the pass steps to the pass to shorten the pass. A good measure for a player or coach to determine if this happens is for the receiving player to be out of bounds when the pass is made and to catch the ball inbounds. The receiver catches the ball in triple threat position with a low, wide, base of balance and support.

The passer follows the pass and executes a defensive closeout. The receiver then executes a live ball move and takes two dribbles, executes a rear turn and makes a weak hand pass back to the next player. The sequence continues until the players are told to progress to the next series.

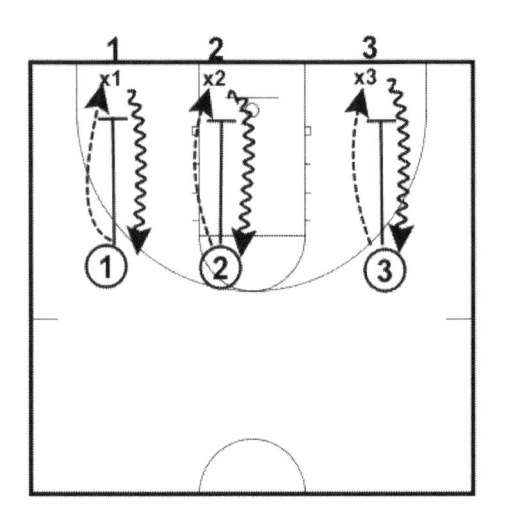

Diagram B

Number 71
Fundamental Lines – Pullback Crossover

Ideal Duration: 30 seconds to one minute total with players rotating after each repetition.

Grouping: Groups of three or four with one ball.

Frequency of Usage: Daily during preseason practice and one or two times a week as the season progresses. Can be used more than once in practice.

This drill teaches:

1) live ball dribble moves such as the direct drive or crossover dribble.
2) long, low, start steps.
3) execution of the pullback crossover.
4) the concept of "going somewhere with your dribble" due to the two dribble limit.
5) rear turns (pivots).
6) flick passing.
7) moving to meet (shortening) the pass.
8) jump catching into triple threat position.
9) use of the shot fake.
10) closeouts.

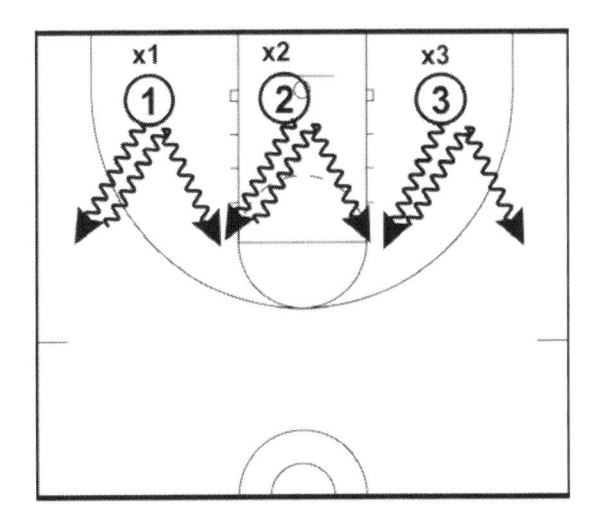

Diagram A

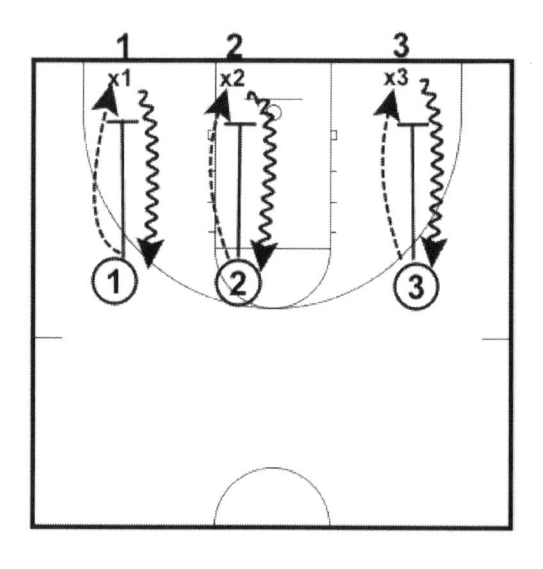

Diagram B

Diagram A depicts the drill with players using the same format as "live ball" but executing a pullback crossover dribble immediately after executing a live ball move.

Diagram B depicts the process of passing back to the next player following a rear turn and closing out for light defensive pressure for the ball handler to work against.

Number 72
Fundamental Lines – Pullback and Go

Ideal Duration: 30 seconds to one minute total with players rotating after each repetition.

Grouping: Groups of three or four with one ball.

Frequency of Usage: Daily during preseason practice and one or two times a week as the season progresses. Can be used more than once in practice.

This drill teaches:

1) live ball dribble moves such as the direct drive or crossover dribble.
2) long, low, start steps.
3) execution of the pullback and go.
4) the concept of "going somewhere with your dribble" due to the two dribble limit.
5) rear turns (pivots).
6) flick passing.
7) moving to meet (shortening) the pass.
8) jump catching into triple threat position.
   9) use of the shot fake.
   10) closeouts.

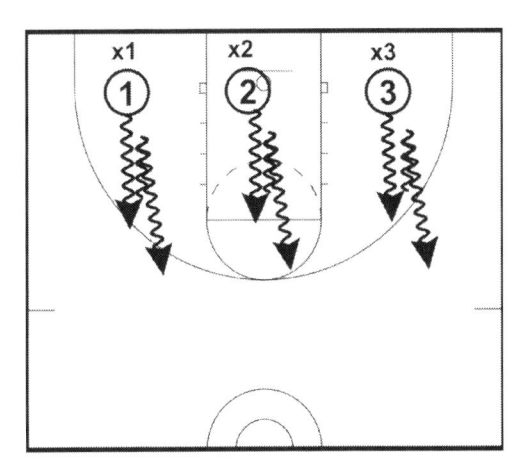

Diagram A

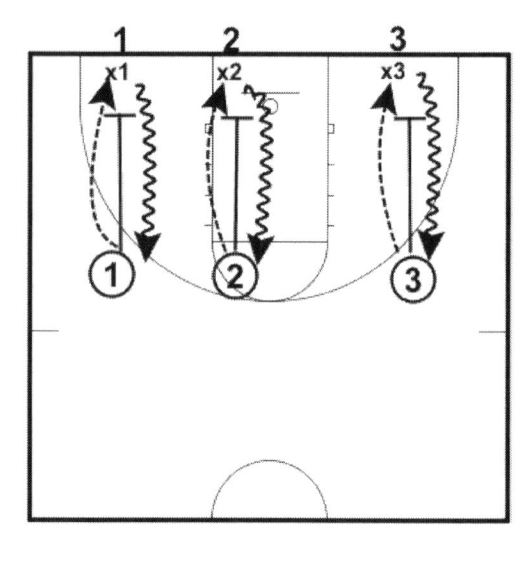

[Diagram B]

Diagram B

Diagram A depicts the drill with players using the same format as "live ball" but executing a pullback and go dribble immediately after executing a live ball move.

Diagram B depicts the process of passing back to the next player following a rear turn and closing out for light defensive pressure for the ball handler to work against.

Number 73
Fundamental Lines – Flick Passing

Ideal Duration: 30 seconds to one minute total.

Grouping: Groups of three to four players with one ball.

Frequency of Usage: Daily during preseason practice and one or two times a week as the season progresses. Can be used more than once in practice.

This drill teaches:

1) flick passing.
2) all basic movement skills.
3) catching the ball with your eyes and hands.
4) communication.

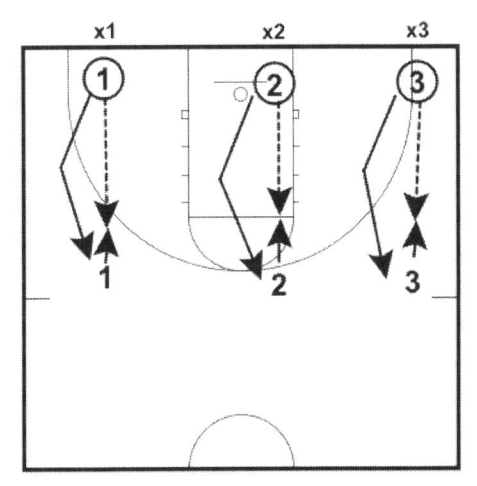

Diagram A

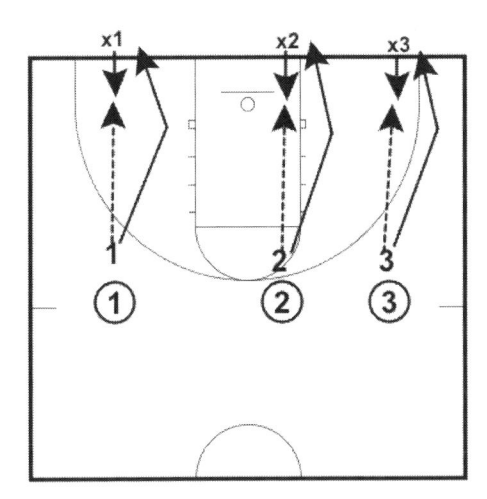

Diagram B

Diagram A depicts the start of the third, and most mentally challenging, phase of the fundamental lines series known as flick passing. Players transition from the live ball series by having a player execute the live ball move followed by two dribbles and pass the ball back to the first player on the baseline.

This sequence must always start with the ball in the group of players with at least two players. The player who just executed the live ball move remains 15 to 18 feet away and awaits a return pass to start the sequence.

Following the transition from one drill to the next, the drill starts with the player with the ball on the baseline passing to the single player opposite. In the examples shown in **Diagrams A and B** the players are using a right hand pass to pass away from the defense.

All groups must start with the same pass. The passer follows the pass with a v-cut and a jump stop and rear turn behind the player who just received the ball. By starting the drill with all players using the same hand to pass with, collisions and injuries will be avoided.

The receiver must take a step to meet, or shorten, the pass. The receiver then repeats the procedure of the passer who initiated the drill. The drill continues until the coach gives the order to change hands being passed with. The drill continues without stopping, players simply change passing hands and the side to which players execute their v-cut. The key rule for players to remember for purposes of safety is to cut to the side of the hand the player passed with.

Number 74
Fundamental Lines – Post Entry Pass

Ideal Duration: 30 seconds to one minute total with players rotating after each repetition.

Grouping: Groups of three or four players with one ball.

Frequency of Usage: Daily during preseason practice and one or two times a week as the season progresses.

This drill teaches:

1) dribble down entry passing into the low post.
2) live ball moves.
3) the concept of "going somewhere with your dribble."
4) rear turns and triple threat.
5) posting up.
6) directing traffic from the post.
7) receiving and chinning the ball in the low post.
8) perimeter post communication.

201 DRILLS FOR COACHING YOUTH BASKETBALL| 150

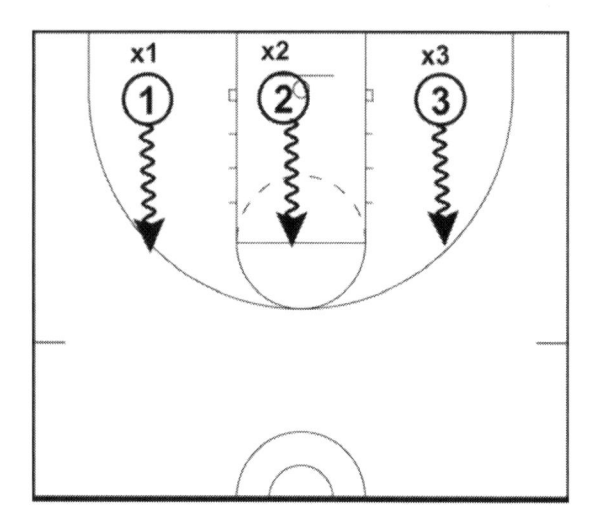

Diagram A

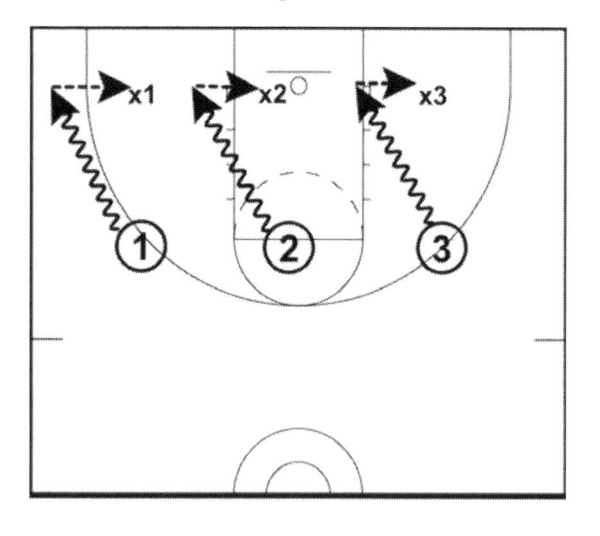

Diagram B

Diagram A depicts the initial live ball move with two dribbles (go somewhere with your dribble). The players execute dribble pick-ups, rear turns and then execute crossover dribbles in the same direction (previously indicated by the coach to avoid collisions).

The players dribble down to the level of the post player with two dribbles and make baseline entry passes to the post players who moved up in line and posted up (**Diagram B**). After making the pass the passers simply go the end of their group's line and the post players repeat the pattern.

UCLA Basic Movement Drills

UCLA Coach John Wooden thought the skills in these drills were so important he included them in every practice, regardless of the stage of the season. The skills covered in these drills include change of pace, v-cutting (change of direction), start steps, jump stops, pivots (turns), step lunges and can include defensive skills such as closeouts.

Why are these drills included in a book on shooting drills? Because without basic movement skills, shooter cannot get open, successfully receive a pass, square-up, pivot and an entire host of skills players must master in order to develop into a great shooter.

Number 75
Change of Pace

Ideal Duration: 30 seconds to one minute total.

Grouping: Mass grouping starting on the baseline and using the entire court.

Frequency of Usage: Daily usage all season.

This drill teaches:

1) the concept of changing pace.
2) basic movement skills while serving as a warm-up activity at the start of practice.

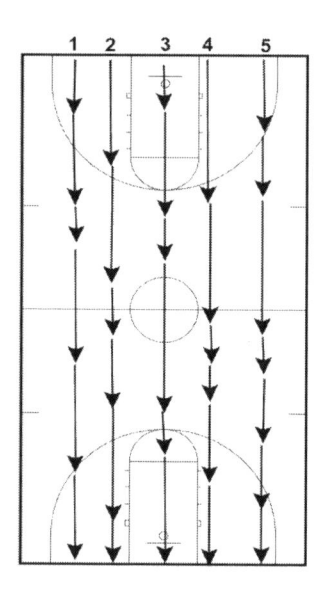

Diagram A

Diagram A depicts the basic alignment used for these drills. Lines of players can be formed across the baseline and the entire court utilized. If space is limited and large numbers of players must be accommodated, the lines can be moved to the sidelines instead. Groups of players as large as 20 to 25 can be accommodated on the baseline in most gyms.

Each set of skills should be executed twice, meaning the players should make a trip down the court and back. *This is an excellent drill to use immediately at the start of practice to warm the muscles prior to stretching.*

Diagram A also shows players executing "change of pace." Change of pace is a concept that actually requires a good deal of practice. Standing still, jogging, accelerating, decelerating and sprinting are all components of changing pace.

Basketball players must master this simple, but not always easy, skill in order to be effective on offense. A key coaching point is to remind players this drill is neither a contest nor a race and standing still is one of the things they must do when executing this drill.

Number 76
V-Cuts

Ideal Duration: 30 seconds to one minute total.

Grouping: Mass grouping starting on the baseline and using the entire court.

Frequency of Usage: Daily usage for the duration of the season.

This drill teaches:

1) change of pace and change of direction.
2) the habit of using hand signals to communicate.
3) the habit of raising both hands to catch a pass when accelerating out of a v-cut.
4) basic movement skills while also serving as a warm-up.

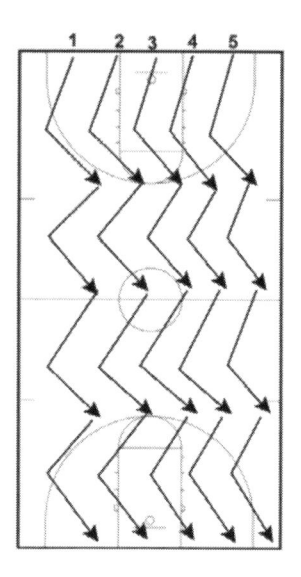

Diagram A

Diagram A depicts the players executing v-cuts en masse. Note, all of the players start by going to their right. This is to prevent injuries due to collision.

Players enter the v-cut (change of direction) moving slowly, plant the foot opposite the direction they intend to cut towards, lower their hips, explode in the opposite direction and quickly raise their hands to provide an appropriate hand target for the passer. If players do not master this skill, they will not be able to properly utilize screens to get open in any offense.

Players move on their own, v-cutting as they move down the court. The next line starts when the preceding line is about 15 feet down the court. Players must "cover distance," meaning moving horizontally at least 15 to 17 feet, and the cut must be at an angle, not a curve.

If the player does not cover 15 to 17 feet horizontally, the defense will have an easy time recovering and denying the cutter the ball. Cutting with a curve and not an angle does not produce a sharp, defined change in direction. This poor technique will also allow a defender to make an easy recover and deny a pass to an offensive player..

Number 77
Starts/Stops/Turns

Ideal Duration: 30 seconds to one minute total.

Grouping: Mass grouping starting on the baseline and using the entire court.

Frequency of Usage: Daily usage for the duration of the season.

This drill teaches:

1) start steps which are used for direct drives, crossovers, stepping to pass the ball and stepping to meet the ball when receiving.
2) jump stops in triple threat position.
3) the basics of the four types of pivots.

Start steps, jump stops (stops) and turns (pivots) are practiced as the last drill in the movement drill series and are depicted in **Diagram A**. Players execute a long, low start step from a triple threat stance. Players may execute either a direct drive or a crossover step as indicated by the coach or simply decide for themselves which to practice.

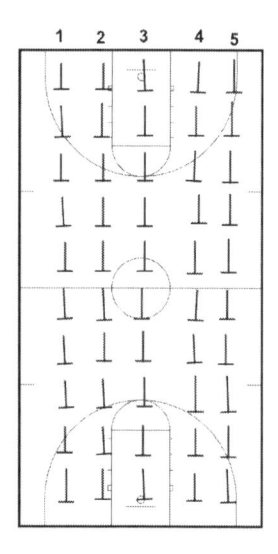

Diagram A

Players execute a hop off the foot used to make the long, low start step. Players then execute a jump stop off the hop, making certain the hop is neither overly long or high and both feet come in contact with the court at the same time, allowing for either foot to be used as a pivot foot. Players land softly and in a triple threat stance.

After landing, the player executes a turn or pivot. There are two basic types of turns that can be executed on either foot. A front turn, or pivot, is a turn made towards the front of the player. A rear turn is made towards the rear of the player. Turns can either be left or right footed.

A turn is executed by lifting the heel of the foot to be pivoted on. At the same time the player shifts slightly more weight to the pivot foot and uses the ball of the foot as the pivot point. The opposite leg is "whipped" around, providing the momentum to complete a 180-degree turn. The player must stay low through out the entire turn.

The key to this is for players to maintain a low, wide base while turning and to keep their head centered between the knees and the chin level. Standing up during a pivot is the worst mistake a player can make in executing a pivot as the player will turn slower and lose balance, requiring more time as the player returns to a good triple threat stance with a wide, low base of body support.

Players move down the court executing long, low start steps, jump-stops followed by turns. Of all the movement skills, this series is the most important. Once the preceding group has made two sets of starts, stops and turns the next group may begin.

Number 78
Step Lunges

Ideal Duration: 30 seconds to one minute total.

Grouping: Mass grouping starting on the baseline and using the entire court.

Frequency of Usage: Daily usage for the duration of the season.

This drill teaches:

1) long, low start steps.
2) body balance.
3) develops upper body strength.
4) basic body movement skills while serving as a daily warm-up.

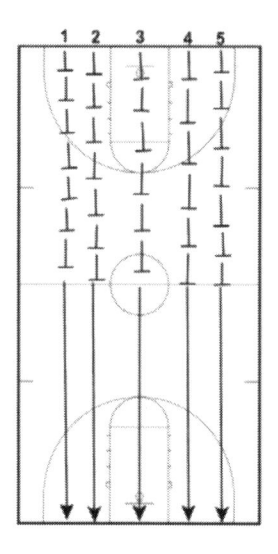

Diagram A

Diagram A depicts players executing step lunges. While not a skill that will be used during a game, step lunges emphasize long, low steps and help players develop balance, flexibility and the long low and straight step required for either a direct drive or a crossover move.

Players should have their hands up, palms out, elbows are extensions of their shoulders and the backs of the player's hands should be visible. This further enhances balance and helps to develop the proper hand positioning when a player is posting up. Once the players reach half court they jog to the other end of the court.

Number 79
Backdoor Cuts

Ideal Duration: 30 seconds to one minute total.

Grouping: Mass grouping starting on the baseline and using the entire court.

Frequency of Usage: Daily usage for the duration of the season.

This drill teaches:

1) proper execution of a backdoor cut.
2) proper execution of a v-cut.
3) the use of hand signals to communicate.
4) proper use of change of pace combined with change of direction.
5) basic movement skills while serving as a daily warm-up.

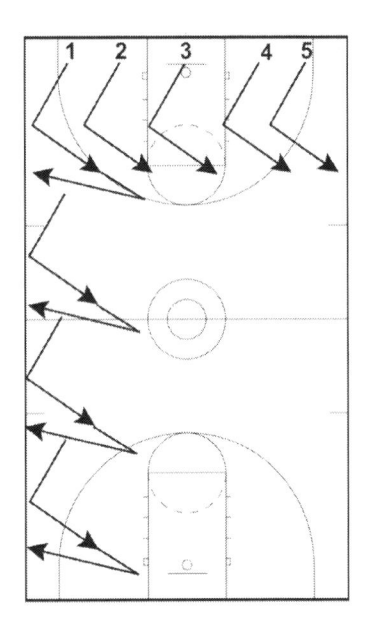

Diagram A

This drill is executed in a fashion very similar to how v-cut drill is executed. Again, please note all cutters cut to the right to start to prevent collisions.

Diagram A depicts all five players in the group starting but after the first v-cut players 2-5 have been omitted for purposes of clarity. After executing a v-cut the player slows and using a clinched fist to indicate a backdoor v-cut executes the movement, in slow and out fast.

As the player accelerates out of the backdoor v-cut the player must extend a hand to indicate the direction the player is cutting in while verbally calling for the ball.

Once all of the players have gone the drill is repeated. This time all of the players cut to their left on the first cut so the backdoor cuts in the opposite direction can be practiced.

Number 80
Circle-up Drill

Ideal Duration: Two minutes maximum duration.

Grouping/organization: Groups as large as 12 players at one goal will work. Use more than one goal for multiple groups when as many players as 24 or 36 total players must be accommodated. Can be executed with or without each player having a ball.

Frequency of Usage: Daily practice.

This drill teaches:

1) Use of the inside foot to face-up to the goal ready to shoot.
2) Footwork in preparing to shoot.
3) Balance when squaring up.
4) Dribble pick-up when squaring up to shoot.
5) Footwork for squaring up to shoot off the pass.

6) Teaches the use of both the left and right foot to square up for a shot.

Diagram A depicts the initial alignment for the players. In this example the players do not have a ball. The coach indicates the direction the players are to walk or run in (there will be collisions if this is not done). On the first whistle the players walk or run in the indicated direction.

On the second whistle, the players plant the heel of their inside foot with the toe of that foot turned in to face the goal. The players then pivot on that foot and square up facing the goal in triple threat position, ready to shoot the ball.

Some key elements for each player to check their feet to determine if they are correctly squared up, was all movement stopped so there will be no drifting when the shot is taken and are the knees bent adequately to shoot with the shooter's head centered between the knees (**Diagram B**).

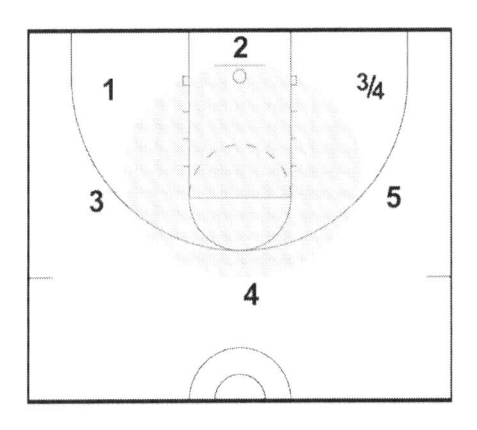

Diagram A

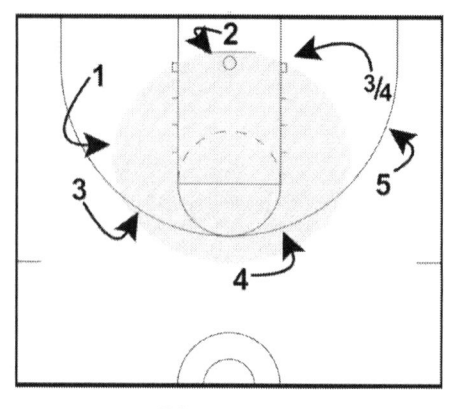

Diagram B

CHAPTER EIGHT

Basic Ball Handling Drills for Point Guards and Perimeter Players

Number 81
Mass Ball Handling

Ideal Duration: Two –eight minutes maximum duration.

Grouping/organization: Groups as large as 25 players on one half court will work. Ideally each player will have a ball. If this is not feasible have players work in pairs and rotate use of the ball every thirty seconds.

Frequency of Usage: Daily practice or as needed. Can be used as part of the daily warm-up process.

This drill teaches:

1) basic dribbling skills (power, control, push-pull and crossover dribble)
2) basic dribbling stance (head up, chin level, arm bar, straight back, head centered, feed hip width apart, knees bent).
3) develops the ability to dribble without watching the ball.

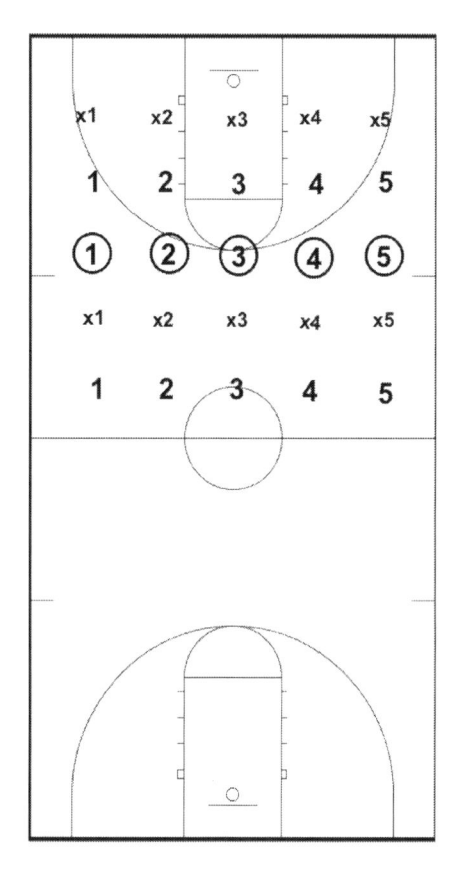

Diagram One

The formation of players shown in **Diagram One** depicts a formation to use for basic ball handling drills. Each player can have a ball or pairs of players can share a ball. The coach has the players execute on command whatever stationary ball handling drills the coach wants performed.

Number 82
Two Ball Passing

Ideal Duration: Two minutes maximum duration.

Grouping/organization: Groups as large as 12 players at one goal will work. Use more than one goal for multiple groups when as many players as 24 or 36 total players must be accommodated. Can be executed with or without each player having a ball.

Frequency of Usage: Daily practice.

This drill teaches:

Two players face each other 12-15 feet apart, each with a ball. The players pass with their right hand to start the drill, "ripping the ball" to the right side to pass away from the defense. This is also to prevent the balls from striking each other during the drill. The players continue passing with the right hand until either they or the coach indicate a change to the left hand.

The passes must be quick, crisp, flat and right on the target. The players should pass as quickly as possible and catch the ball with their eyes while remaining in a triple threat stance. Also of importance is a long, low start step with each pass to put zip on the pass. The players must recover after each pass to keep their spacing.

Once players have obtained a level of skill with two ball passing, a third ball can be added to the drill to increase the challenge. All types of pass can be used in the drill, bounce passes, overhead passes and chest passes.

Number 83
Two Ball Dribbling

Ideal Duration: Two-five minutes maximum duration.

Grouping/organization: Can be used as a tool for any drill involving ball handling.

Frequency of Usage: Daily practice.

This drill teaches:

1) Develops excellent hand-eye coordination.
2) Forces the development of both hands while dribbling.
3) Dramatically increases the concentration of the ball handler.
4) Increases the difficulty of any ball handling drill.

Each player starts with two balls. The balls can be of different sizes, different materials and different levels of inflation. The player can dribble both balls in a stationary position with knees bent and work to walking then running while dribbling both balls.

Every type of dribble should be worked on. The most difficult skill players can work on is two dribble the ball in rhythm and then out of rhythm. Also difficult to perform is to dribble one ball waist high with the knees bent and dribble the other ball below the knees.

Number 84
Back to Passer

Ideal Duration: Two minutes maximum duration.

Grouping/organization: Partners with a ball. Spread out in as wide an area as possible.

Frequency of Usage: Daily practice.

This drill teaches:

1) Hand-eye coordination.
2) Catching the ball with the eyes.
3) Using verbals to communicate a pass has been made.
4) Quickly locating a ball that has been passed.

This drill can be challenging. Players partner up and obtain a ball. The player without ball turns his or her back to the player with the ball.

The player with the ball passes the ball and then calls the name of the player whose back is turned. The player must spin around, locate the ball, step to shorten the pass, block and tuck to physically catch the ball while catching ball with the eyes. The drill continues for about one minute.

Number 85
Live Ball Dribble Move Shooting

Ideal Duration: Three-five minutes maximum duration.

Grouping/organization: Groups as large as 12 players at one goal will work. Use more than one goal for multiple groups when as many players as 24 or 36 total players must be accommodated. Can be executed with or without each player having a ball.

Frequency of Usage: Daily practice.

This drill teaches:

1) Dribbling skills in a variety of speeds and use of locations.
2) Teaches attacking the basket with the dribble and finishing the play with a lay-up.

Players are grouped in two lines at half court or in four lines at half court, using both goals to allow more players to have repetitions in a shorter amount of time.

The player starts their turn with a live ball move, a long, low start step used as a direct drive or a crossover step. Shot and pass fakes can be used as well. Just beyond the 3-point line the player executes a dribble move such as a hesitation move, an in-out dribble, a crossover dribble or a stutter step move.

The player then drives to finish with a lay-up or a short jump shot. The player retrieves his or her rebound and then dribbles out of bounds to the end of the opposite line.

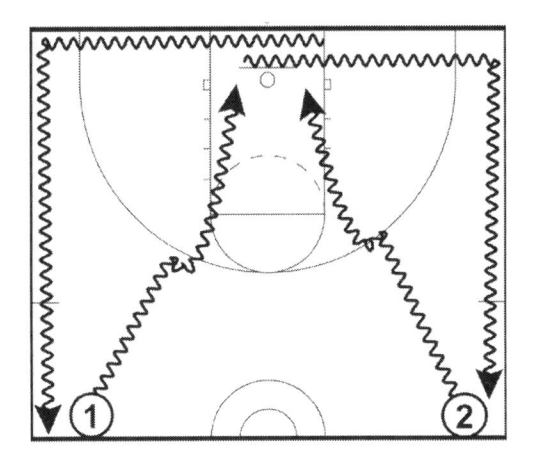

Live Ball Dribble Move Shooting

Number 86
Dribble Tag

Ideal Duration: Three-five minutes maximum duration.

Grouping/organization: Can accommodate large numbers of players. Each player must have a ball. Can be done as a two-ball dribble drill. Start with a well defined area and decrease the area as the drill progresses

Frequency of Usage: Daily practice.
This drill teaches:

1) Game-like ball handling skills.
2) Competition.
3) Players to keep their head up and to view the court and area around them.
4) Forces players to protect their dribble with their body and arm bar.

This drill is just plain fun. Every player has a ball and starts the game inside the designated area. Players are eliminated form the game when:

- a player loses control of their dribble
- picks their dribble up.
- has their ball stolen from them.
- steps out of the designated area.

Players may not pick up their dribble to deflect an opponent's ball nor may they commit a foul. As the number of players decreases the area players may dribble should be decreased as well. The game continues until there is a winner.

Number 87
3-to-1

This is not a drill but rather a teaching concept. Players should practice their weak hand dribbling three times as much as their dominant hand dribbling. When practicing, when the hand being used to dribble with does not matter, players should be required to use their weak hand.

CHAPTER NINE

Shooting Practice

Develop an Integrated System of Teaching of Skills, Concepts and Tactics

Like pieces of a puzzle, when each piece is in its place, the picture is complete. The same can be said of teaching the game of basketball. It does not matter what you the coach know, it matters what your players know and have mastered, the good basketball habits your players have established as a result of good teaching, hard work and repetition.

The best programs in any sport have an integrated system. Every concept taught to players fit both the overriding purpose of the program and the offensive and defensive systems. The terminology used fits like a glove and each drill teaches only concepts, skills and tactics that fit the overall grand scheme of the program. There is no wasted time in practice as a result and the very nature of the carefully crafted puzzle fitting together eliminates any possible doubt or indecision from creeping into the minds of the players during a game.

If the skill, concept, drill or tactic does not serve a clear purpose in the overall system, eliminate it. Less is more. Refine each item in the integrated system, insuring clarity and purpose.

Execution of Fundamentals At Game Speed Is Essential

Fundamentals are key for any phase of the game for a player, and a team, to be successful. This is especially true for the offensive phase of the game. Well executed offense will yield open shots, clear driving lanes to the goal and the ability to score large amounts of points in a short period of time, so does the opportunity to make bad passes, travel or mishandle a ball.

Players, and coaches, must understand this aspect of offensive basketball. The key to maximizing the positive aspects while negating or reducing the negative aspects is to mast the fundamentals at "game speed."

Practice Against the Clock

The ability to play with a sense of urgency for the duration of the game is essential. One of the best ways to build this habit so this becomes the norm and not a source of stress for players during a game is to practice against the clock.

Every possible drill that can be run for time and in some way made competitive should be modified to include the time element. Creating a game-like atmosphere in practice allows players to adjust to the pressure of always pushing the break and playing with a sense of urgency.

Keep Appropriate Records

It is a time consuming practice but you will never regret having the data on hand. This information can be used for motivational purposes, evaluating players, practice sessions, drill selection, starting assignments and if necessary, to deal with parents. Players love to look at their statistics, even if the numbers are based on practice sessions.

The single most important reason to keep these numbers handy and posted is accountability. Players do not do what their coaches tell them, they do what their coaches emphasize. Posting stats of performance in practice tells players in a subtle, and not so subtle way, that practice matters and they are always being evaluated for effort, improvement and performance.

Planning To Work With Your Shooters

Simply providing one standard workout for developing shooters would be counterproductive and against my approach to coaching and sharing information with other coaches.

Every program and every player is different. Different approaches may be required to fit the program and the player. In fact, over the course of the many years spent in developing shooters, my approach to developmental workouts changed depending on the players available and the needs of the team for the coming season.

The first considerations in planning a workout program are developing individual shooting technique followed by shooting volume. How will players be guided in the process of developing shooting technique? How many shots do the players need to take in the off-season, pre-season and in-season?

Range Testing

The first step in the entire process should be an accurate range test. This will help the player and coach identify with a degree of accuracy the actual shooting range of the player and any identifiable flaws or tendencies in the player's shot.

Rules of Range Testing

Every player in the program should be range tested and a record of the results kept. This is a valuable tool for identifying areas of needed improvement, the actual range a player can shoot from with a degree of reliability and objective measure to be used to convince both the player and parent of what the player's actual shooting range and ability is.

The range test is a valuable motivational tool in the process of developing shooting ability. Players have an easily identifiable standard of achievement and a clear idea of what to work on in order to improve and be "green lighted" for an increased shooting range.

Players are not allowed to shoot beyond their established range in games and scrimmage situations unless specifically instructed to do so.

Players are allowed to shoot beyond their established range during shooting drills when instructed to do so in order to develop the range of their shot.

Players may re-test at designated times during the course of the season. Any player who is able to improve his or her range test score is then "green lighted" to shoot from the improved distance.

Range Testing Procedure

Sample Range Test Chart

The range test chart shown is a sample. The numbered circles are shown in lieu of the paired dots to show distance. The first circle is 6-8 feet, the second circle as at 10-12 feet, the third at 15 feet and the fourth and final just beyond the 3-point line. Again, the range test chart shown is just a sample. The distances can be made shorter and more "layers" added to the test.

Once a range test has been decided upon, make a master range test chart and duplicate as many copies as needed. Be sure to add a chart to record the final field goal percentages the player achieved at each distance.

The test starts on the right side of the goal with the player taking two shots from each pair of dots. The player shoots all ten shots at that distance, moving in a semi-circle around the goal before moving back to the next distance in the test. If a player makes a shot, circle the dot.

If the player misses the shot, record the miss as long, short, left or right by making a tiny hash mark indicating how the shot was missed. This information can be invaluable in analyzing possible flaws in the player's shot.

For example, if the majority of hash indicators are on the top of the dot and slanted to the right, it is an indication the player misses long and to the right. Feedback can then be given to the player on how to correct the flaw in the shot.

In addition to learning of consistent flaws in a shooter's technique, it is also possible to determine where on the court the player is the most effective. If the player misses on consistently on the left side of the court but makes 70% or 80% of the shot attempts on the right, the coach now knows to run sets for that player on the right side of the court.

For a player to "pass" a distance in the range test, the player must make 60% of the shot attempts at that distance. Why 60%? The player is not tired, not being defended, is shooting under optimal shooting conditions and game slippage has to be allowed for.

Keep Records

Always keep copies of the player's range test results. This is a valuable source of information that can serve as a record of improvement or sadly, proof positive of a player's limitations in a parent coach meeting.

Know Your Players

The information gained in the range test can be invaluable for a coach when planning offense, inbounds plays, last second shot sets and player roles.

CHAPTER TEN

Warming Up The Shot: The Shooting Progression

Number 88
Shadow Shooting

Players partner up with a ball at a goal. More than one group may shoot at a goal. The ball is placed on the court and players take turn "shadow shooting" without a ball. The partner who is not shooting watches and makes suggestions about possible corrections in technique for their shooting partner. Two or three repetitions each are enough for daily practice. By shooting the ball to one another, the focus is on technique and not making the basket. Players are to hold a high, one-second follow through.

201 DRILLS FOR COACHING YOUTH BASKETBALL| 178

SIVILS | 179

Number 89
Shadow Shooting With a Ball

The second step in the shooting progression is for the players to pick up their ball and shoot the ball to one another. For their target, the players should focus on the piece of the court in between their partner's feet. The partner should allow the ball to strike the court if possible. Again, the partner's offer constructive criticism if needed while shadow shooting with a ball. The shooters should shoot the ball as high as the top of the backboard while performing this exercise. Like shadow shooting without a ball, two or three repetitions are sufficient for daily practice. Players are to hold a high, one-second follow through.

Number 90
Straight Line Shooting

The focus of this portion of the shooting progression is shooting the ball on a "shot line." While this can be done against a wall or any flat surface so the ball will rebound directly back to the shooter, the idea surface is the edge of the backboard as shown in the photograph above and to the right.

Players like the challenge of shooting the ball against the edge of the backboard. Failure to do so will result in the ball rebounding at an unusual angle, letting the player know the ball did not follow a straight shot line.

By not concentrating on "making the basket" the shooter focuses on keeping the ball straight and developing the techniques necessary to have a consistently straight shot line. Players are to hold a high, one-second follow through.

Number 91
Green Light Shooting

Players like to come into the gym and immediately begin launching 3-point shot attempts. If the first shot goes in the player often thinks, "this is going to be a good shooting day!" If the first shot is missed, the player will often think the opposite, "this is going to be a bad shooting day!"

The truth is the how the brain perceives things will go that day will often play a role in the success or failure of the shooter that practice or game.

The purpose of Green Light Shooting is to both warm up the shot while working on good shooting technique and to have immediate success shooting, helping the brain to think this session will be a successful one.

The first partner makes 20 shots from 2-3 feet from the goal. The shots should be clean swishes with no iron or backboard. The partner rebounds. After the first partner has made 20 shots, the second partner shoots.

Both shooters work their way around the goal in a semi-circle and then back to their starting point. For post players an exception can be made and all 20 of the shots are bank shots.

If only one drill in the entire shooting progression can be done on a daily basis in practice, this is the drill to use. Players still hold a high one-second follow through and coach each other while doing Green Light Shooting.

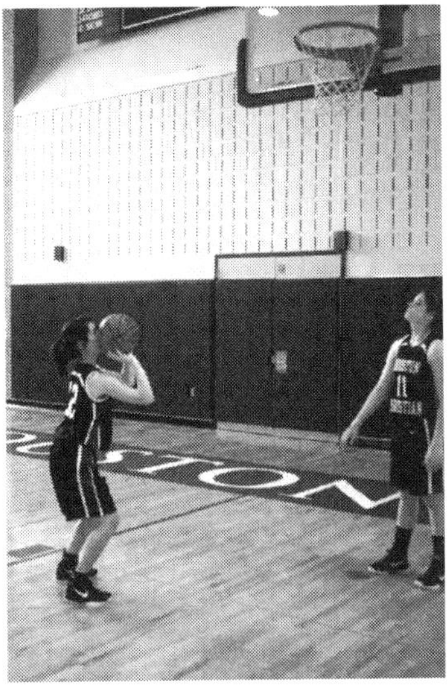

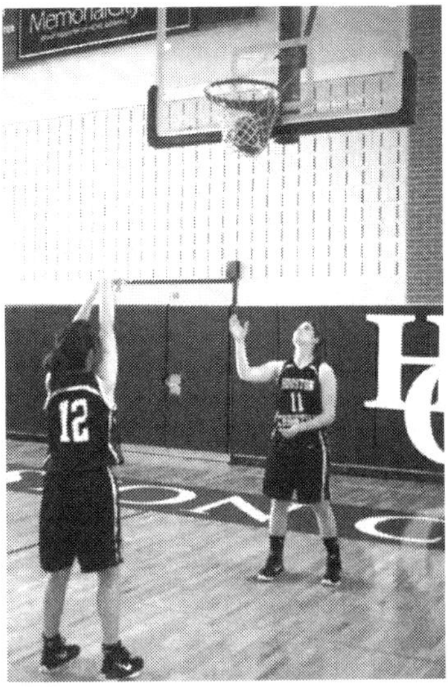
12
11

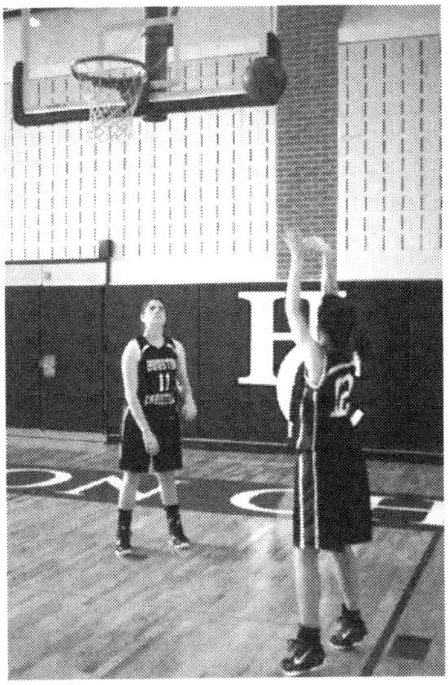
11
12

Number 92
Grooving the Shot

Grooving the shot is the most time consuming portion of the shooting progression. The first shooter takes a shot from three feet in front of the rim. If the shooter swishes the shot, makes it cleanly with no rim or backboard, the shooter takes one large step backwards.

If the shooter misses the shot, the shooter takes a step forward. If the shooter makes the shot, but not cleanly, the shooter takes another shot from the exact same spot.

The shooter works his or her way back in a straight line from the goal until he or she has reached his or her maximum range. The partner then repeats the process while the first shooter rebounds.

The ideal location is directly in front of the rim. If there are too many groups of shooters for each group to use this location, working from the baseline or at a 45-degree angle are fine, simply insist the shooters work in a straight line as they work their way to the maximum of their shooting range.

The Shooter is working to increase distance with each made/swished shot.

If the shooter misses, the shooter must move forward one step.

201 DRILLS FOR COACHING YOUTH BASKETBALL | 186

If the shooter makes the shot, but hits the rim or backboard, the shooter remains in the same location and shoots again.

CHAPTER ELEVEN

Lay-Up Drills

Free throws and lay-ups win games. It is that simple. Lay-ups should be practiced on a daily basis with an emphasis placed making 100 percent of all lay-ups attempted, regardless of whether or not a foul has been committed, contact made or the lay-up has been attempted at maximum speed. Lay-ups must be practiced from every possible angle a lay-up can be taken.

Number 93
One Bounce Lay-ups

Ideal Duration: Two minutes per player.

Grouping/organization: Can be done with partners and a ball, one player and ball or in groups.

Frequency of Usage: Daily practice early in the season. Can be used once a week after games start. Can be scheduled two or three times a practice to build to transition from a slow drill or activity to a more active or intense activity.

This drill teaches:

1) players how to coach themselves to correct mistakes in lay-up technique.
2) proper footwork for the lay-up in an easy to understand and correct method.
3) correct usage of the outside hand when shooting a lay-up.
4) how to use the backboard when shooting lay-ups.

This is the best teaching drill for lay-ups I have ever found! Each player can coach him or herself and make the needed corrections. The ultimate goal for each player is to be able to shoot a one-bounce lay-up from behind the 3-point line.

The player is allowed three steps and one bounce of the ball. The first step must always be with the inside foot. The ball is always dribbled and shot with the outside hand. Note, the words left and right are not used, only inside and outside. This makes the cognitive part of the exercise less complicated. The thought process is the
same with the only variable that changes is the side of the goal the lay-ups is being executed from.

If the player takes two or four steps, a mistake has been made in footwork. If the player takes two or more dribbles a mistake has been made in footwork or ball handling.

Note how far back the shooter has started in the photographs below. For beginning players, the starting distance should be as close as is required for the player to be able to successfully execute the lay-up. As the player becomes more skilled the distance should be increased until the player can execute a one-bounce lay-up starting from behind the 3-point line.

Note also the player chins the ball after the last dribble. This makes it extremely difficult for the defense to strip the ball without fouling and increases the likelihood the player will make the lay-up if fouled.

In the first photograph in the sequence the player has taken her first step with the inside foot and has used her one allotted dribble.

In the third photograph in the sequence the player is taking her second step and has chinned the ball, protecting it in the strongest place she can hold it. In the final photograph the shooter has jumped using her inside leg and is shooting the ball with her outside hand. The diagrams below depict the exact footwork. **Diagram A** depicts a more advanced player who is working to be able to make a one-bounce lay-up from behind the 3-point line. **Diagram B** depicts a player who is just learning how to shoot lay-ups.

Diagram A

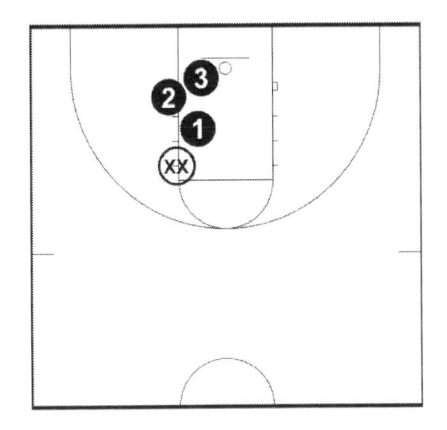

Diagram B

Number 94
One Bounce Power Lay-ups

Ideal Duration: Two minutes per player.

Grouping/organization: Can be done with partners and a ball, one player and ball or in groups.

Frequency of Usage: Daily practice early in the season. Can be used once a week after games start. Can be scheduled two or three times a practice to build to transition from a slow drill or activity to a more active or intense activity.

This drill teaches:

1) players how to execute a power lay-up.
2) proper footwork for the power lay-up.
3) correct usage of the outside hand when shooting a power lay-up.
4) how to use the backboard when shooting power lay-ups.
5) chinning the ball for a power shot.

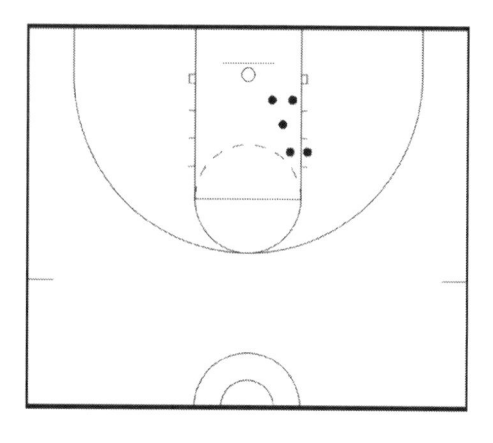

Diagram A

This drill, like one bounce lay-ups, is meant to teach players to coach themselves. As shown in **Diagram A**, the player starts as shown. The first step is always with the inside foot. The player dribbles the ball at the exact same time the inside foot is planted. The toe of the step foot should point at the goal.

The player immediately snaps the ball up to his/her chin with elbows out while executing a quick jump stop, landing on both feet at the same time in a balanced power stance with the chin level. The toes should be pointing at the baseline and the inside elbow should almost be under the net.

The shooter can power up immediately or shot fake before shooting. The shooter obtains his/her own rebound and hustles to the other side of the lane and repeats the drill again.

Number 95
X-Outs

Ideal Duration: Two minutes maximum for two players or one minute for one player.

Grouping/organization: Partners with a ball for two minutes. One player with a ball for one minute.

Frequency of Usage: Daily practice. Can be scheduled two or three times a practice to build to transition from a slow drill or activity to a more active or intense activity.

This drill teaches:

1) attacking the goal for a lay-up from the high post area with only one dribble.
2) "flashing" into the high post area to receive the ball and attacking the goal.
3) footwork for the lay-up.
4) scoring at the rim with contact if partners are used for the drill.

The drill begins with the shooter cutting to fill the high post as shown in **Diagram A.** The player can make a straight flash cut or use a v-cut as shown in **Diagram B.**

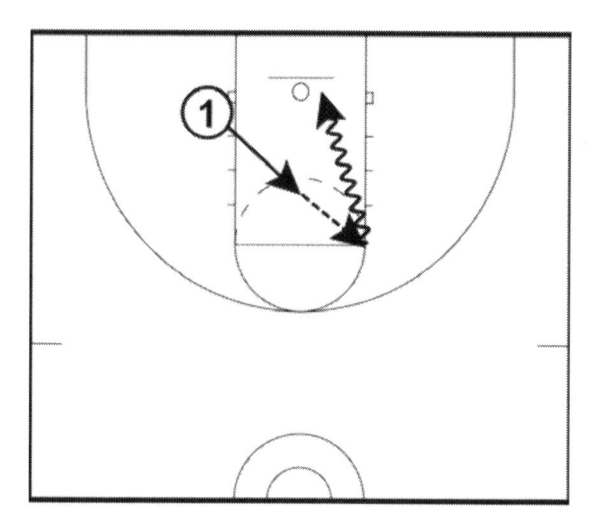

Diagram A

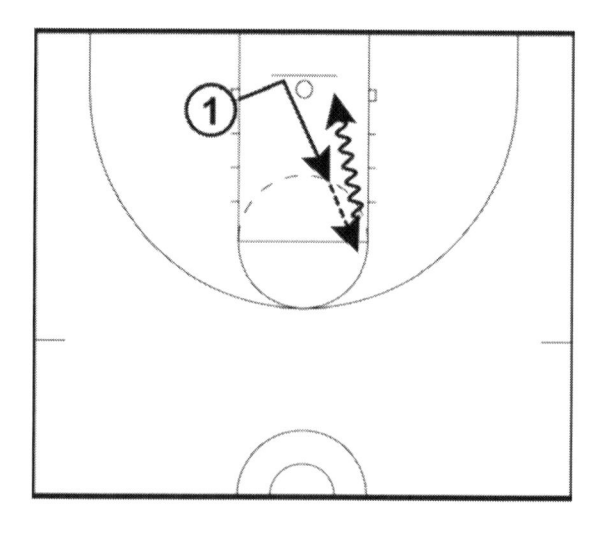

Diagram B

The player carries the ball during the first half of the cut and passes the ball to him/herself. The player must "shorten the pass" by moving assertively to meet the pass. The player catches the ball in the high post facing the sideline and exe cutes a rear turn pivot using the high foot, the foot away from the baseline, to execute the pivot.

The first step is directly to the goal with the toe of the foot pointing at the goal. This first step is also the first step of a "one bounce lay-up." The player obtains the rebound of the make or miss and changes sides of the lane and repeats the skill.

Players keep track of how many lay-ups made in one minute. Records should be kept of the number of makes and posted for the player to monitor his or her progress over the season. It also places an emphasis on the value of and importance of making lay-ups.

If two players are stationed at a goal the player who is waiting can make contact with the shooter to work on scoring lay-ups when fouled. The coach must be careful to provide instruction on the appropriate amount of contact to use to prevent injury or tempers from flaring. At the end of one minute the second player executes the drill.

Number 96
X-Crosses

Ideal Duration: Two minutes maximum for two players or one minute for one player.

Grouping/organization: Partners with a ball for two minutes. One player with a ball for one minute.

Frequency of Usage: Daily practice. Can be scheduled two or three times a practice to build to transition from a slow drill or activity to a more active or intense activity.

This drill teaches:

1) attacking the goal for a lay-up while driving across the lane with only one dribble.
2) "flashing" into the high post area to receive the ball and attacking the goal.
3) footwork for the lay-up.
4) scoring at the rim with contact if partners are used for the drill.
5) proper technique for shooting a lay-up when driving across the front of the rim.
6) flashing from different angles on the court into the high post area and then attacking the rim on the opposite side of the lane.
7) players to use their imagination in practicing their skills.

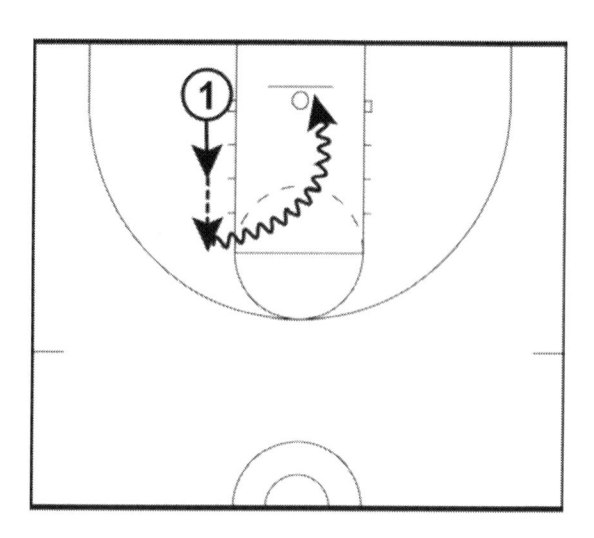

Diagram A

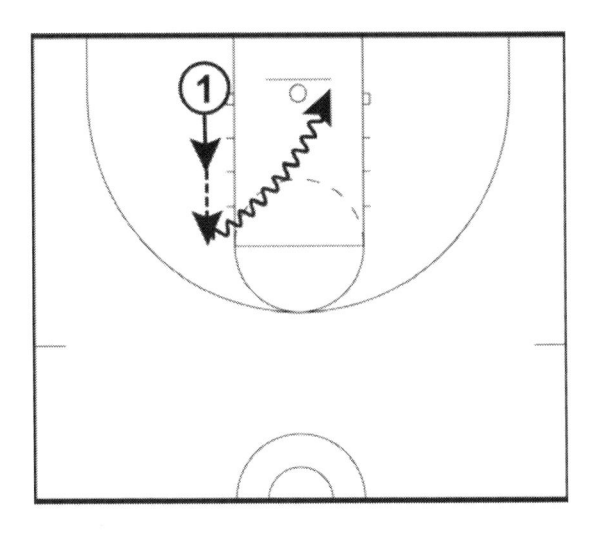

Diagram B

This drill, X-Across is very similar in organization and execution to the X-out drill. **Diagram A** depicts the start of the drill with the player flashing into the high post area from the ball side low post. The player could flash from the opposite side of the lane from the low post or high post.

Again, the player starts by carrying the ball and then passing the ball to him or herself by tossing the ball out with backspin. The player must "shorten the pass" by assertively moving to meet the pass. In this example the player has flashed up the lane to receive a pass from the top area of the court.

Of key importance in this drill is learning to "circle" the rim. Note in **Diagram A** the shooter has "circled the rim" and upon release of the shot all of the shooter's momentum is heading directly at the rim. In **Diagram B** the shooter has not "circled the rim" and all of the shooter's momentum is heading directly at the baseline at a 45-degree angle to the rim. This cause the shooter to have a tendency to miss the shot short, meaning the ball will hit the rim on the short side of the shot causing a miss.

The shooter must aim high and soft off the glass with the ball impacting the backboard just to the inside of the corner of the square painted on the glass or directly above the middle of the square. This can be a difficult shot to make due to the approach angle, making it essential players both circle the rim and use the glass correctly.

Number 97
Partner Lay-ups

Ideal Duration: Three minutes total with each player shooting for a maximum of 1.5 minutes.

Grouping/organization: Partners with a ball. Two groups, if careful, can go at the same goal.

Frequency of Usage: Daily practice. Can be scheduled two or three times a practice to build to transition from a slow drill or activity to a more active or intense activity. Can also be used to work on pull-up jump shots for the mid-range game.

This drill teaches:

1) Shooting lay-ups from all angles.
2) Shooting lay-ups while fatigued.
3) Driving from the 3-point line to the goal in one dribble.
4) Using the shot fake before driving.
5) Live ball moves.

Diagram A depicts the basic pattern of Partner Lay-ups. The shooter, #1, drives for a lay-up. #2 rebounds the lay-up while #1 cuts hard to the other side of the court. #1 receives the pass by meeting the pass and assuming the triple threat position behind the three-point line.

#1 then drives the basket again, repeating the process as depicted in **Diagram B**. **Diagram C** depicts how the shooter must vary the attack approach on each lay-up.

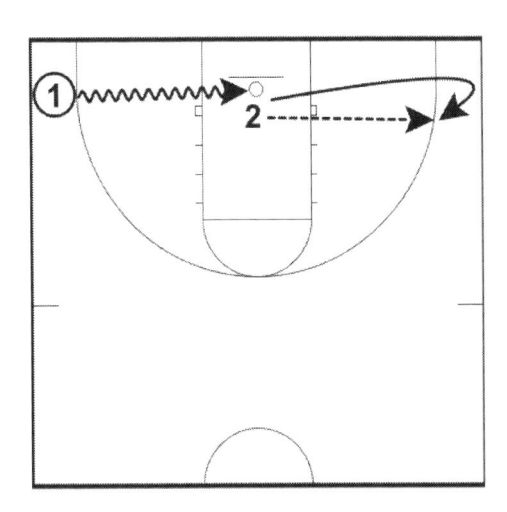

Diagram A

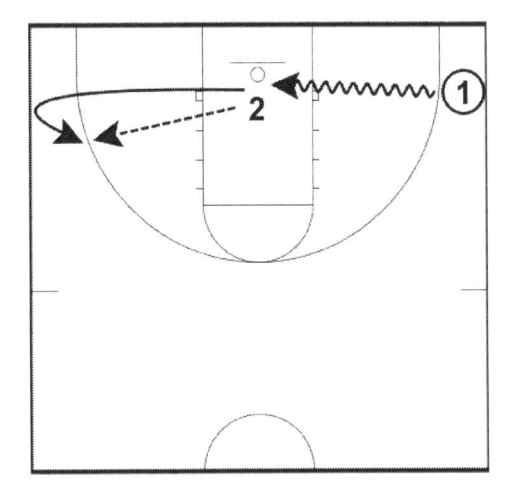

Diagram B

Key coaching points include the following: the shooter tries to execute the drive with traveling with only one dribble, the ball must be shot high soft off the glass and the drive must be initiated from the triple threat position with a long, low start step.

The players work against the clock, starting with one minute and working up to 1.5 minutes. The rebounder keeps track of the number of made lay-ups and missed lay-ups. A target number of lay-ups for the players to make should be set prior to the start of the drill.

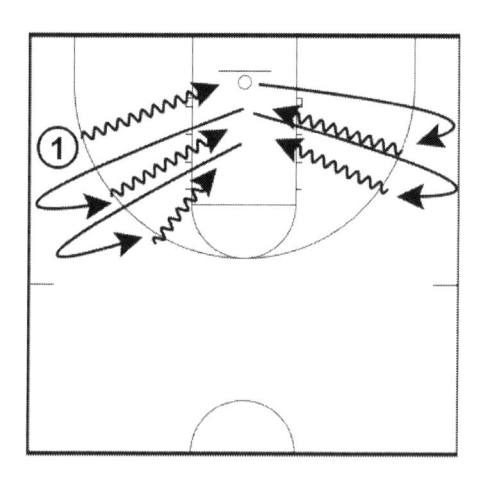

Diagram C

Number 98
Backdoor Lay-ups

Ideal Duration: 2-4 minutes total duration

Grouping/organization: 4 to 6 players per goal is ideal. Use as many goals as space allows. If a token defender is going to be added to the drill to teach recognition, 6-8 players per goal is ideal.

Frequency of usage: Depending on your offense and the importance of the backdoor cut to your execution, this drill can be used on a daily basis or once or twice a week.

This drill teaches:

1) Timing between the ball handler and the cutter.
2) Communication and recognition between the ball handler and the cutter as to when the backdoor cut will be utilized.
3) Recognition of over-play denial by the defense on the part of the cutter and the ball handler.
4) Passing down the lane line on backdoor passes (this allows the cutter to have room to catch the ball and shoot a short bank shot or take a lay-up depending on how the help defender plays the backdoor cut and pass).
5) Driving the backdoor to create the passing lane.
6) Conditioning
7) Catching the backdoor pass and finishing the play by scoring.
8) Proper offensive spacing.

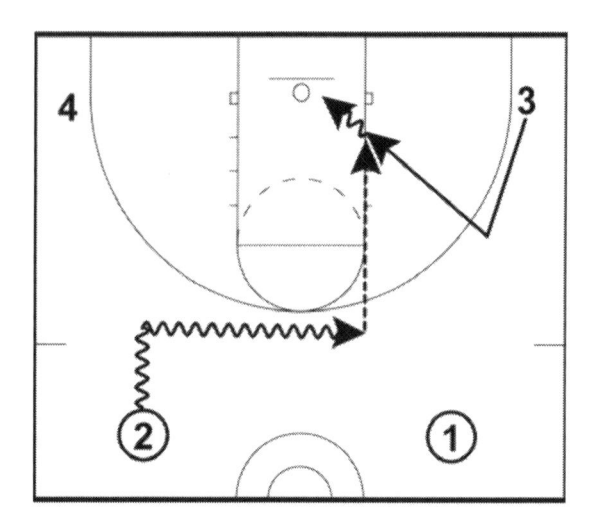

Diagram A

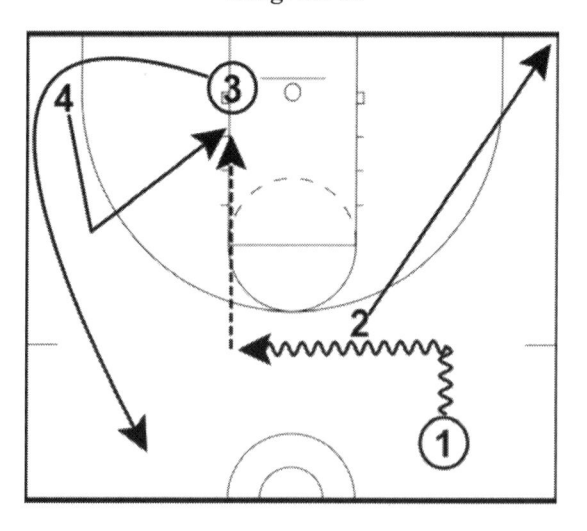

Diagram B

Number 99
Two Line Lay-ups

Ideal Duration: 2-4 minutes

Grouping/organization: Two student assistants or players as passers. Divide the post players into groups and organize as depicted in Diagram A.

Frequency of usage: Daily or as needed. This is a much more realistic drill for lay-ups than the "traditional" two line lay-ups drill.

This drill teaches:

1) cutting to get open in the high post.
2) receiving the ball.
3) proper footwork.
4) the habit of facing up and looking under the net.
5) driving to the goal with one dribble.
6) finishing at the rim.
7) both running and power lay-ups.
8) cross the lane lay-ups can be practiced as well.
9) excellent drill for teaching playing the high post.

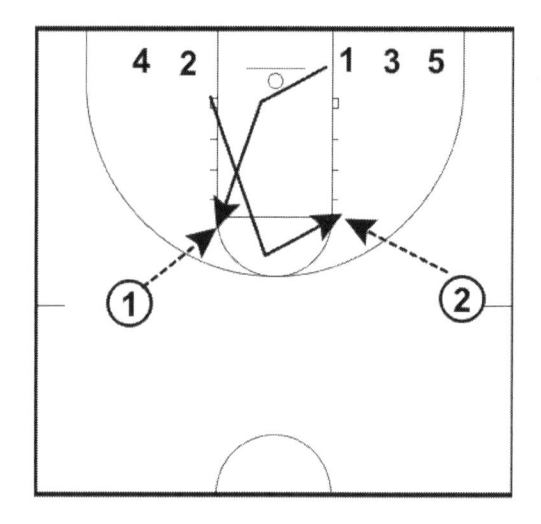

Diagram A

Unlike most versions of two line lay-ups, this drill is highly productive and efficient, working on several skills at the same time. **Diagram A** depicts how the drill is set-up. Coaches or players can act as the two passers.

The cutters make v-cuts to get open in the high post. Notice the different type of v-cut taken by each of the two cutters. It is important for safety reasons to utilize two different v-cuts in order to prevent injuries due to collisions.

NOTE, this is not the primary reason why two different v-cuts are used. The shooters are practicing getting open against a single defender.

In a game, if the defender is playing below the line of the ball (the imaginary line between the ball and the offensive player), the cutter must first take the defender down and then v-cut up towards the ball. If the defender is playing above the line of the ball, the cutter must first take the defender up and then cut under the defender.

In **Diagram A** #1 is working against a defender who is playing below the line of the ball and makes a down v-cut. #2 is working against a defender who is defending on or above the line of the ball and makes an up v-cut. The cutter must provide the correct hand target for the passer, call for the ball and meet the pass.

Upon receiving the ball the shooter can either execute a drop step to the goal and shoot a one-bounce lay-up or square up on the inside foot, shot fake, and drive for a lay-up. Be sure to alternate the v-cut used by each of the two lines. Both power lay-ups and running lay-ups can be practiced with this drill.

After making the lay-up the shooter rebounds the ball and passes back to the passer the shooter received the ball from as shown in **Diagram B**. The shooter then moves to the end of the opposite line.

To make the drill as efficient as possible, keep the groups at each goal to no more than 4 to 6 players with two passers if more than one goal is available for practice. Stress technique and execution.

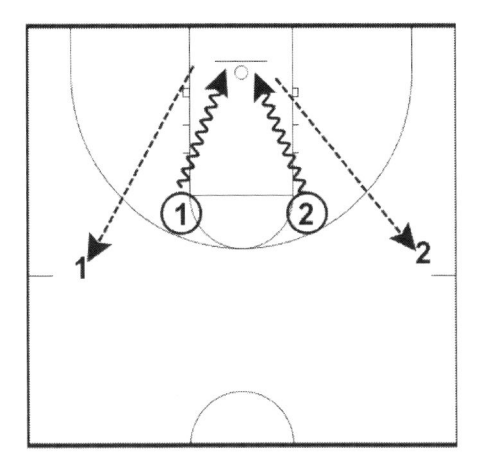

Diagram B

CHAPTER TWELVE

Free Throws

"65 percent of all points scored by the winning team in the final two minutes of a game are scored at the foul line."
- Pete Gillen -

Number 100
Plus Four — Minus Two

Ideal Duration: This drill can take up to 10 minutes to complete.

Grouping/organization: Ideally groups of no more than three players with a ball at a goal. The smaller the group, the quicker the drill will be completed.

Frequency of usage: Daily or as needed.

This drill teaches:

1) making free throws in a competitive situation.
2) the ability bounce back and concentrate after missing a free throw.

The drill is designed for each player to win or lose. Establish a reward for winning and a consequence for losing to make the drill have something at stake for the shooter.

Making a free throw earns a score of +1. Missing a free throw earns a score of -1. The objective is to win by scoring a +4. If a player produces a score of -2 at any point in the "game" the player loses.

The drill/game can be adapted to fit the level of skill of the shooter. Plus two – minus two is an example of an adaptation for a weaker shooter or a middle school shooter just learning the game. Plus eight – minus two would be an example of an advanced free throw shooter who needs to be challenged.

Players shoot two free throws and rotate. To make the game even more challenging, the two free throws can be treated as a one-and-one. If the player misses the first free throw, the player loses the opportunity to shoot the second free throw.

The drill can also be made more competitive by having the players at each goal compete to see who can reach +4 first. Devise a way to break ties if all of the shooters reach +4 during the same "rotation."

Number 101
Free Throw Swish

Ideal Duration: This drill can take up to 10 minutes to complete.

Grouping/organization: Groups of three players and a ball at most.

Frequency of usage: Daily or as needed. This is a great individual workout drill for free throw shooting.

This drill teaches:

1) concentration of technique.
2) concentration of swishing the free throw, not just making it.
3) creates a sense of urgency while practicing free throws.
4) is more challenging than most free throw shooting drills.

This drill works exactly like Plus 4 except for the way the drill is scored. Missing a free throw still results in a -1. Making a free throw but drawing contact with the rim or backboard, no matter how slight, is scored as a 0. In order to score a +1 the free throw must be swished!

Keep records of the player's scores for this drill.

Number 102
Team Free Throw Bonus Competition

Ideal Duration: 5-7 minutes or less.

Grouping/organization: The entire team participates. The players may shoot at one goal or be divided into groups and shoot at a number of goals.

Frequency of usage: Daily or as needed.

This drill teaches:

1) making the first free throw in a one-and-one.
2) increased concentration when shooting free throws.
3) the importance of each player's free throw attempts to the overall team success.

Each team member shoots a one-and-one free throw. In order to shoot the second free throw, the player must make the first free throw attempt. The team must make a specified number of free throws as a group or suffer a negative consequence such as a pre-specified number of push-ups or sprints. For example, if a twelve player team is required to shoot 75% as a group, the players would need to make 18 out of 24 free throws.

Number 103
80% Free Throw Shooting

Ideal Duration: 2 to 4 minutes.

Grouping/organization: Groups of three players and a ball or less.

Frequency of usage: Daily or as needed.

This drill teaches:

1) to focus on technique and not results (making the shot).
2) building good technique habits.
3) players to correct their own shooting flaws or mistakes.
4) players to be able to coach their teammates in regard to shooting technique.

This drill will seem odd due to the fact the objective is NOT to make free throws. Instead the focus is purely on technique.

When players focus only on making a free throw and not shooting technique, bad habits can form and existing poor habits cannot be broken, or at best are difficult to change.

80% Free Throw Shooting also teaches players WHAT to focus on when shooting a free throw (all free throws should be treated as high stakes, pressure free throws). Sport psychologists have found by focusing on technique and not making the free throw, shooters experience more success in actually making free throws, particularly so-called "clutch" or "pressure" free throws.

The coach designates one aspect of the free throw shot. For example, keeping the ball straight (shot line). It is perfectly acceptable to miss the free throw long or short. It is also acceptable to make the free throw. The goal is for the free throw attempt to be perfectly straight 80% of the time.

What is NOT acceptable is to miss left or right or to make the free throw but with a shot line that was not straight.

Like any other drill involving free throws, keep records. Have players shoot a total of 10 free throws. If the shooter has a partner, the partner can judge if the designated element of technique as correct. If not, the shooter must do this on his/her own.

Number 104
Daily Shooting for 75%

Ideal Duration: 2-3 minutes

Grouping/organization: Groups of 2 or 3 players and a ball at each basket. Groups may be larger if necessary.

Frequency of usage: Daily all season.

This drill teaches:

1) the value of each individual free throw.
2) the importance of each free taken over the course of a game.

Each player in the group is allowed to shoot two free throws and then rotate. Each player shoots two free throws twice for a total of four free throws.

The player then tells a student assistant coach his/her total for the day. That total is recorded and posted each day. The goal for all players is to make 75% of their free throws. This translates into making 3 out of the 4 free throws attempted.

Players no longer have the advantage of shooting 10 or 25 free throws and getting in a shooting groove. Each individual free throw really counts!

Not only should each daily total be charted, but a continuous graph showing the average of the player over time must be maintained and posted. This simple and quick drill really drives home just how important each individual free throw really is in determining the outcome of a game.

A variation of this drill, which should be done daily, is to have the players shoot one-and-one instead of two free throws. If the player misses the first free throw, the player does not get to shoot the second free throw, automatically guaranteeing the best possible free throw percentage for the day is a mere 50% (assuming the player makes the other two free throws).

Number 105
Situational Free Throws

Ideal Duration: 30 seconds to 1 minute.

Grouping/organization: line up to shot a free throw in a game situation. Explain time, score and scenario before the designated shooter shoots the free throw.

Frequency of usage: daily and throughout practice. Insert this drill at random times during practice, either mid-drill or in between drills.

This drill teaches:

1) shooting free throws under game-like conditions.
2) shooting free throws under pressure and requires players think about tactics and strategy following the free throw attempt.
3) preparation for real game situations.
4) adaptability.

Simply call a foul, even if it is made up, in the middle of a drill or in between drills and have the players immediately line up for a free throw.

Designate the shooter and give a 10-12 second description of time, score and scenario. The shooter must make (or miss) the free throws. Be sure to make clear if the free throw is a one-and-one, two shot foul or one shot foul.

This is a great drill for practicing a wide range of game situations such as breaking a press, setting a press, protecting a late game lead, making key free throws in a close game, etc.

Number 106
Free Throw Challenge

Ideal Duration: 3-5 minutes a day

Grouping/organization: Partners with a basketball.

Frequency of usage: Daily for the duration of the challenge series.

This drill teaches:

1) shooting free throws in a competitive situation.
2) competition.
3) free throw shooting.
4) focusing on technique rather than outcome (this is how you win)

This drill is really a traditional "ladder tournament." The drill runs over a pre-determined and announced number of days. Players are paired up for the first day and all the pairings are posted. The goal of the competition is to hold the number one spot on the rankings at the end of the tournament/drill.

Each day players compete within each pairing by shooting a predetermined set of numbers (5 or 10 free throws). The winner advances and "moves up" the challenge list and the loser moves down. Each day the new pairings of players compete with winners and losers again moving up and down the list.

A tie breaking procedure will need to be determined. It can be as simple as sudden death. The first player to miss a free throw in the event of a tie loses.

Make a big deal out of this event, keep records of past winners and have some sort of prize for the winner. Over time this drill will take on some meaning for the players. It is also important to have a consequence and a reward for that specific days winners and losers that goes beyond moving up or moving down the list.

Number 107
Free Throw League

Ideal Duration: 3-8 minutes a day depending on time of the year.

Grouping/organization: Depending on your total number of players available, create teams of 4 to 5 players. Try to make the teams balanced if possible. Each team only lasts the duration of the league and then new teams will be formed.

Frequency of usage: Daily for the duration of the league. Great for both in-season and off-season practice.

This drill teaches:

1) the value of each free throw to the entire team's effort.
2) competing as a team.
3) free throw shooting in a competitive environment.

This is a league competition. The champion will not be the best individual free throw shooter, but the best free throw shooting TEAM! Every day each team shoots and records the required number of free throws. Players report the number of made free throws out of the required number of attempts.

The league champion can be determined in a variety of ways. Each days free throws made total can be added up and the daily rankings are determined by which team has made the most free throws overall.

Another way is to pit teams against each other in head-to-head competition. Score the competition like the sport of ice hockey. The winning team receives two points in the standings. The losing team receives zero points and in the case of a tie in "regulation," after the tie has been broken, the winning team receives two points and the losing team receives one point. Standings are based on point totals derived from direct, daily team competition.

I prefer the second method. It introduces more competition and players are always shooting for something. Achieving a tie and "going into overtime" means at least one point can be earned in the standings.

Number 108
Shoot Two (or One or Three)

Ideal Duration: 1-2 minutes

Grouping/organization: Groups of three, or smaller, and a ball at a goal.

Frequency of usage: Daily or as needed.

This drill teaches:

1) shooting free throws in a game-like situation.

Stop practice in the middle of a drill or between drills and give your players 10 seconds or less to group themselves with a ball at a goal. Tell them to shoot two free throws, one free throw or three free throws. You can also tell them to shoot a one-and-one. If they miss the first they do not get to shoot the second. Record the results and add up the total for the team. The players as a group must make a pre-designated number.

By shooting in these seemingly random combinations, you are creating a game-like scenario. Players practice free throws by shooting a large volume at one time or two at a time but in rotations. Seldom do they actually practice shooting free throws like they would in a game, two at a time (two shot foul or a technical), one free throw (foul on a made basket) or three free throws (foul on a 3-point shot attempt).

Number 109
Scrimmage Free Throws

Ideal Duration: 30 seconds

Grouping/organization: Game situations – use your normal free throw alignments.

Frequency of usage: Anytime you scrimmage in practice.

This drill teaches:

1) game situations involving free throws.

Always have your weakest free throw shooters shoot the free throw. This is also a great way to start fast break drills or pressing drills.

Number 110
Make Three in a Row – Score 65

Ideal Duration: 5 minutes

Grouping/organization: Groups of three and a ball at each goal.

Frequency of usage: Daily or as needed.

This drill teaches:

1) free throw shooting.
2) the ability to make three free throws in a row.
3) group free throw responsibility.

Put five minutes on the clock. The goal is for the entire team to make 65 strings of 3 free throws in a row. Each player shoots free throws until the player either makes 3 in a row or misses a free throw.

If a player makes three in a row, the player shouts "3" and the "point" is recorded by a student assistant. If a player misses, the next shooter takes his/her place.

This great drill comes from Coach Don Meyer.

CHAPTER THIRTEEN

Developmental Shooting Drills

As I mentioned earlier, this book is NOT about how to shoot per se. It is not meant to be an instructional guide for a specific shooting system. The drills in this book are meant to be tools to teach the shooting system you, the coach, believe to be the best approach to shooting. Having said that, the developmental drills in this chapter are excellent tools to teach any system of shooting. Adapt these drills as necessary to fit the system you are teaching.

Number 111
Line Shooting

Ideal Duration: 2-4 Minutes

Grouping/organization: Ball and a partner on a line on the court.

Frequency of usage: Daily or as needed.

This drill teaches:

1) focus on correct shooting form (not on making or missing).

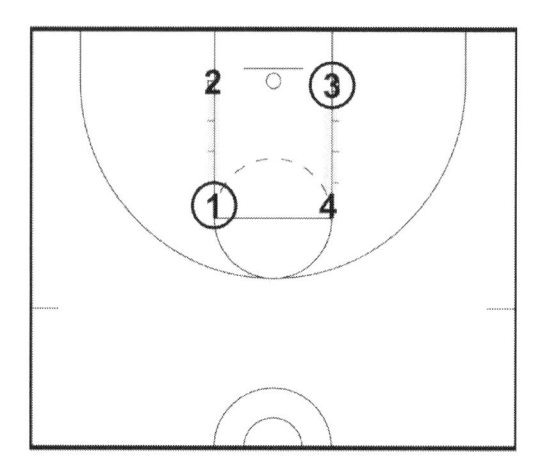

Diagram A

The purpose of this developmental drill is for players to learn correct technique. Players overwhelmingly focus on makes and misses. If they make a shot with poor technique, players think this is the method they should shoot with.

Line shooting takes the make or miss element out of shooting. Each set of players finds a line on the court. The players square themselves to the line and shoot the ball to their partner who lets the ball hit the court. The object is to hit the line dead center. If the ball hits the line it counts as a make. If the ball misses the line it counts as a miss.

For the first minute or so the players just shoot the ball back and forth to work on technique while coaching each other (teaching point: have your players hold a high, one second follow through on every shot, regardless of shooting system).

After a minute or two the competitive aspect of this drills starts. Have the players keep score and see how many makes each pair can make in one minute and record the results.

Number 112
Mass Shooting (Shadow)

Ideal Duration: 3-5 minutes

Grouping/organization: See **Diagram A**. Can be done with a ball and without a ball.

Frequency of usage: Daily early in the season or off-season then as needed.

This drill teaches:

1) shooting form.
2) players how to coach themselves and their teammates.

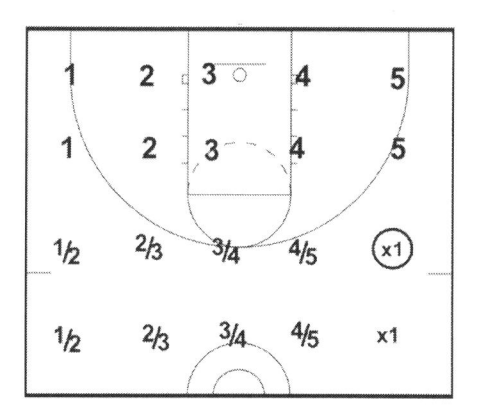

Diagram A

The focus of this drill is on form and technique. Players are spread out with partners as shown in Diagram A. This drill can be done with or without balls. Always start without balls. Simply have the partner who has the ball set it on the court.

The players face their partner and on command perform specific shooting skills and techniques en masse or one partner at a time with the other player providing verbal feedback to help their partner correct any mistakes. Executing the skills of shooting in this manner can be done slowly or at game speed. Whole-part method can be used as well.

After several minutes the ball can be picked up and the players shoot on command or on their own initiative. The ball should be allowed to hit the court and the shooters should hold a high one-second follow through to allow their teammate to see any flaws and to provide feedback.

Number 113
Dribble Pick-Ups

Ideal Duration: 2-5 minutes

Grouping/organization: In lines, or at goals, with each player in possession of a ball.

Frequency of usage: Daily or as needed. Great for off-season.

This drill teaches:

1) the proper technique (as determined by your shooting system of choice) to pick up the ball from a dribble and be able to shoot with correct form.

Each player takes one hard dribble with the dominant hand and snaps it up to the shooting pocket with hand placed correctly on the ball while taking a one-two step forward. Players can be organized in lines similar to the ones used in UCLA Drills and move down the court or they can be in lines at all six goals and work for short distances.

After working with the strong hand (dominant hand) players should repeat the process with their weak hand.

Number 114
Triple Threat Off the Pass

Ideal Duration: 2-4 minutes

Grouping/organization: Partners with a ball spread throughout the gym.

Frequency of usage: Daily or as needed. Great for off-season work.

This drill teaches:

1) preparing to shoot off the pass.
2) "shortening" the pass (meeting the pass by stepping to it).
3) proper timing for catching, footwork and shooting in rhythm.
4) catching in triple threat position.
5) player communication (visual and verbal) when passing and receiving.

Players spread out roughly 15 to 17 feet apart and pass the ball to each other. The passer calls the name of the receiver and the receiver calls for the ball. The receiver offers a shooting pocket as a target for the passer who focuses on accuracy of passing.

The receiver/shooter watches the ball all the way into the shooting pocket (catches the ball with his/her eyes) and executes a step plan to shorten the pass. Upon catching the ball the shooter must be in perfect triple threat position ready to shoot. The passer offers verbal feedback for corrections or to let the shooter know the skill was executed perfectly.

Number 115
One Hand Shooting (Groove Your Shot)

Ideal Duration: 1-3 minutes

Grouping/organization: Each player has a ball or can work with a partner.

Frequency of usage: Daily

This drill teaches:

1) basic shooting technique.
2) players how to correct flaws in their own shot.
3) players, if working with a partner, how to provide feedback to another shooter.
4) players to warm-up their shot.

This simple drill is a good way to practice technique and to warm-up a shot. The player does not use their balance hand, forcing the player to shoot with correct form. This drill should not be performed more than 5 feet from the goal and no closer than 3 feet from the goal.

The player makes five to seven shots from one spot and then moves in a semi-circle around the goal. The player holds a high one-second follow through on each shot.

Number 116
One Pass Shooting (Head On)

Ideal Duration: 2-4 minutes

Grouping/organization: Partners and a ball at a goal.

Frequency of usage: Daily or as needed. Excellent drill for off-season work as well.

This drill teaches:

1) shooting off the pass.
2) preparing to receive a pass and shoot.
3) shooting rhythm for shooting off a pass.
4) footwork for shooting off a pass.
5) shortening (meeting the pass by stepping to it) the pass.

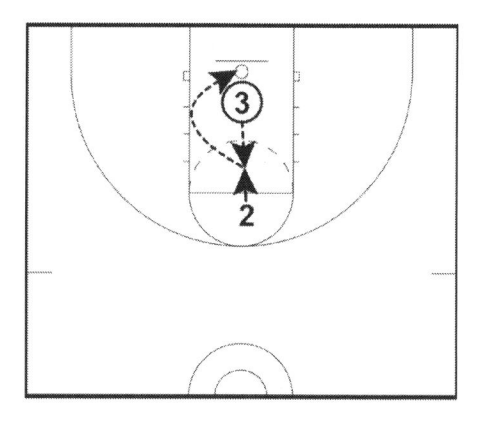

Diagram A

The passer stands directly under the goal with the shooter lined up as if preparing to shoot a free throw. The shooter calls for the ball and offers a shooting pocket as a target. The passer calls the shooter's name and passes directly to the shooting pocket.

The shooter uses a one-two step (or a jump stop if that is the desired technique), catches the ball in perfect triple threat, shoots in rhythm and holds a high, one-second follow through. The passer also acts as a rebounder. After five or six shots the players rotate roles.

Number 117
One Pass Shooting With ¼ Face-up

Ideal Duration: 2-4 minutes.

Grouping/organization: Partner's with a ball at a goal.

Frequency of usage: Daily or as needed. Excellent off-season drill.

This drill teaches:

1) shooting off the pass.
2) preparing to receive a pass and shoot.
3) shooting rhythm for shooting off a pass.
4) footwork for shooting off a pass.
5) shortening (meeting the pass by stepping to it) the pass.
6) squaring-up upon receiving the pass.

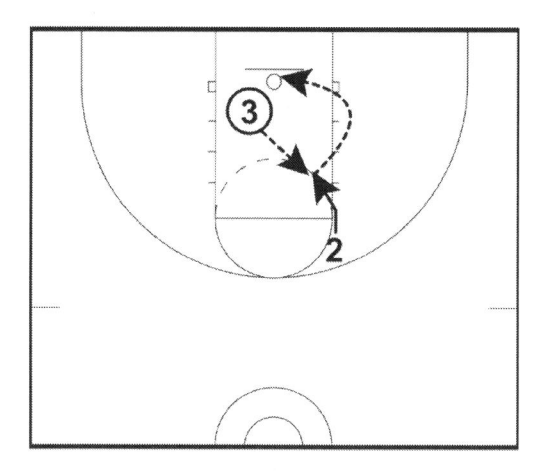

Diagram A

The passer stands directly under the goal with the shooter lined up as if preparing to shoot a free throw. The shooter calls for the ball and offers a shooting pocket as a target. The passer calls the shooter's name and passes directly to the shooting pocket.

The shooter uses a one-two step (or a jump stop if that is the desired technique) stepping with the inside foot first, catches the ball and steps with the second foot, squaring-up (facing-up) in perfect triple threat, shoots in rhythm and holds a high, one-second follow through. The passer also acts as a rebounder. After five or six shots the players rotate roles.

Number 118

One Pass Baseline Shooting With Face-up

Ideal Duration: 2-4 minutes.

Grouping/organization: Partner's with a ball at a goal.

Frequency of usage: Daily or as needed. Excellent off-season drill.

This drill teaches:

1) shooting off the pass.
2) preparing to receive a pass and shoot.
3) shooting rhythm for shooting off a pass.
4) footwork for shooting off a pass.
5) shortening (meeting the pass by stepping to it) the pass.
6) squaring-up upon receiving the pass.

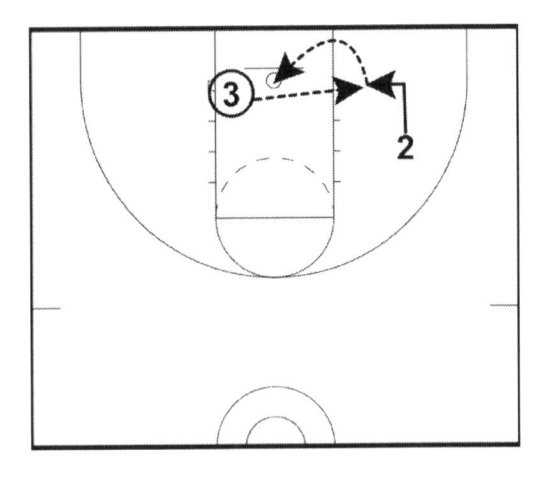

Diagram A

The passer stands directly under the goal with the shooter lined up as if preparing to shoot a free throw. The shooter calls for the ball and offers a shooting pocket as a target. The passer calls the shooter's name and passes directly to the shooting pocket.

The shooter uses a one-two step (or a jump stop if that is the desired technique) stepping with the inside foot first, catches the ball and steps with the second foot, squaring-up (facing-up) in perfect triple threat, shoots in rhythm and holds a high, one-second follow through. The passer also acts as a rebounder. After five or six shots the players rotate roles.

Number 119
One Bounce Shooting Head On

Ideal Duration: 2-4 minutes (more if a player is practicing alone)

Grouping/organization: Each player has a ball.

Frequency of usage: Daily or as needed.

This drill teaches:

1) shooting off the dribble.
2) technique for a dribble pick-up.
3) using either hand for a dribble pick-up into triple threat.

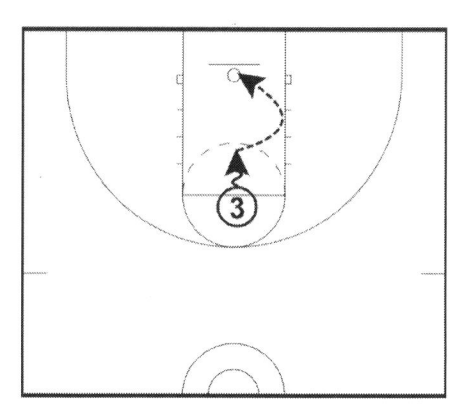

Diagram A

This drill can be done with a partner but is easily done with one player. The player lines up in a direct line with the free throw shooting spot. The player starts in a triple threat stance, takes one hard dribble while stepping with one foot. The ball and the step foot should contact the court at the same time. The player executes a dribble pick-up while taking the second step, finishing in perfect triple threat, shoots the shot in rhythm and holds a high, one-second follow through.

Number 120
One Bounce Shooting With ¼ Face-up

Ideal Duration: 2-4 minutes (more if a player is practicing alone)

Grouping/organization: Each player has a ball.

Frequency of usage: Daily or as needed.

This drill teaches:

1) shooting off the dribble.
2) technique for a dribble pick-up.
3) using either hand for a dribble pick-up into triple threat.
4) squaring-up (facing-up) off the dribble.

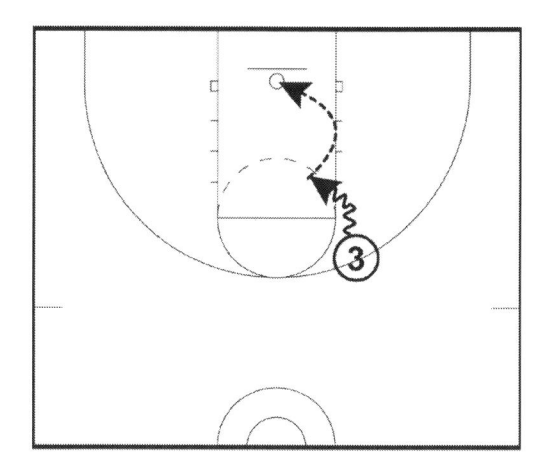

Diagram A

This drill can be done with a partner but is easily done with one player. The player lines up in a direct line with the free throw shooting spot. The player starts in a triple threat stance, takes one hard dribble while stepping with one foot. The heel of the step foot should come in contact with the court in such a way that the player's toes are pointing directly at the rim.

The ball and the step foot should contact the court at the same time. The player executes a dribble pick-up while taking the second step, squares-up (faces-up) finishing in perfect triple threat, shoots the shot in rhythm and holds a high, one-second follow through.

Number 121
One Bounce Baseline Shooting With Face-up

Ideal Duration: 2-4 minutes (more if a player is practicing alone)

Grouping/organization: Each player has a ball.

Frequency of usage: Daily or as needed.

This drill teaches:

1) shooting off the dribble.
2) technique for a dribble pick-up.
3) using either hand for a dribble pick-up into triple threat.
4) squaring-up (facing-up) off the dribble.

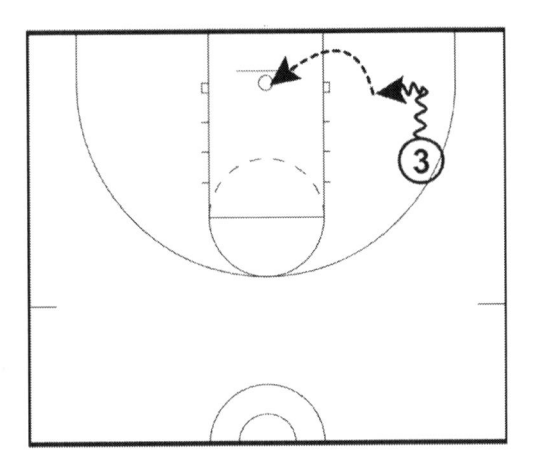

Diagram A

This drill can be done with a partner but is easily done with one player. The player lines up in a direct line with the free throw shooting spot.

The player starts in a triple threat stance, takes one hard dribble while stepping with one foot. The heel of the step foot should come in contact with the court in such a way that the player's toes are pointing directly at the rim.

The ball and the step foot should contact the court at the same time. The player executes a dribble pick-up while taking the second step, squares-up (faces-up) finishing in perfect triple threat, shoots the shot in rhythm and holds a high, one-second follow through.

Number 122
Bank Shot Range Shooting

Ideal Duration: 3-6 Minutes

Grouping/organization: Ball and a partner or single player with a ball.

Frequency of usage: Daily or as needed. Excellent drill for off-season work.

This drill teaches:

1) shooting technique and form.
2) shooting bank shots (off the backboard).

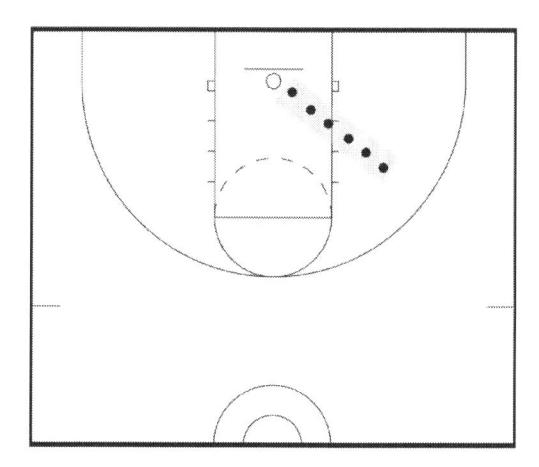

Diagram A

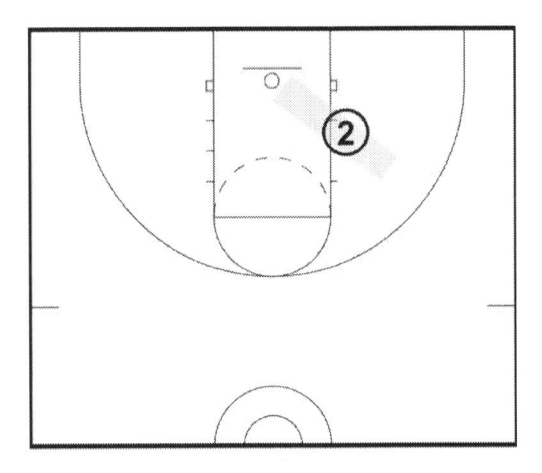

Diagram B

This drill is designed to help players learn to use the backboard when shooting any shot under 12 feet at an angle ranging from 45° to 30° to the backboard.

The player starts three feet from the rim and "kisses" the ball high and soft off the glass, using the top, ball side corner of the square on the backboard. After making five shots, the player takes one small step back and repeats the process until the player has reached a distance of 12 feet from the goal.

The drill can be done on one side on one day and the other side on the next practice session. The player can also return to the drill later in practice and repeat the drill on the other side of the rim.

Number 123
Footwork Jump Shooting

Ideal Duration: 3-5 minutes

Grouping/organization: Can be done in lines, as a single player, or as a mass group. Each player should have a ball.

Frequency of usage: Daily or as needed. Excellent off-season drill.

This drill teaches:

1) using foot fakes to create space for a shot.
2) being squared up and in triple threat with knees bent after the use of the six inch foot fake.
3) simple six inch foot fakes and recovery such as a:
- jab fake.
- direct drive fake.
- crossover fake.
- jab, recover, crossover fake.

Some coaches do not believe in the use of foot fakes to create space due to the fact so many players have trouble returning to perfect triple threat and being squared-up to shoot. This is certainly a concern.

This drill can be done with players in lines, in mass and on command or by an individual player. When done in lines or individually, the player can shoot the ball without dribbling after executing the foot fake and recovering properly.

When done in mass the players do not shoot the ball but rather focus on correctly performing the designated foot fake on command and then recovering properly.

Number 124
Shot Fake Shooting

Ideal Duration: 3-5 minutes

Grouping/organization: Can be done in lines, with a partner or individually.

Frequency of usage: Daily or as needed. Excellent off-season drill.

This drill teaches:

1) the use of the two-inch shot fake.
2) recovering to perfect triple threat after a shot fake.
3) not taking the bend out of the knees during a shot fake.
4) shooting after the shot fake.

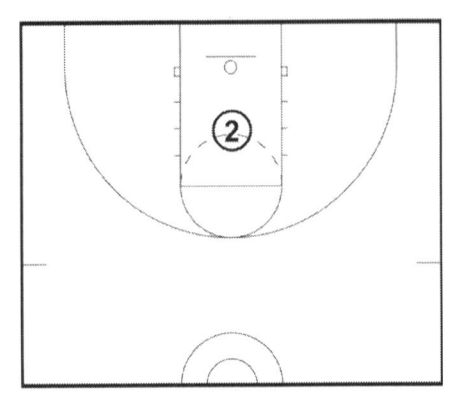

Diagram A

The player executes a two-inch shot fake without taking the bend out of the knees. The player then shoots a stationary jump shot. The player should work from 6 to 8 feet from the goal when performing this drill, shoot five shots and then relocate to shoot again.

Number 125
Count the Steps – Triple Attack

Ideal Duration: 2-4 minutes maximum. Once the player has mastered the footwork one minute is enough time.

Grouping/organization: Partners with a ball at a minimum. Using a student assistant or coach can allow groups of up to four or five players work efficiently.

Frequency of usage: Daily or as needed. Daily in the off-season to develop footwork for shooting.

This drill teaches:

1) precise footwork for perimeter players.
2) driving against the grain.
3) catching the ball ready to shoot.
4) the habit of using an exact number of steps each time for specific offensive cuts.
5) consistency in footwork.
6) 3-point shooting.
7) finishing at the goal when driving.

In addition to working on the 3-point shot, the focus of this drill is footwork. The so-called "triple cut" is a common cut used in many 3-point plays as well as motion oriented offenses. The shooters start with their inside foot directly under the rim facing the sideline. In the example shown in **Diagram A** the shooter is facing the left sideline.

The shooter makes a tight curl cut, counting steps. The shooter works hard to cut at game speed and take the exact same number of steps each repetition. This helps the shooter to develop good footwork and consistency in the cut and the shot.

In addition to working on the 3-point shot, the counter move of driving against the grain can be practiced as well (**Diagram B**).

A token defender can be added to pressure the cutter to work on decision making as well. If the defender gives the shooter enough space the shooter takes the 3-point shot. If the defender crowds the shooter, the shooter executes a two-inch shot fake and drives against the grain.

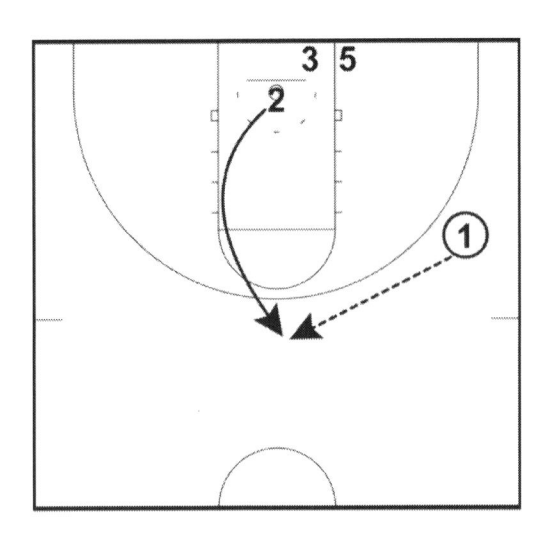

Diagram A

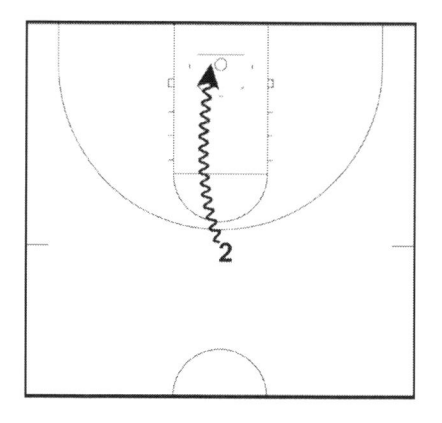

Diagram B

Number 126
Count the Steps – Baseline Dribble Off or Baseline Cut

Ideal Duration: 2-4 minutes maximum. Once the player has mastered the footwork one minute is enough time.

Grouping/organization: Partners with a ball at a minimum. Using a student assistant or coach can allow groups of up to four or five players work efficiently.

Frequency of usage: Daily or as needed. Daily in the off-season to develop footwork for shooting.

This drill teaches:

1) precise footwork for perimeter players.
2) catching the ball ready to shoot.
3) the habit of using an exact number of steps each time for specific offensive cuts.
4) consistency in footwork.

5) 3-point shooting.
6) finishing at the goal when driving.
7) shot fake, one dribble and mid-range jump shot.
8) recognition of a baseline dribble off to create space (very effective zone attack tactic).

This drill uses the same approach as the one described in Count the Steps – Triple Attack. This time the cutter makes a game speed cut to the corner, again counting steps from the foot directly under the goal.

A variation of this drill can include adding the two-inch up fake and driving to the middle for either a lay-up or pull-up jump shot.

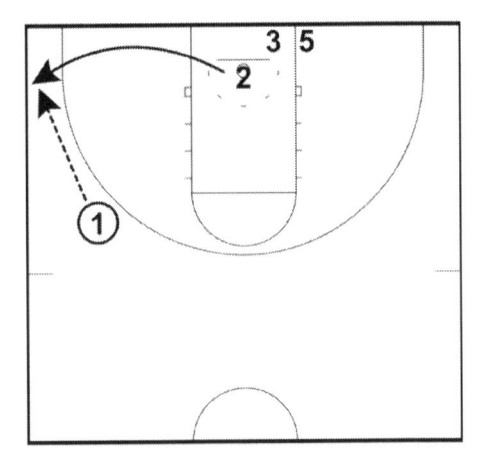

Diagram A

Number 127
Screening Progression

Ideal Duration: 2-4 minutes once the skills and progression have been learned.

Grouping/organization: Groups of 3 with a ball or groups of two with a student assistant or a coach.

Frequency of usage: Daily or as needed.

This drill teaches:

1) the footwork and technique of screening effectively.
2) the footwork and technique of cutting off screens effectively.
3) recognition of being screened for and the type of cut to use.
4) recognition of when a screen should be set and what type of screen to use.
5) the footwork necessary to be ready to catch and shoot when receiving a pass.

Great shooters will be heavily defended, both when in possession of the ball and without. This requires the ability to get open in order to receive the ball. Of what use is a great shooter who cannot use screens to get open?

Successfully shooting of a screen requires good footwork, proper execution of screening and cutting techniques by two players, recognition by every player involved on offense, the ability to communicate with hand signals and finally the ability to shoot off the pass. The screening progression drill is designed to practice all of these essential skills at once.

The drill can be done with or without defense, though in the learning stages it is essential the offense have success and master the small details involved, requiring the defense to be absent from the drill. Defense may be added in stages, starting with token pressure and working up to game intensity.

The drill is a sequenced progression of screens and cuts, hence the name of the drill. The sequence is as follows: down screen, flare screen, back screen, pin screen and re-screen (**Diagrams A** through **D**).

The re-screen, setting a particular type of screen followed by the appropriate matching screen, for example, a down screen followed by a flare screen, can be changed each practice session. The cutter shoots each time after coming off the screen taking a total of five shots before rotating to be a passer, screener or rebounder as determined by the coach.

A variation of the drill is to use two passers, passing to the screener reinforcing the concept of being a second cutter. A Shoot-A-Way™ can be used as well to ease the process of running down missed shots and making certain the passers have enough balls to keep the screener and cutter moving at a constant pace.

The screen progression can be done with or without shooting the ball. If time is important, perform the progression without shooting.

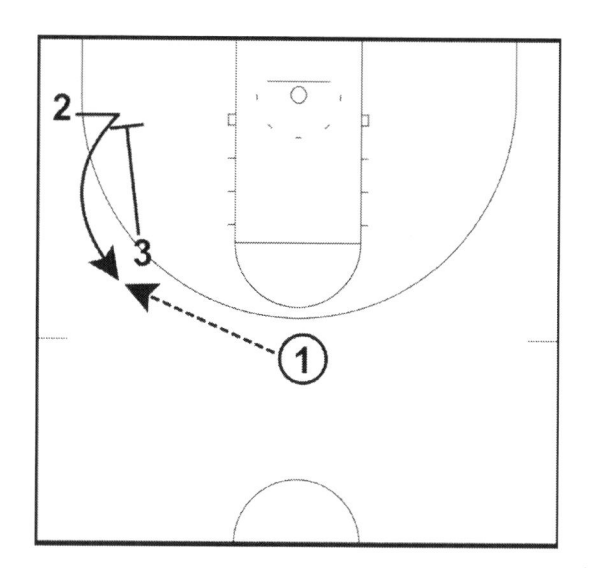

Diagram A

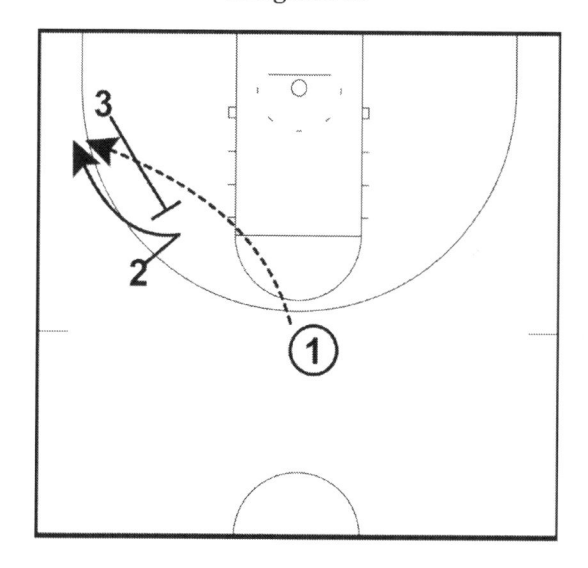

Diagram B

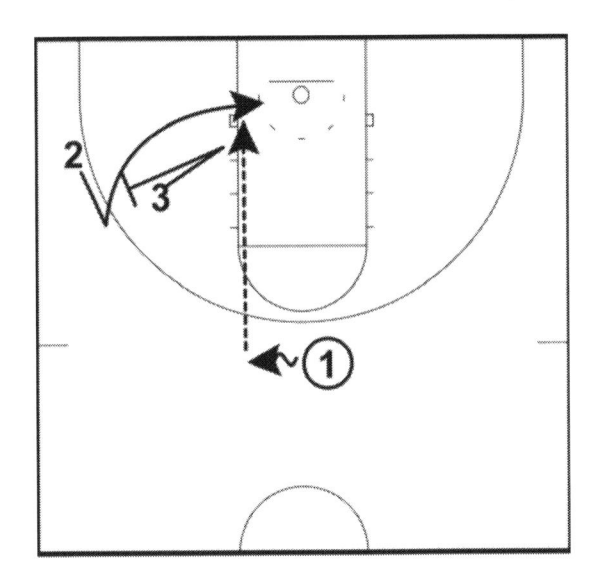

Diagram C

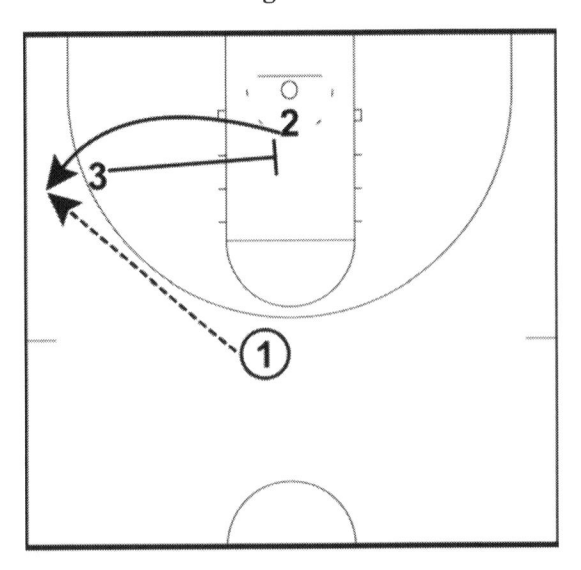

Diagram D

CHAPTER FOURTEEN

General Shooting Drills

Number 128
Rapid Fire Shooting

Ideal Duration: Two minutes total with shooters rotating after every five shots.

Grouping/organization: Partners with a ball. May have more than one group at a goal.

Frequency of Usage: Daily practice. Can be scheduled two or three times a practice to build to transition from a slow drill or activity to a more active or intense activity.

This drill teaches:

1) Grooving a shot from one specific location.
2) Meeting the pass.
3) Executing proper footwork prior to catching the ball.
4) Be ready to shoot as soon as the pass is caught.

Rapid fire shooting is not an offense specific drill. It is meant to allow players to work on shooting form and have multiple shoots in a short period of time. **Diagram A** shows the basic set-up. While it is ideal to shoot from the foul line, more than one set of partners can shoot at a single goal.

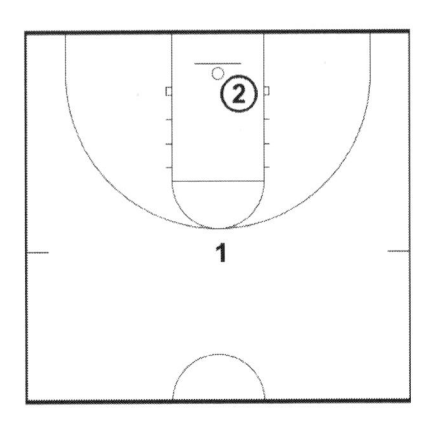

Diagram A

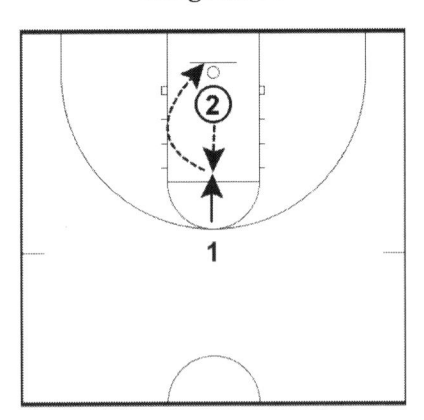

Diagram B

Diagram B shows #2 passing to #1 who steps into the pass, catches the ball in triple threat position and shoots a fifteen foot jump shot with good form and holds a high, one second follow through. #2 rebounds the shot attempt while #1 moves back to the top of the three-point line to repeat the process.

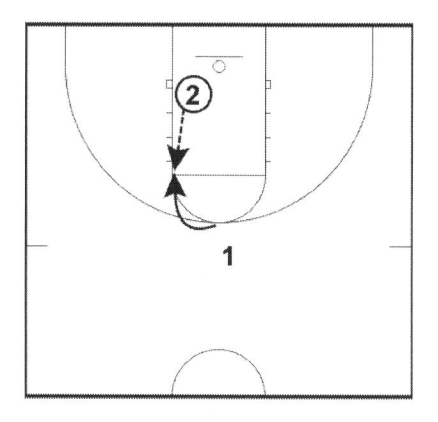

Diagram C

Diagram C depicts the drill run from a slightly different angle. #1 is must turn into the shot and practice the appropriate footwork and balance prior to shooting a shot where the approach has not been head on to the goal. #1 curves into the shot during the approach.

Number 129
Machine Gun Shooting

Ideal Duration: 3-5 minutes.

Grouping/organization: Three players and a ball at a goal. If space is limited, two groups can go at one goal. Simply have one group on each side of the goal.

Frequency of usage: Daily or as needed.

This drill teaches:

1) cutting.
2) passing.
3) footwork.

4) setting up for the shot off the pass.
5) shooting.
6) offensive rebounding.

Machine Gun Shooting is a drill that can be adapted to offensive specific shots. The drill also allows for multiple shots in a rapid succession. Diagram A shows the basic alignment for the drill. #1 is the passer, #2 is the shooter and #5 is the rebounder.

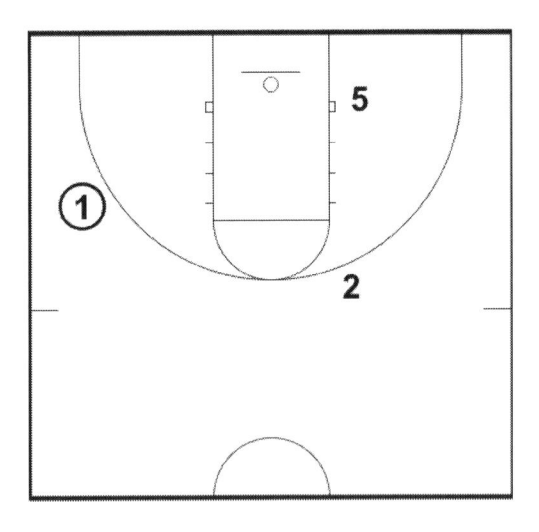

Diagram A

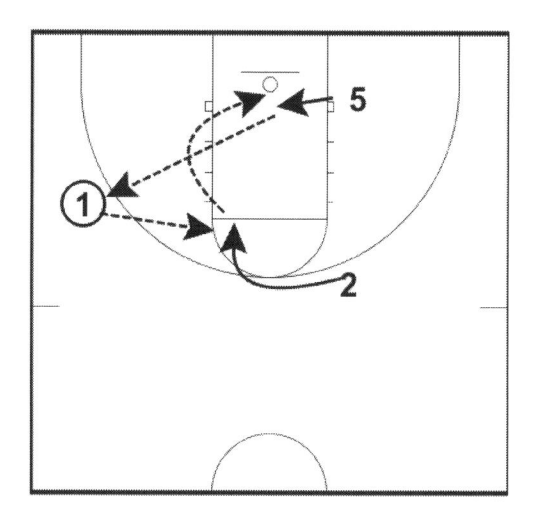

Diagram B

Diagram B shows the basic workings of the drill. #2 executes a correct curving approach to meet the pass from #1. #2 then takes a jump shot. #5 rebounds the shot attempt and passes the ball to #1.

The options for #2 are numerous. #2 could cut back to the initial starting point for a return pass or cut to another area on the court where a shot from the offense is obtained. The positioning of the passer #1 can be relocated to fit a location on the court where a pass would come from in the flow of the offense used.

Number 130
Four Corner Shooting

Ideal Duration: 5-8 Minutes

Grouping/organization: See Diagram A

Frequency of usage: Daily or as needed. This is a great drill to start practice after warm-ups and stretching. It gets the players moving and involves lots of technique work. Every player has a ball during this drill.

This drill teaches:

1) footwork.
2) shooting.
3) organization.
4) communication.
5) ability to follow directions.
6) passing.
7) catching.

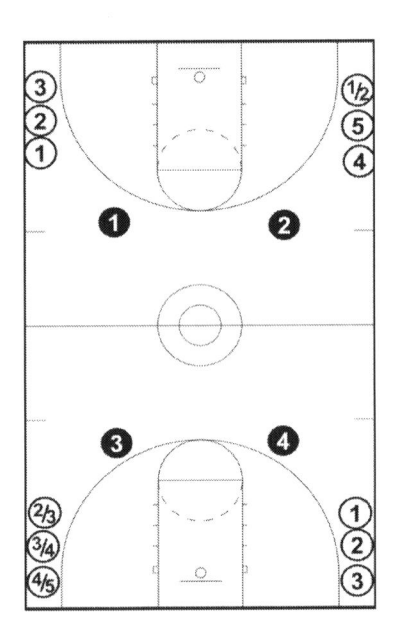

Diagram A

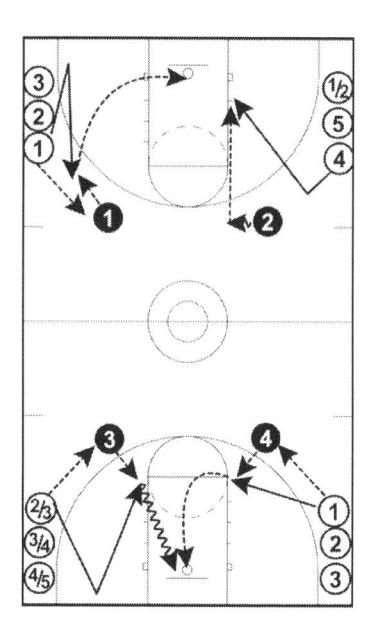

Diagram B

At each goal the first player in line passes the ball to the coach who tells that player what cut to make as well as the type of shot or drive the coach wants while the ball is in the air. The coach then passes the ball to the player after the player's cut. The player must score or finish the put back in one attempt and then rotate to the next goal to the right with the ball. Each coach can work on one cut, move and shot for the duration of the drill or change it each repetition.

Number 131
Three Man Motion Perimeter Shooting

Ideal Duration: 3-5 Minutes

Grouping/organization: Groups of three and a ball at a goal.

Frequency of usage: Daily

This drill teaches:

1) motion movement.
2) working as a unit.
3) cutting and screening.
4) spacing.
5) a wide range of shots.
6) offensive rebounding.
7) floor balance.

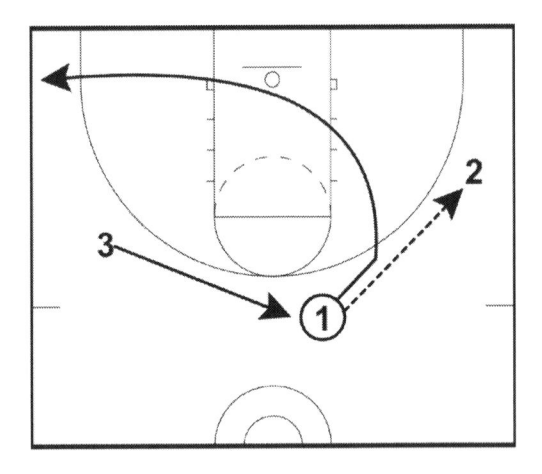

Diagram A

Players may not shoot until the pre-designated, by the coach, number of passes has been made. If so desired, a pre-designated number of screens can be the restriction. Suggestions for additional restrictions include:
- any player can shoot the shot.
- a specific player must shoot the shot.
- a specific shot must be taken.
- a specific cut off a specific screen must be used to obtain the shot.

Number 132
Three Man Motion Blocker/Mover Shooting

Ideal Duration: l3-5 Minutes

Grouping/organization: Groups of three and a ball at a goal.

Frequency of usage: Daily

This drill teaches:

1) motion movement.
2) working as a unit.
3) cutting and screening.
4) spacing.
5) a wide range of shots.
6) offensive rebounding.
7) floor balance.
8) second cutting.
9) screening for the designated shooter.

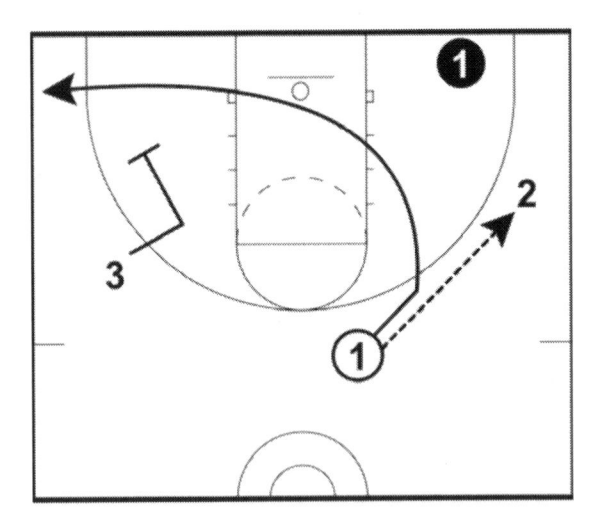

Diagram A

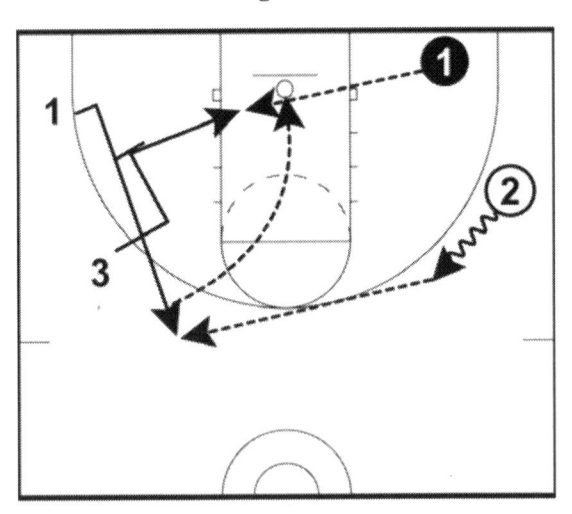

Diagram B

For coaches who use Coach Dick Bennett's Blocker/Mover style motion offense, this is a great drill to practice the necessary coordination between the mover (cutter and shooter) and the blockers (screeners). In these two diagrams, #1 is the mover, or designated shooter.

Note a coach passes the ball to the blocker, #3, who set the down screen for the blockers. It is important to reward the blockers with a shot in this drill as blockers spend so much time getting the same player (the mover) open for a shot.

Also, in many cases the player who will be open against excellent defensive teams is not the mover, due to the defense helping on the mover, but the blocker. Getting to shoot after setting numerous screens builds the habit of second cutting, which will create shots for blockers in actual games.

Number 133
32-Point Drill

Ideal Duration: This drill can take up to 15 minutes in its unmodified form.

Grouping/organization: Partner's with a ball at a goal. Two sets of partners may shoot at one goal.

Frequency of usage: As needed.

This drill teaches:

1) passing.
2) offensive rebounding.
3) preparing to shoot upon receiving the pass.
4) shooting from different locations on the court.
5) 3-point shooting.
6) use of the shot fake.
7) mid-range jump shot.
8) driving from the 3-point line with a one dribble limit.
9) shooting lay-ups.
10) shooting free throws.

The 32-Point Drill works on 3-point shooting, the mid-range jump shot and lay-ups. At the conclusion of the drill, the shooter must make two free throws. This drill can take some time so be sure to plan accordingly. There are two simple variations. Scoring for the drill is as follows: 3-point shots are worth three points, the mid-range jump shot is worth two points and the lay-up is worth one point. The two free throws are worth one point each.

The five 3-point shooting spots are utilized. The shooter attempts a 3-point shot, followed by a shot fake, one dribble pull-up 15 ft. jump shot. The third and final shot is a lay-up, utilizing if possible one dribble from the 3-point line. The shooter works from all five of the 3-point shooting spots.

The first, and most time consuming variation of the drill, requires the shooter to score on all three shots at each of the five spots and finish by making two free throws. The total score will be 32 points. Score is kept by the shooter and totals can be recorded when finished. This can be an excellent competitive shooting drill.

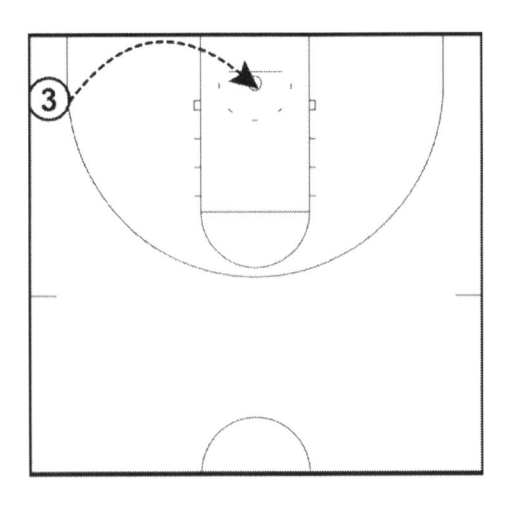

Diagram A

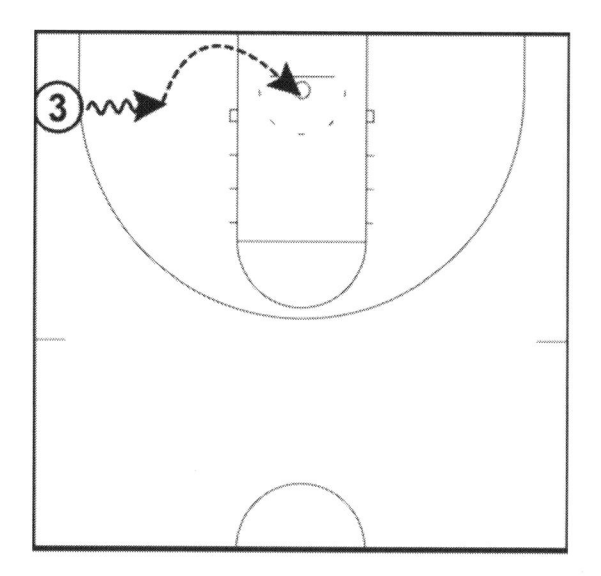

Diagram B

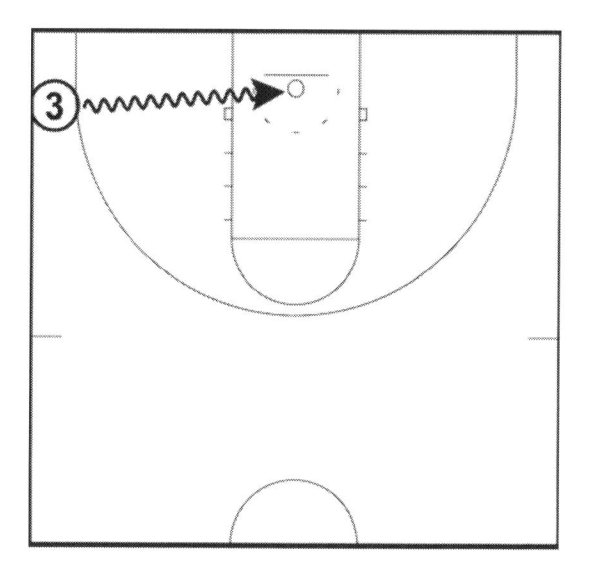

Diagram C

Number 134
Modified 32-Point Drill

Ideal Duration: 5 to 7 minutes in its modified form.

Grouping/organization: Partner's with a ball at a goal. Two sets of partners may shoot at one goal.

Frequency of usage: As needed.

This drill teaches:

1) passing.
2) offensive rebounding.
3) preparing to shoot upon receiving the pass.
4) shooting from different locations on the court.
5) 3-point shooting.
6) use of the shot fake.
7) mid-range jump shot.
8) driving from the 3-point line with a one dribble limit.
9) shooting lay-ups.
10) shooting free throws.

The Modified 32-Point Drill works on 3-point shooting, the mid-range jump shot and lay-ups. At the conclusion of the drill, the shooter must make two free throws. This drill can take some time so be sure to plan accordingly.

There are two simple variations. Scoring for the drill is as follows: 3-point shots are worth three points, the mid-range jump shot is worth two points and the lay-up is worth one point. The two free throws are worth one point each.

The five 3-point shooting spots are utilized. The shooter attempts a 3-point shot, followed by a shot fake, one dribble pull-up 15 ft. jump shot. The third and final shot is a lay-up, utilizing if possible one dribble from the 3-point line. The shooter works from all five of the 3-point shooting spots.

In its modified form, the shooter is only allowed on shot from each of the 15 shots required in the drill plus two free throws. The maximum score is 32 points. The same scoring system is used as in 32 Point Drill.

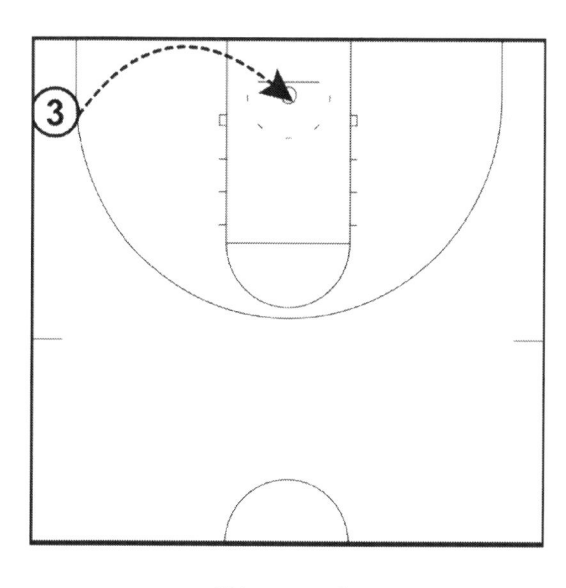

Diagram A

201 DRILLS FOR COACHING YOUTH BASKETBALL| 260

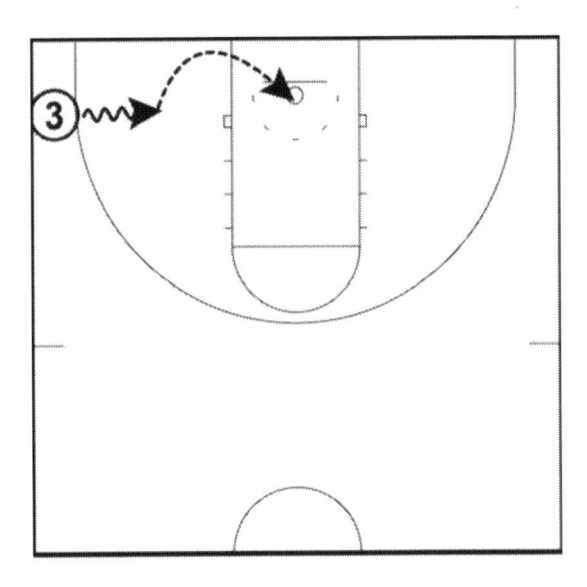

Diagram B

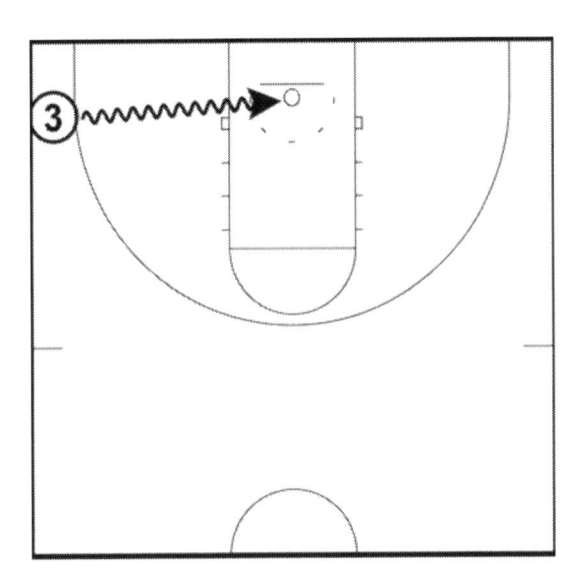

Diagram C

Number 135
Fan the Ball — Two Perimeters and a Post

Ideal Duration: 2 to 4 minutes maximum.

Grouping/organization: Groups of three players with a ball.

Frequency of usage: Daily or as needed.

This drill teaches:

1) feeding the post skills.
2) fanning the ball out to perimeter players for shot attempts.
3) feeding the post and moving for an open shot.
4) sliding into an open passing lane opposite the post player for a shot attempt.
5) 3-point shooting.

The objective of this drill is to practice feeding the post and fanning the ball out for 3-point shot attempts, either by passing diagonally opposite or using feed the post and move. The drill can be executed with or without defense. Organization can be done in lines or using groups of three at every goal if space and facilities permit. **Diagram A** and **Diagram B** depict how the drill should be executed.

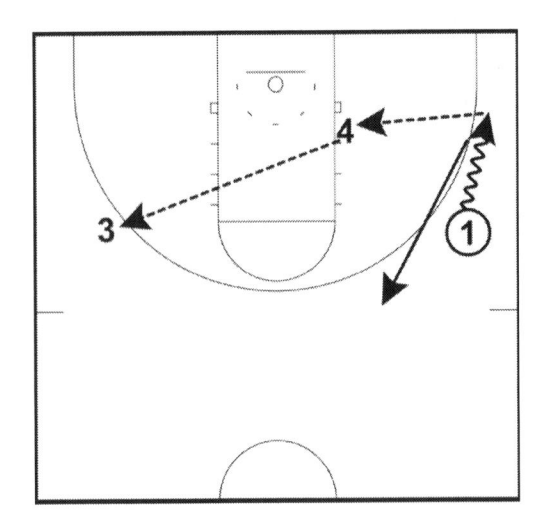

Diagram A

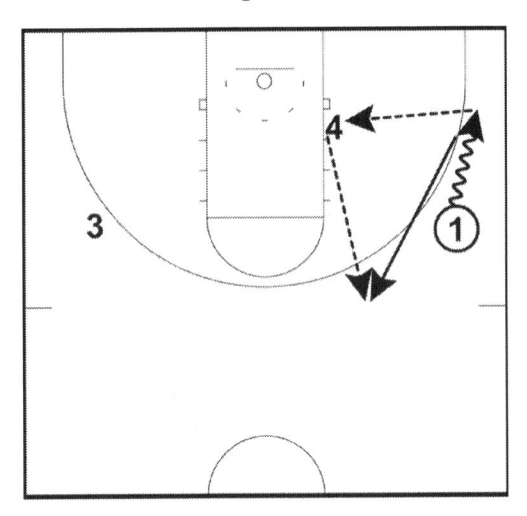

Diagram B

Number 136
Beat the All Star

Ideal Duration: 3-5 minutes

Grouping/organization: Can be done with a single player with a ball, in pairs or a group of three players with a ball.

Frequency of usage: Daily in the off-season and for fun occasionally during the season.

This drill teaches:

1) shooting in a competitive setting.
2) free throws.
3) a wide variety of jump shots.

The first shot of the game for each player is a free throw. If the player makes the free throw he/she scores a +1. A miss is scored as -3. Each made lay-up is worth +2 and each made jump shot is worth +1. Any missed shot after the free throw is -2. Players may attempt a maximum of two lay-ups. The jump shots are taken from designated spots. The first player to reach 10 points wins. Players shoot until they miss if more than one player is playing "beat the All Star." After a missed shot, the next player shoots.

Number 137
Two Minute Shooting

Ideal Duration: 2 minutes per player (ideally) and six minutes total.

Grouping/organization: Groups of three players with a ball at each goal. Players shoot from five spots designated by the coach. The spots may vary depending on the needs of the team or player.

Frequency of usage: Daily or as needed.

This drill teaches:

1) shooting from a variety of locations on the court.
2) shooting off the pass.
3) offensive rebounding.
4) passing to the shooting pocket.

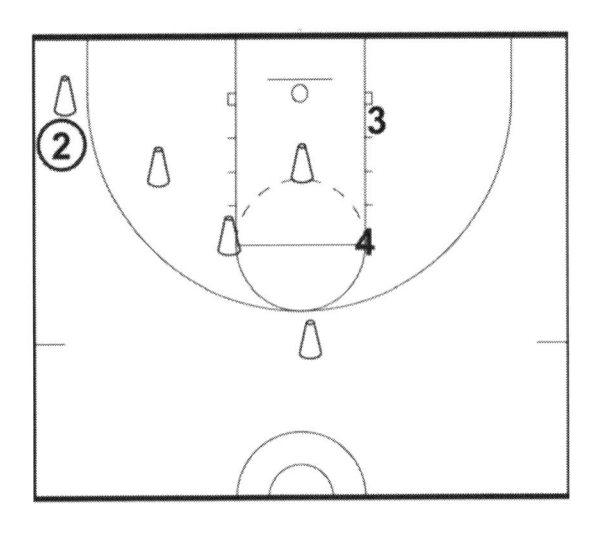

Diagram A

The shooter shoots, the rebounder recovers the ball and passes to the passer who passes to the shooter. The shooter must MAKE five shots from each of the five spots!

The goal is to make 25 shots in 2 minutes. If the shooter makes 25 shots in less than two minutes, the shooter receives a +1 for every second under 2 minutes. If it takes the shooter longer than 2 minutes to make 25 shots, the shooter receives -1 for every second over 2 minutes. The shooter or group of shooters with the best score wins the drill/competition.

Number 138
Three Pass Partner Shooting

Ideal Duration: Two minutes

Grouping/organization: Partners with a ball. One pair of shooters per goal is ideal but if necessary two pairs of shooters may work at the same goal.

Frequency of usage: Daily or as needed.

This drill teaches:

1) offensive movement.
2) working with a teammate on offense.
3) shooting off cuts.
4) footwork.
5) preparing to shoot of the pass.
6) passing to a shooter's shooting pocket.
7) shooting from a variety of spots.
8) shooting at game speed.
9) offensive creativity when working with a teammate.

201 DRILLS FOR COACHING YOUTH BASKETBALL| 266

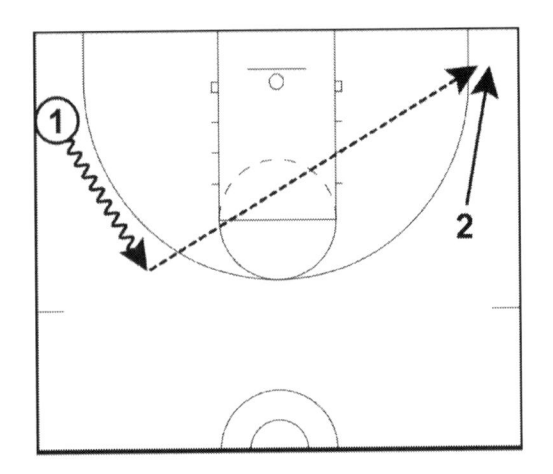

Diagram A

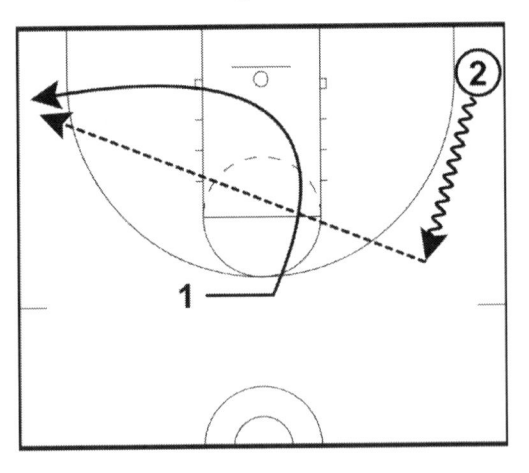

Diagram B

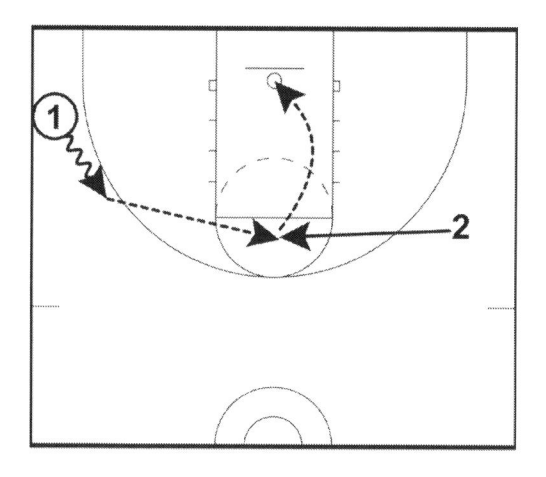

Diagram C

Diagrams A through **C** depict one three pass sequence. The possible combinations are limitless and bound only by the player's imaginations and ability to properly execute cuts, particularly those used in the team offense. **Diagram A** depicts the first cut and pass.

Diagram B depicts the second cut and pass as the players work together. **Diagram C** depicts the third and final cut and pass, after which #2 takes a shot. #2 follows the shot as the players properly re-space and the sequence begins again.

Since the first pass will be made by #2, #1 will take the shot in the second sequence. Be patient with your players the first one or two times this drill is used. It is a fantastic drill for motion-oriented offenses.

Number 139
Three Pass Shooting With Screening

Ideal Duration: 2 minutes

Grouping/organization: Groups of three players with a ball at a goal.

Frequency of usage: Daily or as needed.

This drill teaches:

1) offensive movement.
2) working with a teammate on offense.
3) shooting off cuts.
4) setting and using screens.
5) reading screens
6) footwork.
7) preparing to shoot of the pass.
8) passing to a shooter's shooting pocket.
9) shooting from a variety of spots.
10) shooting at game speed.
11) offensive creativity when working with teammates.

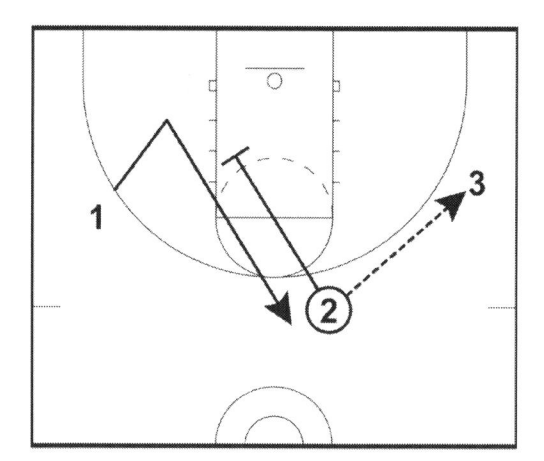

Diagram A

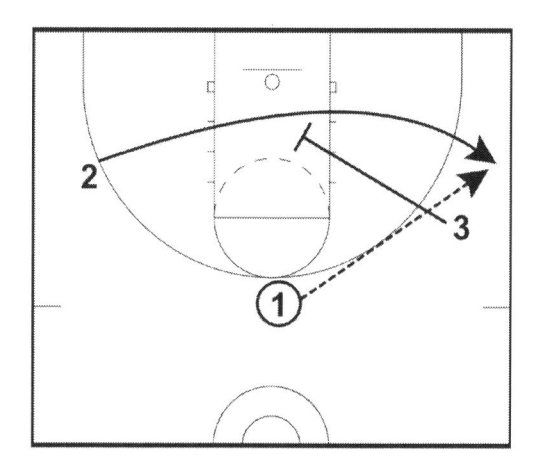

Diagram B

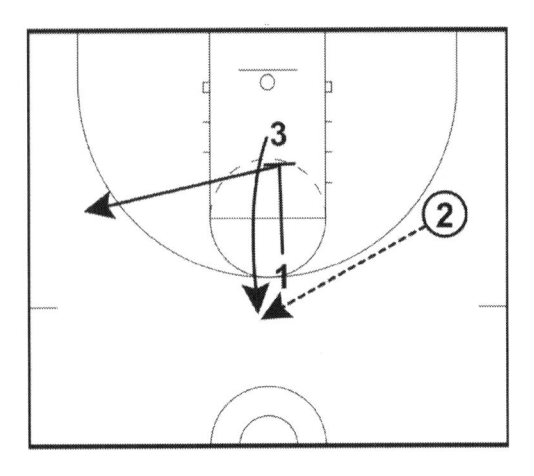

Diagram C

Diagrams A through **C** shot a three-pass cutting and screening sequence. Just like two pass shooting, the possibilities are limited only to the player's imagination, restrictions placed by the coach, and the player's ability to work together setting screens, cutting and reading screens. The players must establish a sequence in which they will pass the ball and adhere to it. The shooter obtains the rebound of his/her shot, the players respace, and the sequence begins again with the shooter making the first of the three passes. This drill can be done with three perimeter players or two perimeter players and a post player. It is an excellent drill for motion offense and to work on cutting and screening as well as shooting.

Number 140
Three Cut Shooting

Ideal Duration: 2-4 minutes

Grouping/organization: Groups of 3 players with a ball at a goal.

Frequency of usage: Daily or as needed.

This drill teaches:

1) three basic cuts.
2) shooting off the pass.
3) shooting off a cut.
4) preparing to shoot off the pass.
5) shooting.

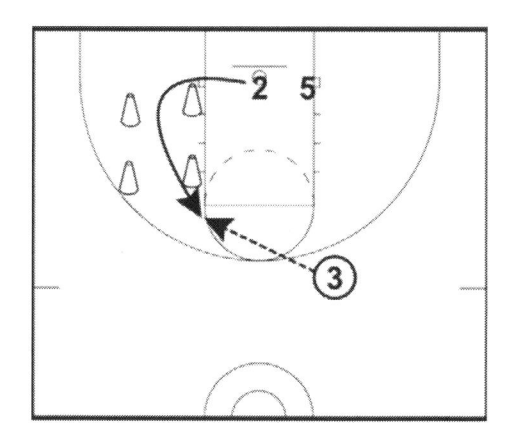

Diagram A

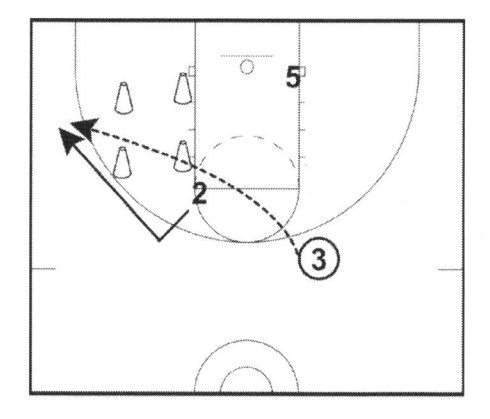

Diagram B

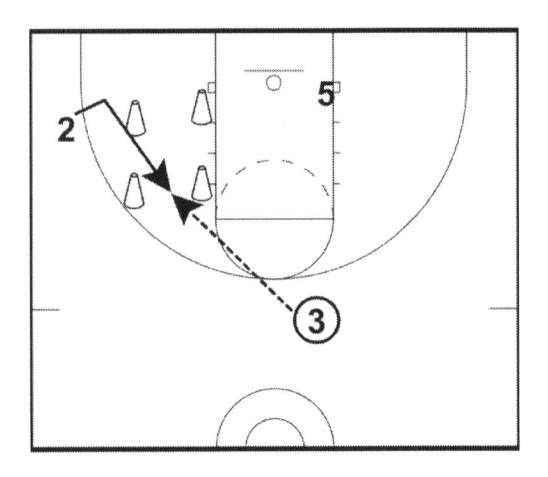

Diagram C

The diagrams depict in order the cutting sequence (curl off a double staggered screen, flare or fade cut, and a pop-up off a down screen). The shooter starts under the rim as shown and uses the cones as screens. #5 acts as the rebounder and passes to #3 who serves as the passer. The players rotate after the first shooter is finished.

Number 141
Second Cutter Shooting

Ideal Duration: 2-4 minutes

Grouping/organization: See Diagram A

Frequency of usage: Daily or as needed.

This drill teaches:

1) the habit of cutting after setting a screen (being a second cutter).
2) looking for gaps in the defense after setting a screen.
3) preparing to shoot off the move.
4) preparing to shoot upon receiving the pass.
5) shooting from various spots.

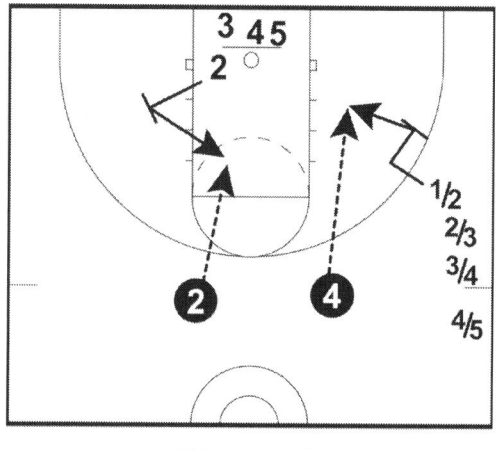

Diagram A

Diagram A depicts players divided into two groups with two coaches or student assistants acting as passers. In each line the first player sets the indicated screen and then executes a second cut, both creating space between the cutter and the screener and "stepping to the shot."

After taking the shot, the shooter can return to the end of his/her line or change lines after rebounding the ball and returning it to the coach. The possibilities for creating second cutting opportunities are limited only by imagination or the continuities of the offense used. This is a great drill for motion offense teams.

CHAPTER FIFTEEN

Competitive Shooting Drills

"It is one thing to be good against a droid, kid. It's another to be good against the living!" - Han Solo to Luke Skywalker in Star Wars

In the game of basketball it is not enough to be able to shoot the ball well. Players have to be able to shoot the ball well in game conditions.

There are many players who shoot the ball well but when the element of competition is introduced to the equation struggle with their shot. As coaches, it is essential to find drills that resemble the competitive aspect of real game competition in order to help players learn to shoot well in competition. Besides, competition is fun!

Number 142
Partner Competitive Shooting

Ideal Duration: Two minutes maximum for two players with each player shooting for one minute and the other player rebounding for a minute then rotating roles. It is also permissible for the players to shoot for two 30-second periods and rebound for two 30 second periods rotating roles twice during the drill.

Grouping/organization: Partners with a ball for two minutes. Two groups may compete at the same goal and every goal in the gym should be used. Mini-competitions can be held between the two groups at one goal. Records should be kept of winners and point scored each time this drill is used. Be creative in using this drill to create tournaments. Ladder format, round robin format, head-to-head format or bracket competitions can be used to make this drill a lot of fun for your players.

Frequency of Usage: Daily practice or once a twice a week.

This drill teaches:

1) shooting while under competitive pressure.
2) rebounding and converting offensive put backs under competitive pressure.
3) accurate passing while tired and under competitive pressure.
4) proper footwork to shoot off the pass.
5) teamwork.
6) strategic thinking as a team.
7) competing while tired.
8) communication.

Scoring system:

Three-point shots = 3 pts.
Two-point shots = 2 pts.
Offensive put backs off missed two-point shots = 1 pt.
Offensive put backs off any made basket = 1 pt.
Offensive put backs off a missed three – point shot = 2 pts.
Note: *For a put back to count the ball cannot touch the court.*

Your players will absolutely love this drill or hate it with a passion! Those who love the drill do so because it is competitive and the players are in control of the strategy of the game while they are competing. Players who hate the drill do so because they dislike the conditioning aspect of the drill or are not competitive by nature. There is no middle ground.

The drill begins as depicted in **Diagram A**. The rebounder is in possession of the ball and the shooter is at half court. Put two minutes on the game clock. The coach starts the drills with a whistle and the shooter attacks. The first three shots each shooter takes must be from the foul line area (**Diagram B**).

Made shots are scored based on the scoring system. After three shots the shooter may select either a two-point shot in the foul line area or a three-point shot above the free throw line extended.

After each shot the shooter must sprint to half court and touch the half court line and sprint back for another shot attempt.

The rebounder is also the passer in this drill. The rebounder must not allow the ball to touch the court. If the rebounder is able to obtain possession of the ball without it touching the court the rebounder, without dribbling, has the opportunity to score an offensive put back. Depending on the type of rebound the rebounder has obtained, the put back is scored accordingly. If the rebounder misses the put back shot there are no second chances.

Players must shout their running score totals as the game progresses. Players must think strategically as they compete. Based on the shooting and rebounding skills that pair of players have, how can they score the most points possible in the time available and win?

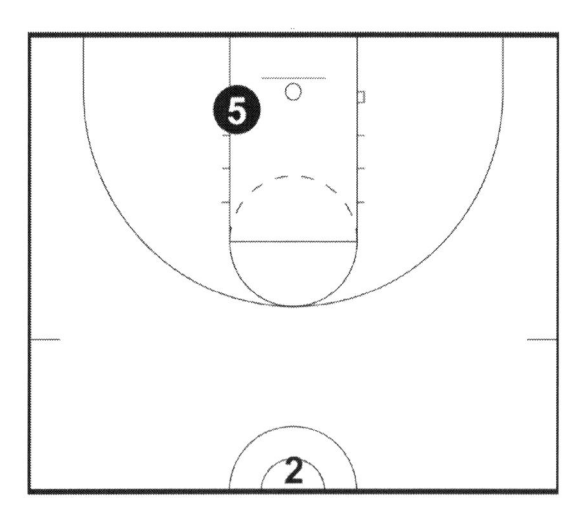

Diagram A

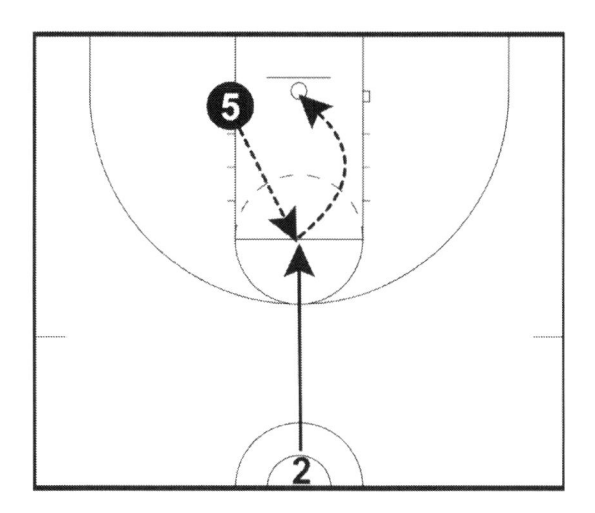

Diagram B

Diagram C depicts the shooter later in the contest. The shooter has taken the mandatory three shot attempts from the foul line area and for strategic reasons is not taking 3-point shot attempts.

Note the shooter v-cut in order to be able to receive the pass squared up for the shot attempt as soon as the ball arrives from the rebounder/passer. Also depicted is the sprint to half court while the rebounder obtains the rebound and makes the put back.

One final note, teams may, if they need to for a strategic reason, skip the put back attempt in the final 15 seconds of the contest.

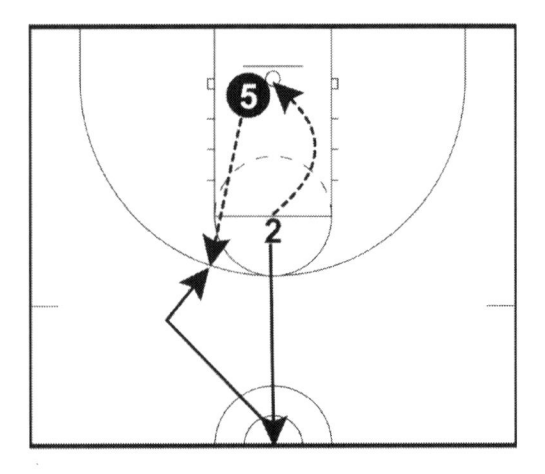

Diagram C

Number 143
4-Up

Ideal Duration: Allow 5-7 minutes for this drill/game.

Grouping/organization: Divide your players into two groups of roughly equal shooting ability.

Frequency of usage: Daily or as needed. This is a great off-season game, end of practice drill or camp drill.

This drill teaches:

1) competitive shooting.
2) teamwork.
3) shooting skills.
4) passing.
5) catching.
6) be ready to shoot upon receiving the ball.
7) offensive rebounding.

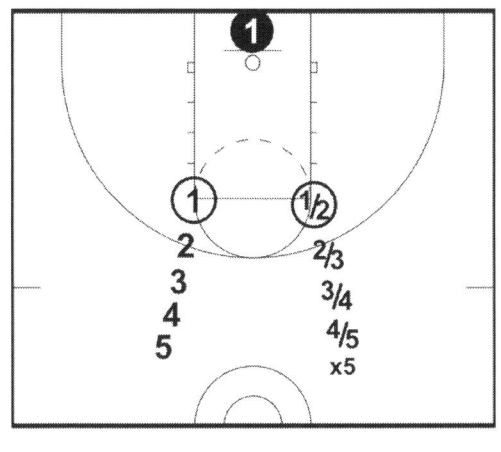

Diagram A

Diagram A depicts the initial organization typical for this drill/game. The coach, who is positioned under the goal keeps score and starts the contest.

The drill is essentially a race to see which team can develop a 4 shot lead, return the ball to the front of its line and have the shooter who made the shot to create the 4 shot lead sprint to the end of the line and every team member to sit down before the opponent can make a shot and reduce the lead to 3 shots.

Scoring works as follows: if the team on the left scores and the team on the right misses, the scoring team is said to be "one up."

If the trailing team scores and the leading team misses the score is now said to be "even." This continues until there is a winner. It can take 5 or 6 minutes to produce a winner if the teams are evenly matched. Should a team be able to score before the team who is 4-up can sit down, the game continues until there is a winner. Scores can go back and forth.

Number 144
Beat the Game Competitive Shooting

Ideal Duration: 6-8 minutes in duration on average

Grouping/organization: This drill requires four balls and a minimum of nine players. The drill starts with three groups of three players with the players moving spots after one minute.

Frequency of usage: Once a week or as needed.

This drill teaches:

1) shooting in competitive situations
2) communication
3) shooting off the pass
4) preparing to shoot off the pass
5) leadership and organization (see drill description)
6) shooting off the cut or move
7) shooting the 3-point shot
8) shooting the 2-point shot
9) shooting off the dribble if necessary

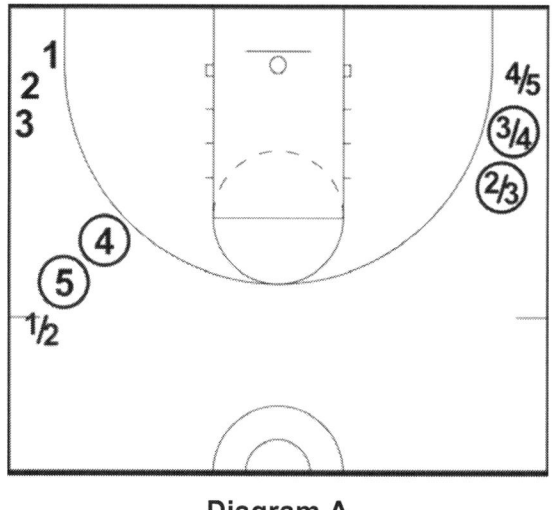

Diagram A

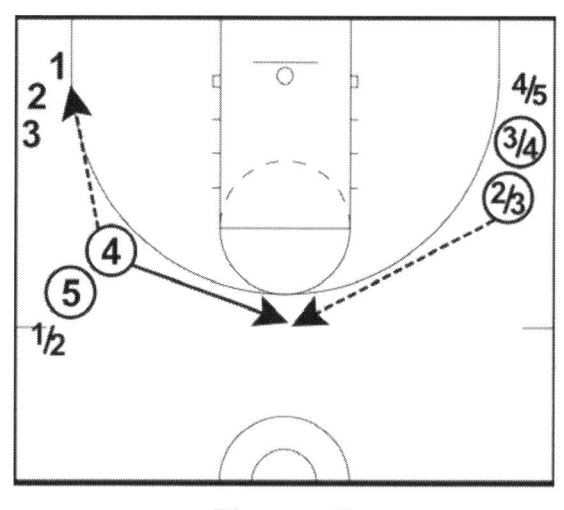

Diagram B

The basic alignment for this drill is shown in **Diagram A**. During the first minute of the drill the rotation is as depicted in **Diagram B**. The ball is passed to the corner for a shot (3-point or 2-point depending on the ability and shooting range of the shooter). The passer cuts hard to the top of the key to receive a pass and takes a shot (again, either 3-point or 2-point depending on the shooter's ability and range). Shooters retrieve their own rebound and pass the ball back to the line where the ball originated. This simple instruction alone will cause considerable confusion. Do

not help them out. The players must communicate and organize themselves for this drill to work. Rotate to the line on the right.

After one minute rotate the spots. **Diagram C** depicts the second set of spots the players will work from. Follow the same directions for the second minute of the drill. **Diagram D** depicts the third and final set of shooting spots. Note the lines have not moved. The location of one set of balls has moved from the corner to the opposite wing.

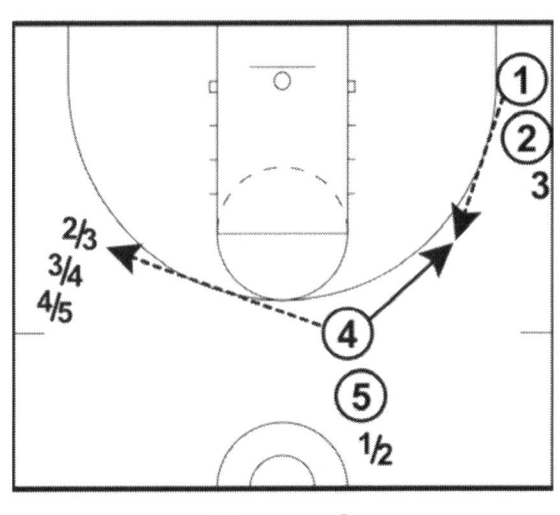

Diagram C

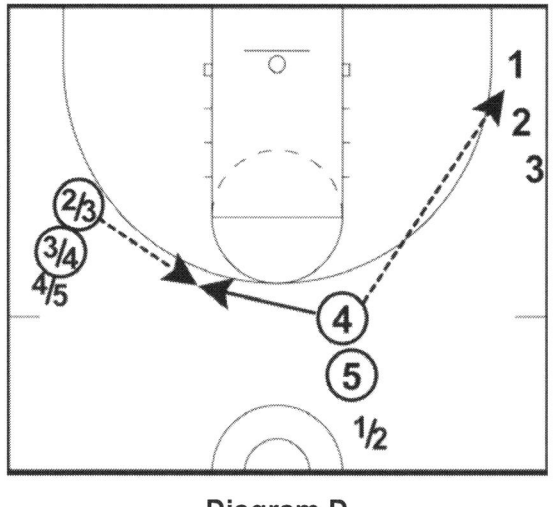

Diagram D

After three minutes call "change." The groups sprint to the other end of the court and the drill repeats itself for an additional three minutes.

Variations:

If you have enough players you can start with two groups, one at each goal on the game court. After three minutes both groups would change ends of the court. Instead of competing against the game the two groups could compete against each other.

Scoring:

3-point shots are worth 3-points.
2-point shots are worth 2-points.
Put backs off missed shots can be worth 1-point if so desired.

Keep score and record the score. Whenever this drill is used, record the score and encourage the players to beat their old high score. A TOP TEN SCORES list can be kept and updated. Players like to compete against their old scores.

This drill will take a few times to master and there will be confusion on the part of the players the first few times this drill is used. Stick with it. This will become a player favorite.

Number 145
Team Competitive

Ideal Duration: 3-5 Minutes

Grouping/organization: Divide players into a minimum of two teams. This drill will work with as many as four teams at one goal. Specify where the teams are to shoot from.

Frequency of usage: Daily or as needed. This drill will be a player favorite.

This drill teaches:

1) competitiveness.
2) preparing to shoot off the pass.
3) shooting.
4) offensive rebounding.
5) passing to a shooting pocket.

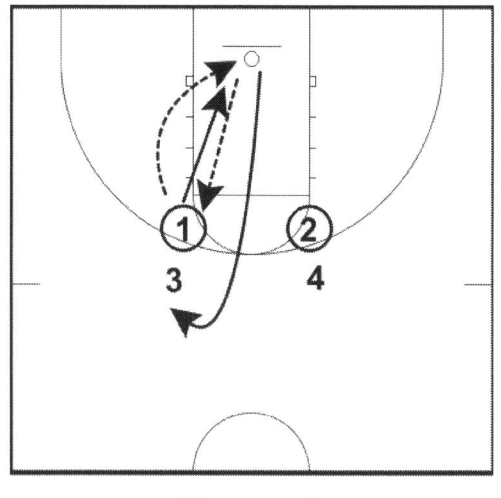

Diagram A

Team Competitive is a great drill to finish practice with. **Diagram A** shows the basic pattern involved. The shooter follows his or her shot, rebounds the shot and passes the ball to the next shooter in line. The first team to reach the pre-determined number wins the game. Players love this simple contest.

Number 146
Two Minute Shooting

Ideal Duration: 2 minutes per player (ideally) and six minutes total.

Grouping/organization: Groups of three players with a ball at each goal. Players shoot from five spots designated by the coach. The spots may vary depending on the needs of the team or player.

Frequency of usage: Daily or as needed.

This drill teaches:

1) shooting from a variety of locations on the court.
2) shooting off the pass.
3) offensive rebounding.
4) passing to the shooting pocket.

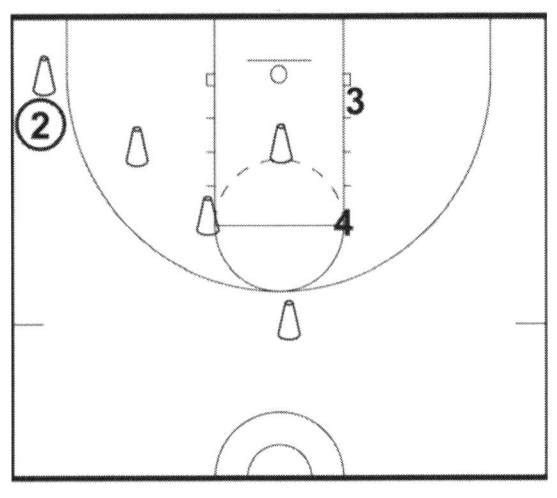

Diagram A

The shooter shoots, the rebounder recovers the ball and passes to the passer who passes to the shooter. The shooter must MAKE five shots from each of the five spots!

The goal is to make 25 shots in 2 minutes. If the shooter makes 25 shots in less than two minutes, the shooter receives a +1 for every second under 2 minutes. If it takes the shooter longer than 2 minutes to make 25 shots, the shooter receives -1 for every second over 2 minutes. The shooter or group of shooters with the best score wins the drill/competition.

CHAPTER SIXTEEN

Three-Point Shooting Drills

Basic Planning for 3-Point Shooting Drills

Diagram A depicts the five primary shooting spots perimeter 3-point shooters should practice from. The spots can vary based on the needs of the offense being used. **Diagram B** shows the area and spots post players who serve as trailers on the fast break must practice from to develop 3-point shooting ability.

201 DRILLS FOR COACHING YOUTH BASKETBALL| 288

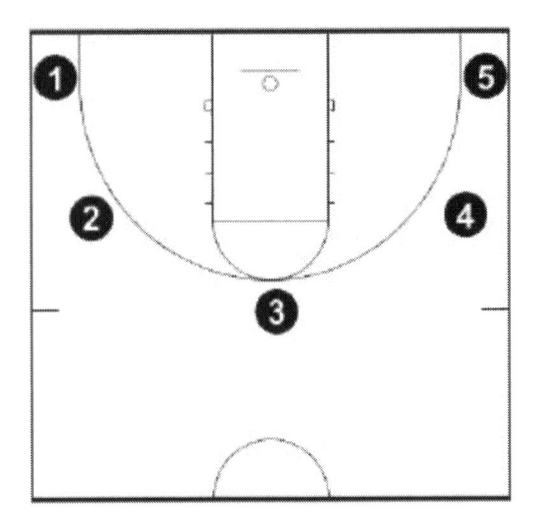

Diagram A

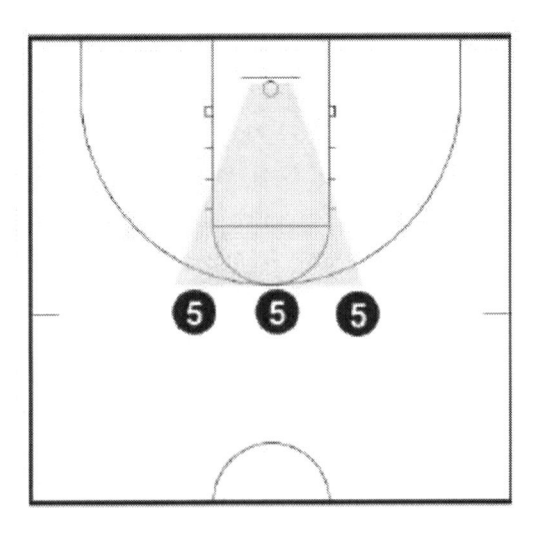

Diagram B

Number 147
3-Point Shoot-out

Ideal Duration: 5 minutes

Grouping/organization: Partners with a ball.

Frequency of usage: Daily usage or twice a week.

This drill teaches:

1) provides a large volume of 3-point shot attempts in a short period of time from the five primary 3-point shooting areas.
2) shooting off the pass.
3) accurate passing to an open and set 3-point shooter.
4) fundamentals of shooting.
5) provides rebounding opportunities.
6) can be used as a competitive drill. At a minimum daily totals should be kept and recorded.

This drill is designed to generate a high volume of 3-point shots in a short period of time. One to five shooters can work at a single time with five players rebounding, one designated rebounder for each shooter.

Players shoot only from the five three-point shooting spots as indicated in Diagram A. The drill should last for five minutes. Players are allotted one minute per spot after which the shooter rotates to the next spot. The rebounder keeps track of the number of shots made. At the end of the session the number of shots made should be recorded.

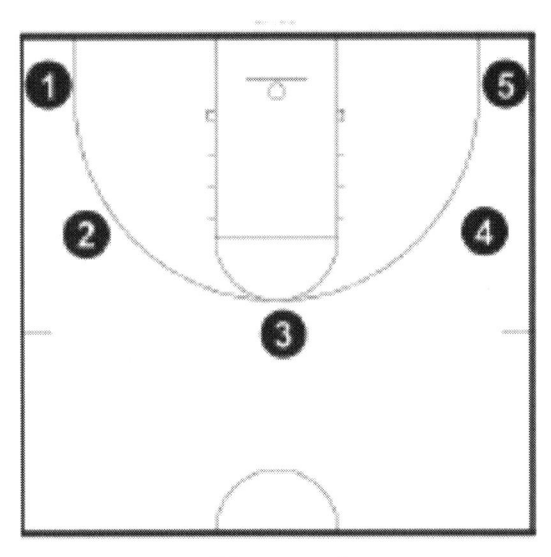

Diagram A

Number 148
Partner Threes

Ideal Duration: Two to three minutes total with constant rotation for the shooters as they work through the progression of types of 3-point shots.

Grouping/organization: Partners with a ball. Two groups may shoot at a goal at the same time if careful.

Frequency of Usage: Daily practice. Can be scheduled two or three times a practice to build to transition from a slow drill or activity to a more active or intense activity.

This drill teaches:

1) All of the tactics that can be used with two player combinations to generate an open 3-point shot.

2) Footwork for shooting.
3) Anticipation and reading offense in order to set up a 3-point shot.

Partner Threes is a simple concept for a drill. 3-point shooters are paired together for the duration of the drill and the sequences involved. One player executes the tactic being practiced and passes to the other player who has executed necessary moves to be open and ready to shoot upon catching the pass. The passer rebounds the shot and passes to the shooter. The two players then switch roles and repeat the process.

Players may shoot a preset number before moving on to the next series in the sequence or await the command of the coach. In Diagram A the players are executing a penetrate and pitch. #1 drives the gap to draw #2's defender. #2 moves up from the baseline to create space and receive the pass from #1. #2 should have feet set, be squared-up, hands ready and prepared to shoot upon catching the pass.

The following diagrams demonstrate the various ways two players can create an open three-point shot attempt. The same drill procedure is used for the entire sequence. Please note an important component of the drill is not just the physical repetition of the skills involved and the tactic being practiced but also the ability to recognize the potential to create such a 3-point shot in a game by using one of the tactics being practiced.

201 DRILLS FOR COACHING YOUTH BASKETBALL | 292

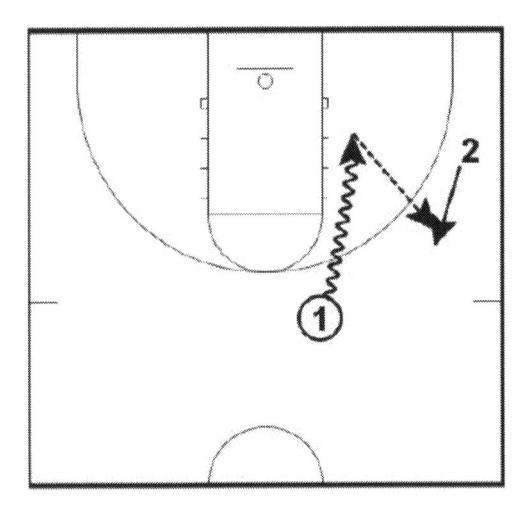

Diagram A (Penetrate & Pitch)

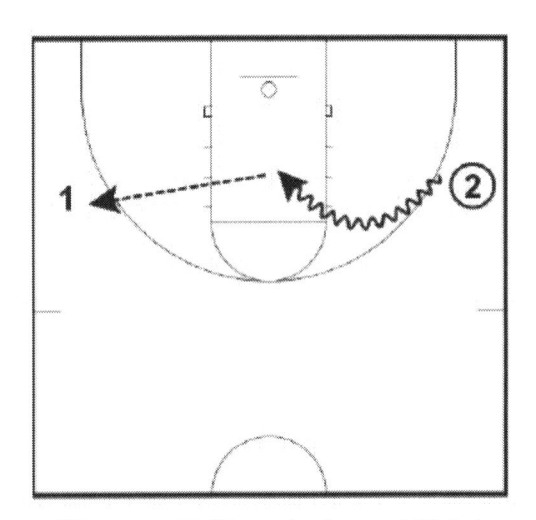

Diagram B (Penetrate and Skip)

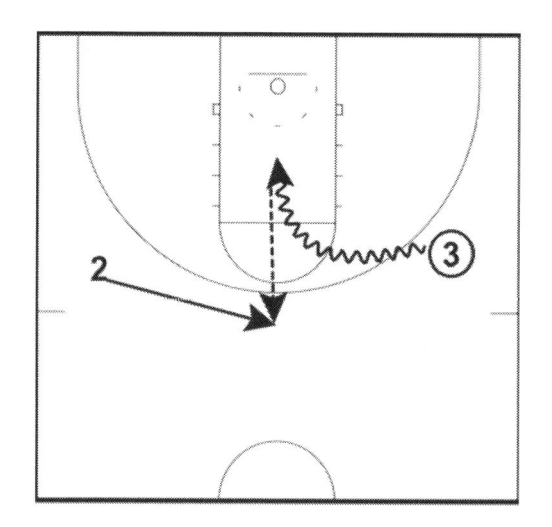

Diagram C (Single Euro)

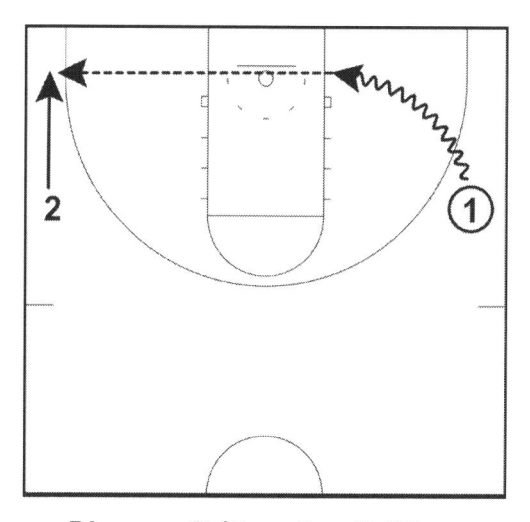

Diagram D (Baseline Drift)

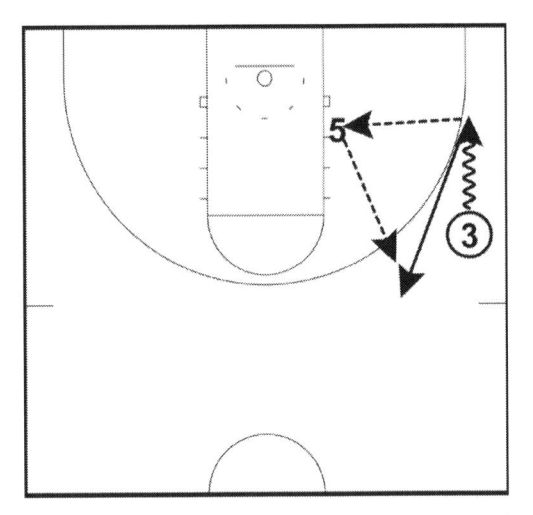

Diagram E (Feed the Post and Move)

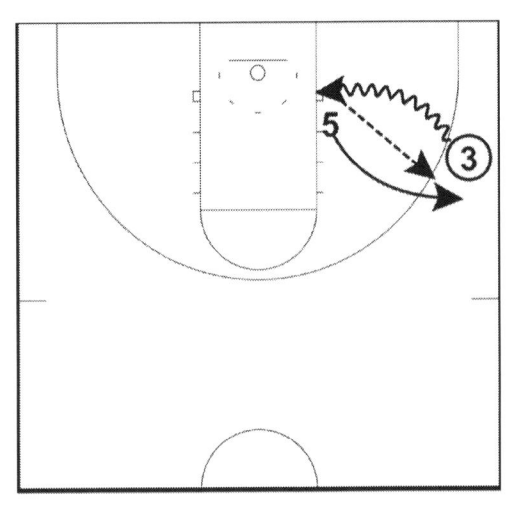

Diagram F (33 Cut)

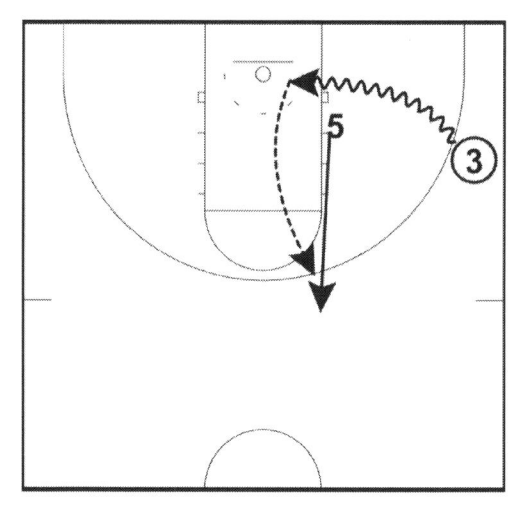

Diagram G (Long I-Cut)

Number 149
Closeout 3's

Ideal Duration: 4-6 minutes total with each shooter shooting 1 to 1.5 minutes each.

Grouping/organization: Groups of four with three balls at each goal.

Frequency of usage: Daily in the off-season or once a twice a week in season.

This drill teaches:

1) shooting accurately with a defender rushing at the shooter.
2) learning to judge when to shot fake and drive.
3) shooting with confidence while under defensive pressure.

The careful planning, great execution, great strategy and tactics can all go out the window due to one hustling defender who refuses to give up. In one brief instant the lone hustling defender can take an otherwise open shot and ruin it for a shooter has done everything correctly.

For this reason, it is essential 3-point shooters develop the ability to shoot an open shot that has suddenly come under defensive pressure.

Closeout 3's is a drill designed to create sudden defensive pressure. Players are organized in groups of four with three of the players having balls.

The first player passes the ball out to the lone 3-point shooter and sprints at the shooter with hands up. The defender secures the rebound and returns to the end of the line. The process continues until the shooter has shot seven shots and then the next shooter replaces the initial shooter (**Diagram A**).

Once a shot has been deflected or blocked, the shooter now has the option of shot faking and driving one dribble and shooting. This is an excellent drill for teaching decision making and learning to shoot with a rapidly approaching defender.

The focus of the shooter should be on the goal and shooting technique. The defender and the possibility of having the shot blocked should not be considered until a defender is able to actually deflect or block a shot.

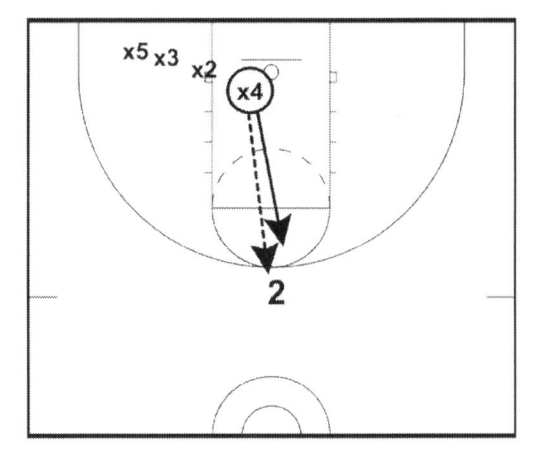

Diagram A

Number 150
Five by Twenty Spot Shooting

Ideal Duration: 7-10 minutes total

Grouping/organization: Partners with a ball. Ideally no more than two groups per goal. Five groups have been depicted in **Diagram A** for the purpose of showing where the shots are taken from.

Frequency of usage: If your team is going to rely heavily on the 3-point shot, this should be a daily drill immediately following the shooting progression. It is part of warming up the 3-point shot and provides a high volume of 3-point shot attempts for each player early in practice.

This drill teaches:

1) basic shooting form.
2) shooting off the pass.

3) repetitions from the five most common, or desired, 3-point shot locations.
4) passing to the shooting pocket, or chin, whichever technique is taught.
5) anticipating the rebound for missed 3-point shot attempts.
6) warming up the 3-point shot.
7) provides a high volume of 3-point shot attempts early in practice.

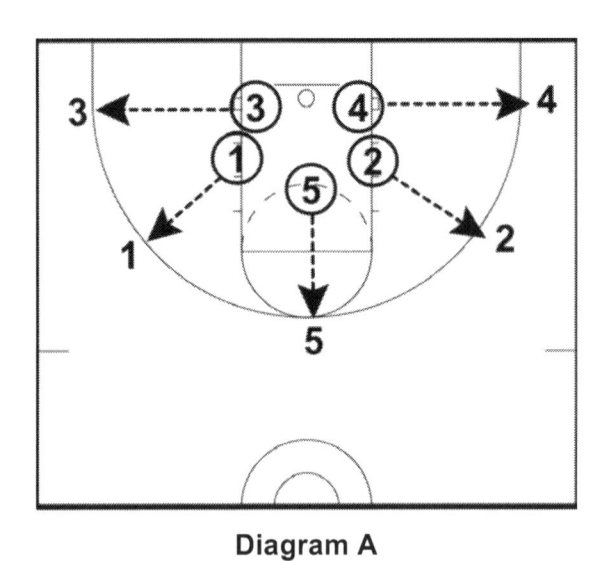

Diagram A

Ideally no more than two groups of two will be positioned at each goal. **Diagram A** only depicts five sets of partners in order to show the five shooting spots. The first shooter takes 20 3-point shot attempts from one of the five spots, keeping track of the total number of made attempts. After 20 attempts, the partners switch. Each player will shoot a total of 100 3-point shot attempts. Student assistant coaches should record and post daily the number of made 3-point shot attempts by each player.

Number 151
Four Line 3-Point Shooting

Ideal Duration: 4-8 minutes

Grouping/organization: Four lines at half court with four basketballs. The four basketballs are located as shown in **Diagram A** at the front of the two interior lines.

Frequency of usage: Daily early in the season and as needed as the season progresses. For the fast break team who by design takes a large number of 3-point shot attempts this is an excellent drill for pre-game warm-ups. It allows for a high volume of shot attempts in a short period of time utilizing many of the tactics and fundamentals that will be utilized in obtaining 3-point shot attempts off the fast beak.

This drill teaches:

1) fundamental footwork for many of the fast break tactics used to obtain 3-point shot attempts.
2) basic tactics for obtaining 3-point shot attempts off the fast break.
3) three point shooting in transition (fast break).
4) essential passing skills in the fast break.
5) essential catching skills in the fast break.
6) shooting the 3-point shot.
7) ball handling skills utilized in the fast break.
8) recognition and communication skills.

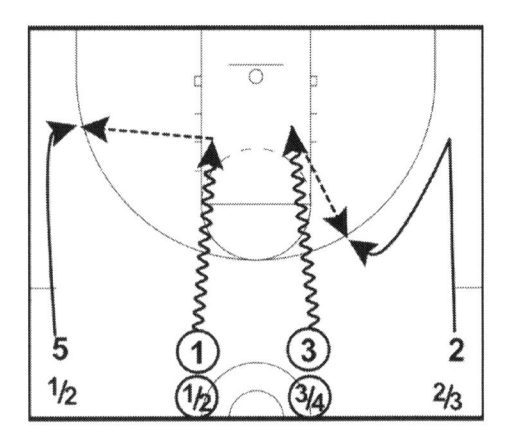

Diagram A

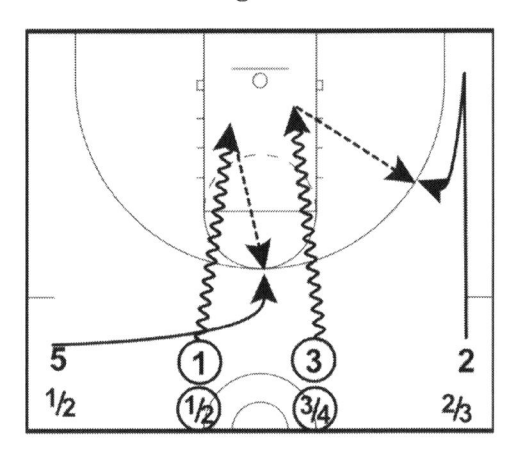

Diagram B

Imagination is the limiting factor in this drill. The drill can be an equal opportunity drill for all players regardless of position as shown in **Diagram A**.

It can also be position specific as depicted in **Diagram B**, requiring players to recognize their position specific cuts and shots.

For example, in my fast break system, the 5 is the designated inbounder, trailer and shoots 3-point shots in transition from the top of the key area.

Note where #5 has cut to for the shot and the fact #1 has executed a "Euro" to generate the appropriate shot for the situation.

Number 152
Two-Ball Threes

Ideal Duration: 2-4 minutes

Grouping/organization: Three players and two balls.

Frequency of usage: Daily or as needed.

This drill teaches:

1) movement concepts, particularly for motion offense teams.
2) passing to a shooting pocket/chin.
3) anticipation and reaction to teammates actions.
4) preparing to shoot before the ball arrives.
5) shooting off the pass.
6) footwork.
7) cutting.
8) 3-point shooting.
9) communication and organization.

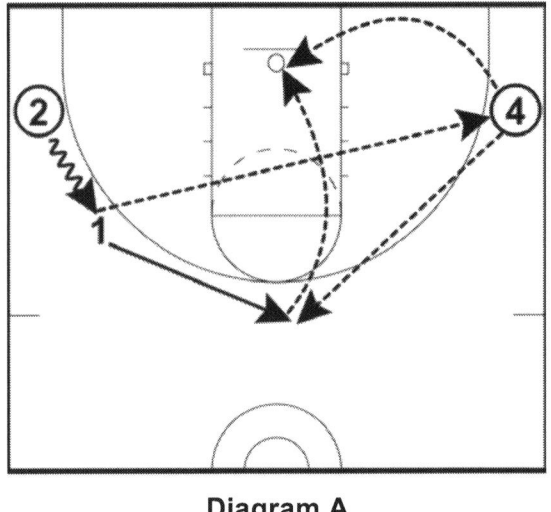

Diagram A

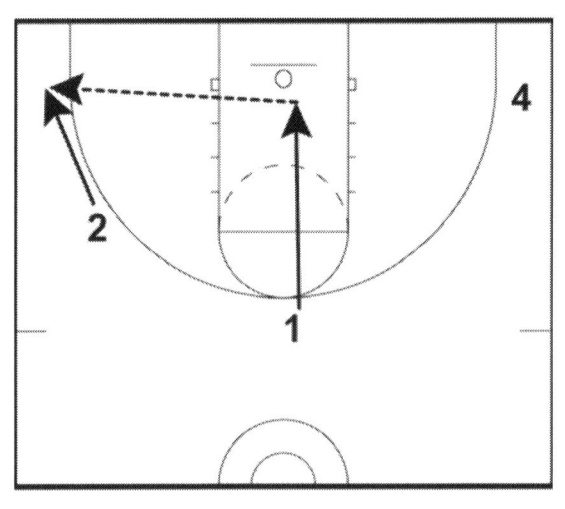

Diagram B

Two-ball three's can seem a little complicated at first to players. It is a great drill to teach creativity, imagination and movement as well as fundamentals and shooting. Diagram A depicts a random initial alignment of players. One simple rule must be complied with for a player to receive a pass to shoot a 3-point shot. The player must cut or move a minimum of 15 feet.

In **Diagram A** the action starts with #1 cutting 15 feet to the top of the 3-point line to receive a pass from #4. #1 shoots a 3-point shot and follows it to obtain the ball. As soon as #4 passes the ball, #2 dribbled off the baseline and made a skip pass to #4 (who did not move, but this will happen sometimes, particularly if you tell your players to work on zone offense concepts). #4 shoots the ball and follows it.

Diagram B shows #1 retrieving the ball he/she shot. #2, the next shooter in the shooting rotation order, cuts 15 feet to the baseline and receives a pass from #1. #2 shoots a 3-point shot and follows to retrieve the ball.

In **Diagram C** #4 pursues his/her shot to the other side of the court. #1 cuts hard to the perimeter on the opposite side of the court. #4 drives the middle for a penetrate and skip pass to #1 who takes a 3-point shot.

The drill continues in this fashion with the players reading and recognizing opportunities. It will take a few attempts over several days for inexperienced players to pick up the concept of moving and reading teammates. Once players grasp what they must do, this drill will become a player favorite. They are allowed to be creative, cut and move, pass, catch, dribble, rebound and best of all, shoot the ball.

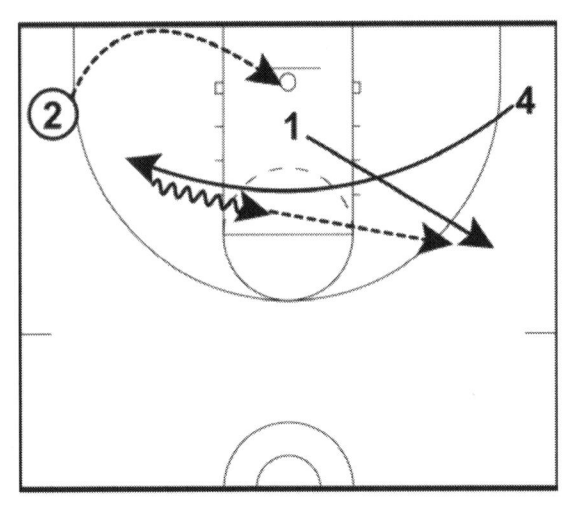

Diagram C

CHAPTER SEVENTEEN

Shooting Drills for Post Play

Post players face difficult challenges in scoring. The defenders are often not only much closer when the post player takes a shot, but the defenders are often in direct physical contact with the offensive player when the shot is taken.

The tallest players on the court will usually be found in the lane area, making it much more difficult to shoot over an opponent. Given all the challenges a post player must contend with, it is essential for the post player to have position specific shooting drills on a daily basis.

Number 153
Duck Cut Shooting

Ideal Duration: One to two minutes total time. Have players rotate after five shots.

Grouping/organization: Partners and a ball is preferable. Can use groups of three and add a defensive player.

Frequency of usage: Daily for all players is good. Particularly good for post players.

This drill teaches:

1) High to low passing and scoring.
2) "Duck cutting" to score against all types of interior defense.
3) Following a high low pass for offensive rebounding position.
4) Following a high low pass for a give and go cut.
5) Making a pass to a cutting high post from the low post area.
6) Reading the low post defender and making the appropriate cut to get open.

Diagram A and Diagram B depict the low post reading the defensive player and making the appropriate "duck cut" to get open. When the defender plays even or below the low post, the offensive player, #4, must v-cut towards the baseline and then step over the defender and slide across the lane (Depicted in **Diagram A**).

If the low post defender plays towards the ball or above the offensive low post, the posts player v-cuts in the direction of the ball and cuts beneath the defensive player (Depicted in **Diagram B**).

The principle being taught is when the defender is playing low, take the defender lower. When the defender is playing high, take the defender higher.

The high low pass must be away from the defense and the cutter must move in the direction of the pass to receive it. This also helps the cutter create enough separation to take a power shot with his/her toes pointed at the baseline after squaring up to the goal (see the information on point blank shooting).

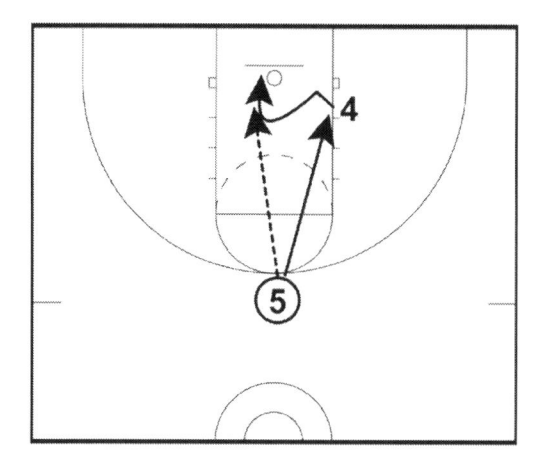

Diagram A

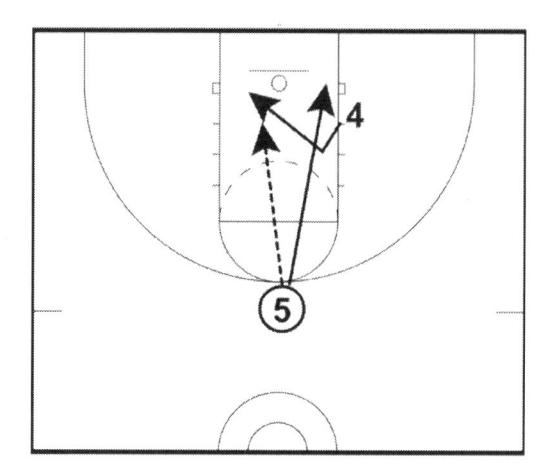

Diagram B

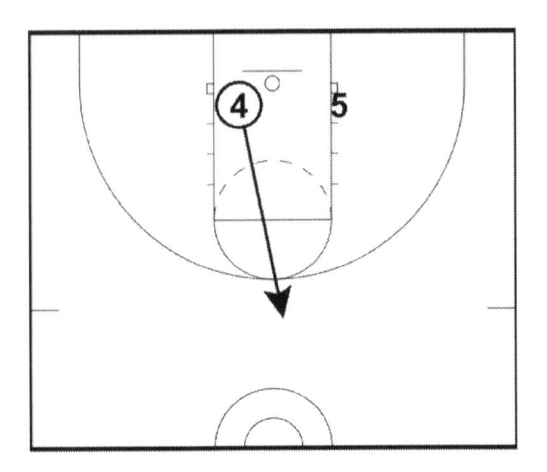

Diagram C

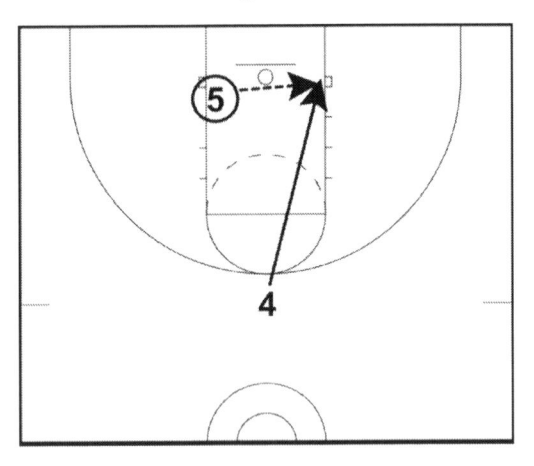

Diagram D

Also note in **Diagrams A** and **B**, #5, the high post makes a back cut to the opposite side of the rim after making the high low pass (**Diagram B**). This habit will consistently position the high post player in the best possible offensive rebounding position as most misses will carom off the rim on the other side. It also creates a back door passing opportunity called a "back half." The back half cut is a great way to prevent the high post defensive player from doubling down on the high low pass (**Diagram D**).

Diagram C depicts the rotation of the drill. After scoring the low post carries the ball and sprints to the high post. The former high post player now occupies the low post and prepares to duck cut.

If groups of three are being used, the defender would become the new offensive low post player and the former high post player would rotate to become the low post defender. Each time a player occupies the offensive low post the player should start from the opposite low post the player started from the last repetition.

When initially learning the drill and skills being worked on, the drill should be done 2-on-0. Later a defender can be added with token defensive pressure and finally the drill can go live on defense.

Number 154
Point Blank Shooting & Point Blank Offensive Rebound Shooting

Ideal Duration: Two minutes total with players rotating turns every 20-30 seconds.

Grouping/organization: Partners and a ball. Can be done in groups of three. Can have multiple groups per goal.

Frequency of usage: Daily for all players.

This drill teaches:

1) Point blank shooting skills.
2) Shooting quickly off an offensive rebound.

3) Using a shot fake.
4) Shooting a contested power shot.
5) Scoring when fouled.

Point Toes at the Baseline

Players are taught to square up to shoot and for nearly every shot, having the shoulders square to the rim or target is the correct technique to use (**Photograph A**). As with many rules, there is an exception. If a player squares up to shot a short-range power shot using the backboard, the shot will most likely by blocked and no foul called (**Photograph B**).

The reason for this is the shooter will show his numbers to the interior defender, giving the defender and excellent look at the ball and time the block (**Photograph B**). If the shooter points his toes at the baseline, the angle of the shooter's body in relationship to that of the defender has now changed dramatically (**Photograph C**).

By pointing their toes at the baseline, the shooter now places his shoulder between the defender and the ball (**Photograph D**). The shooter must now reach across the inside shoulder and arm of the shooter to block or contest a shot. The act of reaching in to block or contest a shot looks like a foul and usually a foul is committed.

To maximize the impact of this adjustment, the wise shooter will try to position the inside shoulder, the shoulder closest to the middle of the lane, just under the net (**Photographs B and D**). This seals the defensive player in such poor defensive position the only way to contest the shot is to foul or interfere with the net resulting in a goal tending violation.

The drill is quite simple. Players are paired with a ball. One player is a defender and the other is the rebounder/shooter.

Each session is 30 seconds in length and then the players switch roles. The defender starts with passive defense and increases pressure up to the point of fouling. The offensive player tosses the ball of the backboard and secures the rebound, points toes at the baseline and executes a point blank power shot. Attention to technique is important.

Photograph A

Photograph B

Photograph C

Photograph D

Number 155
Feeding the Post Skill Progression

Ideal Duration: One minute total for each step in the skill progression.

Grouping/organization: Can be done as shown as a group drill, with partners and a ball (no defense) or in groups of three with a ball (one post defender).

Frequency of Usage: Daily practice. Changing from one end of the court to the other can simulate a fast break situation requiring quick organization, making the drill more game like.

This drill teaches:

1) Post and perimeter coordination in making entry passes to the post.
2) Posting up skills.
3) Reading the defense on the part of both post and perimeter players.
4) Passing skills.
5) Post pass receiving skills.
6) Scoring in the post.
7) Communication skills of post players.

Four ways the defense can play the post:

- On Top
- Below
- Behind
- Dead Front

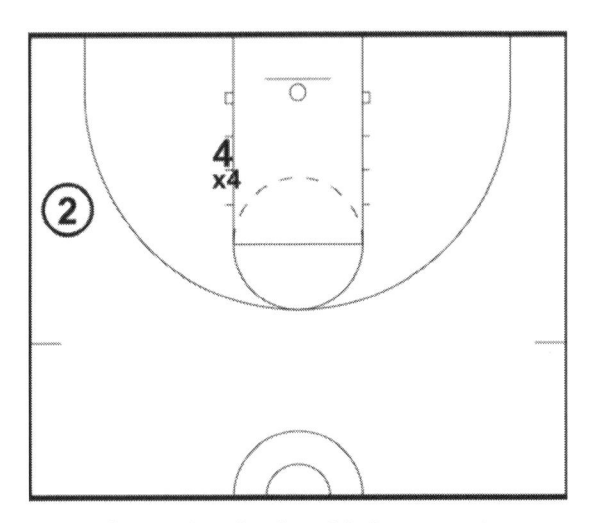

Defense is playing high or on top.

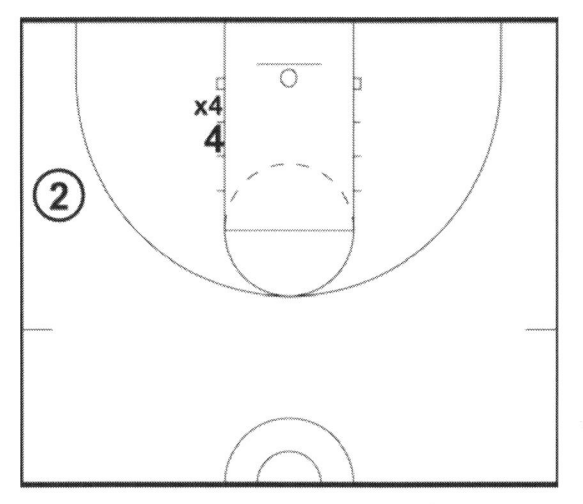

Defense is playing low or on the bottom.

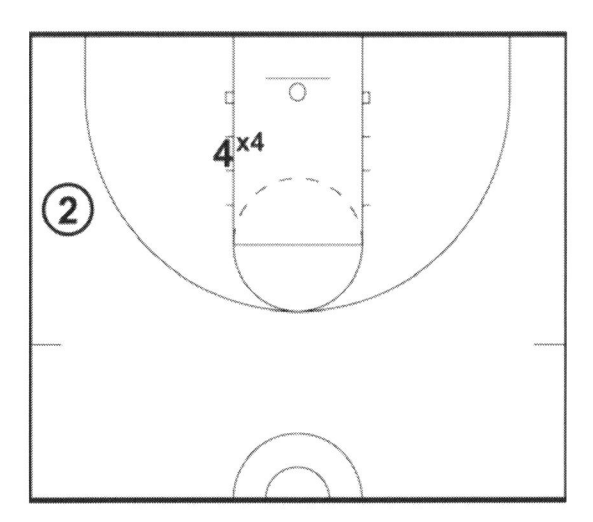

Defense is playing directly behind.

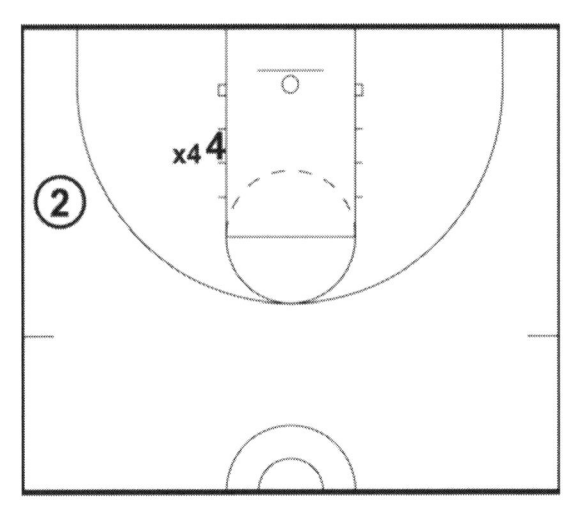

Defense is "Dead Fronting.

Drill Progression Organization

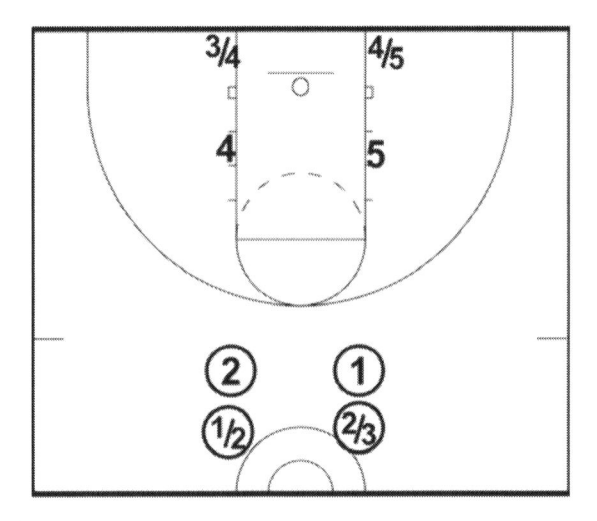

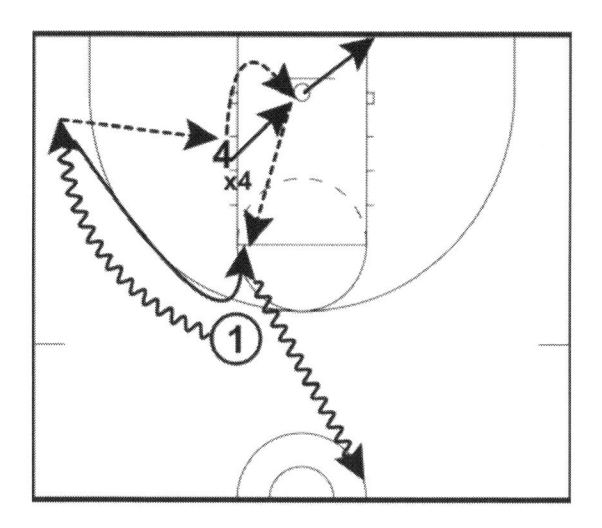

The diagram to the left above depicts how players should be set up prior to the start of the drill. The diagram to the right above depicts the player rotation during the drill. Post players rebound their shot and make an outlet pass to the perimeter player who passed the ball into the post and then go to the end of the other post player line. Perimeter's move to the elbow after feeding the post, receive the outlet pass, turn aggressively and face-up looking under the net and then attack dribble hard to half court before moving to the end of the other perimeter player line.

The Post Feed Progression

Dribble Down with Baseline Feed

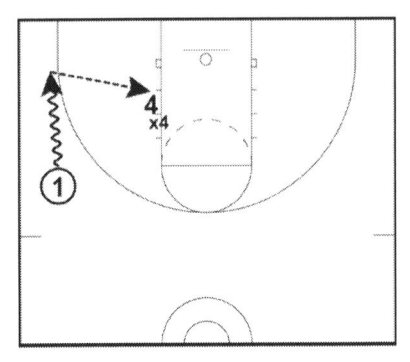

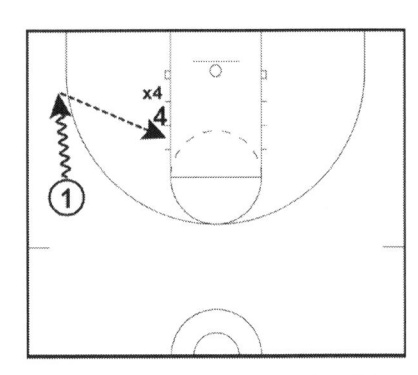

Dribble Down   **Dribble Down and Key the Shot**

Dribble down is the first post feed in the progression. The perimeter player dribbles down to a level "below" the post player and makes a baseline bounce pass back to the post player. The defender is playing on the high side of the post player. The bounce pass on the baseline side communicates to the post player the shot is either a catch and score or a drop step. The key element of recognition for the perimeter player is the location of the defensive player.

Dribble Down and Key the Shot

In the second post feed in the progression the defender hustles to play the baseline side taking away the baseline bounce pass for an easy score.

The perimeter must recognize the change in defense and "rip the ball" to pass to the high side, away from the relocated baseline defender, and "key" the shot by passing to the high side of the post player.

Keying the shot tells the post player the post move must be made by turning away from the baseline and towards the middle. Ripping the ball means the perimeter player rips the ball aggressively across his or her chest to use, in this case, the right hand instead of the left, to make the pass.

Dribble Down and Defense is Behind the Post

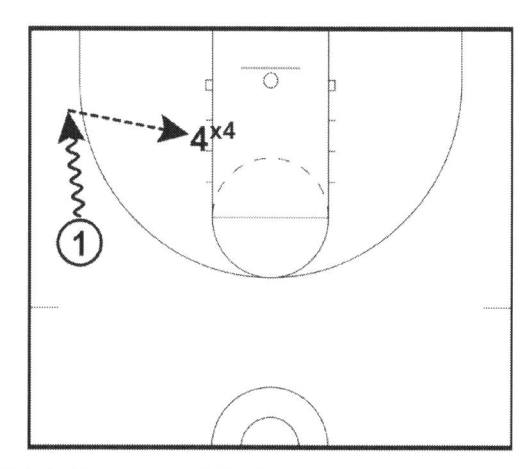

Dribble Down and Defense is Behind the Post

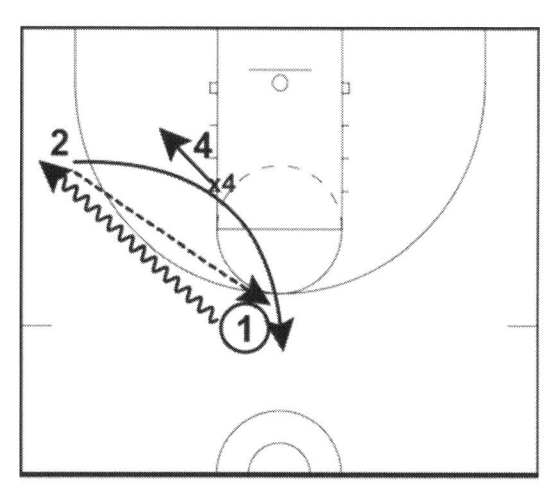

Dribble Loop and Feed From on Top

The next post feed is the dribble down and the defense plays behind. The perimeter must recognize the location of the defender and pass the ball directly to the post player's numbers. This communicates the defender is directly behind and the post must execute a post move of his or her choice to beat the defender.

Dribble Loop and Feed From on Top

An additional perimeter player must be added to the drill for dribble loops. The post defender is playing on the high side. Normally the post player would simply direct traffic to the wing and receive the appropriate post entry pass from the wing. Often the defense will deny this pass. Should this happen, the perimeter players simply execute a dribble loop. The top perimeter with the ball dribbles directly at the wing who makes a loop cut without turning his or her back to the ball and fills the vacated space on top.

In this example, and for the purpose of the drill, the defender fronts the post player. The ball handler rips the ball to pass away from the defender on the ball and the defender of the looping perimeter. The post player seals the post defender out of the lane, establishing arm and leg dominance while directing traffic. The ball is passed to the top perimeter who then makes a two hand overhead pass, not to directly to the post player but just underneath the ball side corner of the backboard.

The post player holds position until the ball is directly overhead and releases to jump and catch the ball. The post player lands with toes pointing toward the baseline in a position to make a point blank power shot.

The reason for the precision air feed pass is to avoid the inevitable help side defender. The pass forces the post player to move to the one location on the court where a charge will not take place and the ball will not be intercepted.

Screen-in and Skip Pass

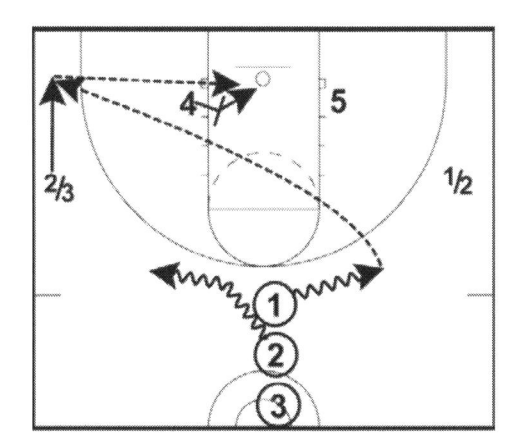

Screen-in and Skip Pass

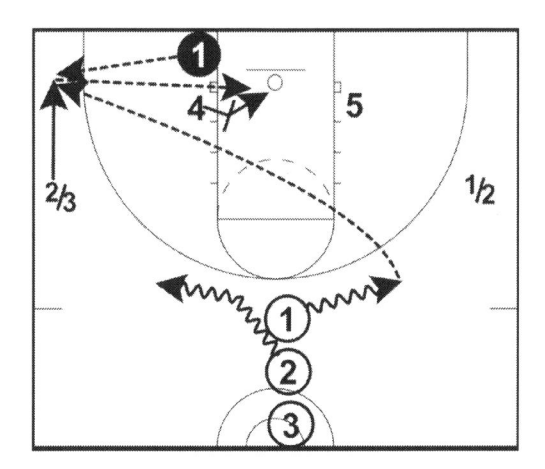

Screen-in and Skip Pass

This step in the progression works on screening in against a zone defense or pin screening a good help side defense. The perimeter lines are adjusted accordingly. On the dribble over and skip pass the post player sets the screen in.

The post sets the screen at an angle that will encourage the defender to closeout on the ball away from the baseline, allowing the baseline entry pass to be used. The post then goes to the next defender and seals the defender under the rim for the post entry pass. Note the required cuts of the perimeter players.

To make the drill more versatile, a coach or student assistant can be added on the baseline side to pass to the perimeter for a 3-point shot attempt after the post feed pass has been executed.

Variations

Start the drill with no defense. When the players have learned the progression and the myriad of small details to be mastered, add defenders to teach recognition.

Once the players have mastered the recognition portion of the drill, after working through the progression allow the post defender to go live. Finally, when the players have mastered the progression and transition to the drill by simply shouting "change" and have the players fast break to the other end of the court and continue the drill as if nothing has happened.

Number 156
Power Put Backs

Ideal Duration: One to two minutes total with players shooting for no longer than 30 seconds at a time. Periods of shooting lasting 15-20 seconds are ideal.

Grouping/organization: Two players and one ball per goal. Can have two groups at one goal.

Frequency of usage: Daily with the drill being inserted one or more times per practice.

This drill teaches:

1) Power shooting from all angles in close to the goal.
2) To rebound, land with proper balance and explode quickly to shoot a power shot.
3) Use of the backboard in close.
4) How to shoot a contested power shot in close to the goal.
5) Reading rebound angles of missed close power shots.
6) The importance of scoring an offensive put back shot.
7) Scoring a power shot when fouled or contested by the defense.

When it is time to use Power Put Backs tell the players to partner up, obtain a ball and start shooting in five seconds or less. Start counting out loud to prompt the players to move quickly and with intensity.

Players should shoot constantly without rotating shooters for a minimum of 15 seconds, then rotate.

The drill starts with the first shooter tossing the ball of the backboard and obtaining a rebound. There is no defense initially. The shooter shoots the rebound and make or miss, rebounds the ball again and shoots again. Each shooter must keep track of the number of made shots the shooter makes. Made shots are to be treated like misses and rebounded out of the net. Long rebounds must be run down and no dribbling is allowed. All shots must be taken without a dribble before shooting.

After both shooters have gone the non-shooting partner becomes a somewhat passive to aggressive defender, contesting the shot and even fouling if so desired. The coach should determine and announce the degree of defensive intensity.

The focus of this drill is less about technique and more about assertiveness, quickness and MAKING the offensive put back.

If time permits during practice have student assistants record the number of makes for each player. If this is a daily drill, post the numbers so players can keep an eye on their totals and work to improve their total, no matter how incrementally, as the season progresses. Remember, the emphasis of this drill is finding a way to find a way to score!

Number 157
10/2 Shooting – Put Backs Count

Ideal Duration: Two minutes maximum per player. Skilled shooters should be able to finish in one minute, allowing two players to shoot in a two-minute period. I learned this great drill from Don Meyer.

Grouping/organization: Partners with a ball is the ideal grouping for this drill. Modify as necessary for your conditions. Ideally one group per goal but two groups per goal is very workable. Also, groups of three players work well if time is available to extend the drill for one minute.

Frequency of usage: This drill is great for daily use in off-season and pre-season workouts. It is a fun "game" for players to play individually as well. During regular season practices once or twice a week is ideal.

This drill teaches:

1) Post players to follow their own shot (some coaches believe any player following their own shot is not a sound concept as it

creates doubt in the shooters mind. I agree with this line of thinking for three-point shooters but not post players. Post players must be super aggressive on the boards at all times and the habit of crashing the boards for every shot must be instilled in post players.).
2) Offensive rebounding angles.
3) Hustle to obtain every rebound.
4) Free throw shooting when tired.
5) Making pressure free throws when tired.
6) Scoring under pressure.
7) Getting open in the high post.

The drill begins with the shooter flashing into the high post to receive a pass from the partner (**Diagram A**). The post player faces up and shoots. After each repetition the shooter passes the ball to the partner and flashes into the high post again.

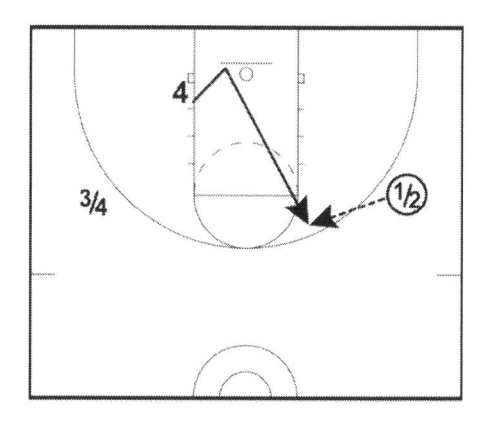

Diagram A

If the shot is made it is scored as one point. The shooter must hustle to prevent the ball from touching the court. Should the ball touch the court, it counts as one of the two permitted misses.

If the shot is made it is scored as one point. The shooter must hustle to prevent the ball from touching the court. Should the ball touch the court, it counts as one of the two permitted misses.

If the shooter misses the shot from the high post, but is able to obtain the offensive rebound without the ball hitting the court, the shooter may shoot one put back shot. If the put back shot goes in, it is scored as one point and the missed shot is "erased" by virtue of the offensive rebound.

If the shooter is able to score 10 points before the "opponent" (missed shots) scores 2 points, the shooter now must make two free throws in a row. If the shooter makes both free throws the shooter wins.

Modifications:

If three players must be used the shooter can alternate the outlet pass and work on receiving the ball from either side of the lane.

If the players are not skilled enough to score 10 points before missing two shots, modify the score needed to win but NEVER eliminate the two made free throws at the end of the game. An example of this modification would be 6-4 or 10-4.

Players can execute this drill by themselves by passing the ball to themselves using a toss with lots of backspin or a toss back device.

Players can also work against the clock and the 10-2 rule in this drill to make it more challenging. Once players are able to have some success working against the clock and the game itself are both challenging and fun making this drill one your post players will love.

CHAPTER EIGHTEEN

Fun Shooting Drills

Number 158
Knock-Out

Ideal Duration: 3-5 minutes

Grouping/organization: All of your players are in a single-file line. Use two balls.

Frequency of usage: Daily or as needed to inject fun into practice. Great camp game.

This drill teaches:

1) shooting under competitive situations.
2) preparing to shoot off the pass.
3) shooting off the pass.
4) offensive rebounding.

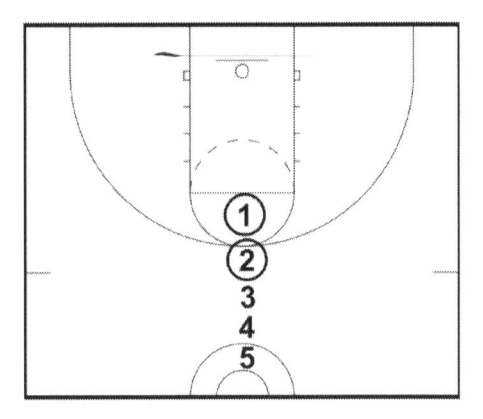

Diagram A

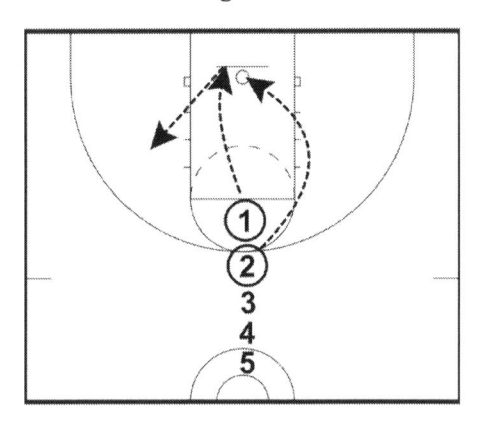

Diagram B

The game starts with the first player shooting. The second player with a ball cannot shoot until the first player has taken a shot. The objective is to "knock out" the player in front of you. In order to do knock a player out, the player in front must have missed his/her shot. If the second shooter makes his/her shot, the player who missed is said to have been "knocked out." The game continues until only one shooter remains. Diagram B depicts the first shooter missing the shot and the second shooter making the shot. The first shooter has been eliminated.

Number 159
Team Spot Shooting

Ideal Duration: 5 minutes

Grouping/organization: Divide the team into two groups. Each group has three balls.

Frequency of usage: Daily or as needed.

This drill teaches:

1) competitive shooting.
2) offensive rebounding.
3) shooting from selected spots.
4) preparing to shoot off the pass.
5) shooting off the pass.

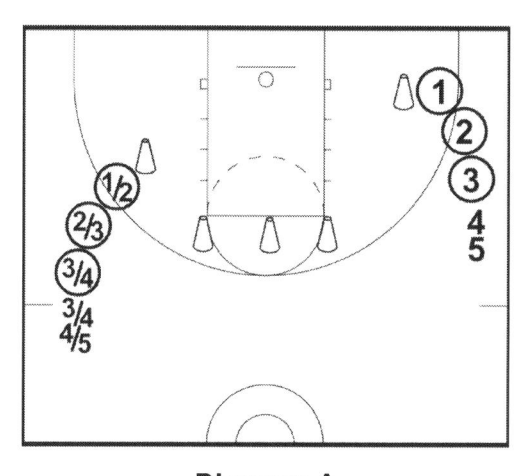

Diagram A

The coach selects five spots for the teams to shoot from and designates how many shots must be made from each of the spots. The shooter shots, follows the shot, obtains the ball and passes back to the next player in line without a ball. When the required number of shots has been made by the team at that designated spot, the team may rotate to the next spot. The team that completes all five spots first wins.

Number 160
Timed Team Range Shooting

Ideal Duration: 5 minutes

Grouping/organization: Divide the team into two groups. Each group has three balls. Use the clock for this drill.

Frequency of usage: Daily or as needed.

This drill teaches:

1) shooting from different distances.
2) competitive shooting.
3) preparing to shoot off the pass.
4) shooting off the pass.
5) offensive rebounding.

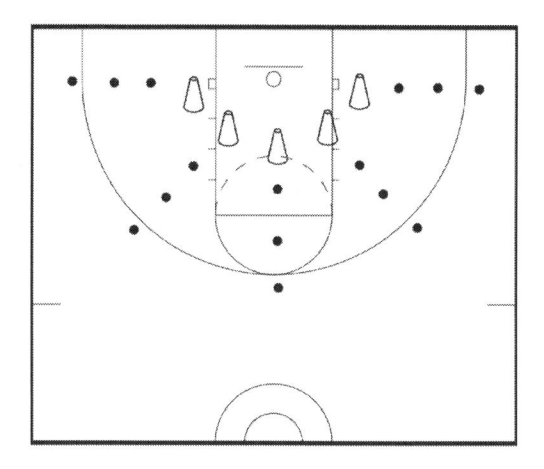

Diagram A

Diagram A shows the "court" for this drill. Divide your players into two groups, each with three basketballs. This drill can be done at one goal but ideally each team will be at its own goal. This drill works against the clock and is scored. The scoring systems is:

- 1 point per made shot from the 1st and 2nd spots.
- 2 points per made shot from the 3rd spot.
- 3 points per made shot from the 4th spot.
- 1 bonus point for finishing a line (five total possible bonus points)
- a perfect score is 75 points.

On the whistle the first shooter shoots from the first spot, follows the shot and passes to the first player in line without a ball. The team counts their point total out loud. In order to advance through the court the team must make the following:

- 4 shots from the 1st spot (4 points total)
- 3 shots from the 2nd spot (3 points total)

- 2 shots from the 3rd spot (4 points total)
- 1 shot from the 4th spot (3 points total)
- 1 bonus point is earned for finishing the line

The team with the highest score win time elapses wins. Keep records of each teams score as well as the total number of wins and losses.

Number 161
Make 25 Don't Miss 2 In a Row

Ideal Duration: 5 minutes

Grouping/organization: Divide your team into two groups, each with three balls. Ideally, each group will have its own goal but it is possible to run this drill at one goal.

Frequency of usage: Daily or as needed.

This drill teaches:

1) competitive shooting.
2) shooting for technique.
3) shooting off the pass.
4) preparing to shoot off the pass.
5) offensive rebounding.

The coach selects where the teams will shoot from. The drill starts on the whistle. The first team to make 25 baskets wins. If a team misses two shots in a row, it must start over with a score of zero. If a team does miss two in a row but can swish the next shoot perfectly, it retains its score and can continue.

An alternative approach to this fun drill is to have one team, raise the number of shots to be made to 35 and have the team compete against the clock to make the required number of shots.

CHAPTER NINETEEN

Two-Minute Intensity Drills

Planning effective, quality practice sessions is a topic that can fill an entire book. This chapter focuses solely on using two-minute intensity drills effectively as part of an overall well planned practice session.

Here are guidelines for using two-minute intensity drills in daily practice sessions:

- When building intensity, start with short bouts and increase the length over time.
- Limit use to no more than three consecutive two-minute intensity drills at a time.
- Use consecutive intensity drills for no more than five minutes total at one time.
- Rest has to be factored into practice sessions.
- Insert "intensity drills" to change the pace of practice physically.
- Insert "intensity drills" to change the pace of practice mentally.
- Limit individual drills to 3-5 minutes.
- Limit team concept drills to 8-10 minutes.

- Always change drills, regardless of drill after 10 minutes.
- If more time is needed for a specific item, split the time into multiple segments.

When building intensity, start with short bouts and increase the length over time.

Physically player's bodies cannot sustain intense physical effort over prolong periods of time. Players also have difficulty maintaining the mental effort required to perform a high intensity task over long periods of time.

Like nearly every other physical and mental task, repetition combined with increasing the length of duration the task must be performed gradually over time will allow players to increase their stamina, both mental and physical, in performing the task.

Let's use as an example one of the drills listed in this book, the 4/4/4 drill. This drill combines placing extreme, relentless pressure on the ball for a total of 12 seconds with handling the ball under extreme ball pressure for 12 seconds.

Each pair of players takes one turn on offense and then one turn on defense. If each player takes two turns each on offense and defense a total 48 to 52 seconds will have elapsed.

Physically and mentally the players will have exerted a large amount of energy in a short period of time. Continuing the drill for another two or three minutes will cause the players to lower their intensity level in order to continue performing the drill. Because the skills and concepts practiced in two-minute intensity drills must be executed with great intensity, this lowering of intensity is precisely the habit we as coaches do NOT want the players to form.

Limit use to no more than three consecutive two-minute intensity drills at a time.

Execution of skills with game level intensity is the desired habit to be created. In order for this to be achieved, the players must perform the skills at game level intensity for the duration of the drill.

In order to ensure the intensity does not reduce due to physical or mental fatigue, limit the use of two-minute intensity drills to no more than three at a time. Preferably the three drills selected will not all last the full two minutes.

Use consecutive intensity drills for no more than five minutes total at one time.

Even with the above guideline of limiting two-minute intensity drills to no more than three consecutive drills, for the same reasons limit the total amount of time dedicated to use of consecutive intensity drills to a total of five minutes of practice time in that particular period of time.

Rest has to be factored into practice sessions.

Rest, or recovery time, has to be built into practice sessions. Following an extremely demanding set of drills, regardless of whether the drills used were of the two-minute intensity variety or other, longer demanding drills, rest has to be built in to allow the players to physically recover.

If this guideline is not followed, fatigue will cause the quality of execution and performance levels to decline. Fatigue will also, depending on the nature of what is being practiced, increase the possibility of injury.

Because basketball requires the ability to perform at high levels of intensity for extended periods of time, start with shorter periods and gradually increase the length of time while demanding players maintain the required level of intensity.

Insert "intensity drills" to change the pace of practice physically.

To jumpstart the intensity of practice following a period of rest or recovery type of drills or work, insert a two-minute intensity drill to the get the players moving again. Follow the two-minute drill with a "normal" drill.

This approach will cause the initial start of the "normal" drill to be smoother and with a higher degree of successful execution as the two-minute drill helped the players refocus both mentally and physically.

Insert "intensity drills" to change the pace of practice mentally.

Intensity drills require mental focus and as the drill and practice progress, an increased level of mental toughness in order to execute the drill correctly. Inserting a two-minute intensity drill can dramatically change the pace of practice mentally.

If a somewhat lengthy period of instruction, review or correction has just taken place, the insertion of a two-minute intensity drill will change the mental pace instantly. It is also a good way to observe which players are capable of mentally changing pace quickly and which are not.

Limit individual drills to 3-5 minutes in duration.

While not directly related to the use of two-minute intensity drills, a good guideline to follow when planning practice sessions is to limit drills that focus on individual skills or individual work on the part of the player to a total of three to five minutes. Change to another drill or activity at the end of the allotted time. Continuing the drill longer than this amount of time loses its effectiveness.

Limit team concept drills to 8-10 minutes.

Just as individual drills lose their effectiveness after three to five minutes, so do drills that incorporate the groups of players working on team concepts. This could be 3-on-3, 4-on-4 or 5-on-5 or working on offense with no defense. Limit the length of this type of drill work to no more than eight to ten minutes.

Always change drills, regardless of drill after 10 minutes.

Regardless of the drill, or activity, after ten minutes players begin to lose focus. Limit any one specific drill or activity in practice to ten minutes in duration, then move on to another drill or activity.

If more time is needed for a specific item, split the time into multiple segments.

There are times when a specific concept, such as half court offense or breaking a full court zone press, need more than eight to ten minutes of practice. Continue to follow the limit of eight to ten minutes of working on the particular concept but schedule additional blocks of time during the practice to work on the concept.

The drills in this chapter could just as easily be placed in another chapter. In fact, some of them are simply because these drills can teach more than one concept. The drills have been inserted in this chapter because while these drills teach other concepts and skills, intensity is what these drill teach best.

These drills also teach concepts that are overlooked yet can make a huge difference, for better or worse, at critical junctures in a game. Remember, players do not do what coaches teach, players do what coaches emphasize. These drills provide an excellent way to emphasize these concepts.

Number 162
Loose Ball Drill

Ideal Duration: 30 seconds minimum to one minute total.

Grouping/organization: Partners with one ball

Frequency of Usage: Daily practice. Can be scheduled two or three times a practice to build to transition from a slow drill or activity to a more active or intense activity.

This drill teaches:

1) Toughness - players learn they can get on the floor without getting hurt
2) Being constantly aware of the possibility of a loose ball

3) Only half the play has been completed when the ball has been obtained, a teammate must get open so possession can be maintained.

4) Intensity
5) Communication
6) Awareness
7) It also places actual emphasis on a concept coaches teach but do not back up with actual action in practice.
   8) Pride in being a gritty team.

As coaches we constantly stress the importance to our players of getting on the floor to obtain loose balls. We praise the one player who consistently dives for the loose balls.

Yet how many times does that one player make the great save to obtain the loose ball, only to turn it over again to the opponent, often for an easy score? Imagine a team where all of your players dive for loose balls AND they never turn the ball over to the opponent!

This can be done by a great one or two minute drill you can insert in practice to crank up the intensity level. This simple ball and a partner drill is called appropriately enough "loose ball drill."

For safety, spread all of your players out around the court and make sure there is plenty of space between pairs. Explain and EMPHASIZE the need to watch for each other for safety reasons.

The drill actually begins with the command to pair up with a partner and a ball. Partner's sprint to an area on the court and start on their own. The first player rolls the ball on the court for the partner to dive on (teach your players how to do this correctly - I suggest talking to your school's volleyball coach about techniques for this) to obtain the loose ball.

The player who rolled the ball must cut 15-20 feet to "get open" and call for the ball. The player who obtained possession of the loose ball, without rolling or traveling, passes the ball to the cutting partner and hops up.

The cutter passes the ball crisply to the diver, who rolls a loose ball for the cutter. Roles are now reversed. The drill should continue for 45 seconds to a minute and then progress to another high intensity drill (See **Diagram A**).

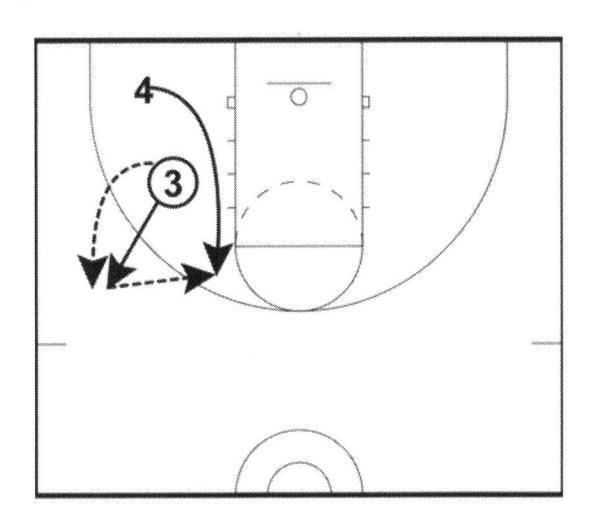

Diagram A

Number 163
Save the Ball Drill

Ideal Duration: 30 seconds to one minute total with players rotating after each repetition.

Grouping: Partners with one ball

Frequency of Usage: One or two times a week.

This drill teaches:

1) Recognition
2) Teamwork
3) Hustle
4) Communication
5) Game awareness

Players spread out around the out-of-bounds line of the basketball court. The player with the ball bounces the ball so it will go out-of-bounds but high enough in the air the other player can save the ball.

The player saving the ball must "run down" the loose ball, jump in the air, catch the ball, attempt to turn and find a teammate to pass to. The partner who initiated the drill with the out-of-bound pass must move in a line perpendicular to the sideline or baseline and call for the ball (**Diagram A**).

If the second player does not move to get open and call for the ball, the player saving the ball should keep the ball and land out-of-bounds if there is no teammate to pass to, toss it towards his/her team's goal if on the defensive end of the court. It is nearly always better to simply hold on the to ball if under the opponent's basket, allowing a set defense to be established rather than a scramble that results in the opponent scoring easily.

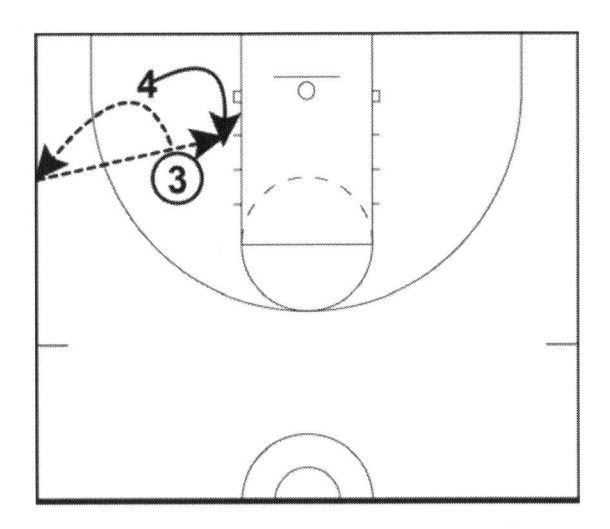

Diagram A

Number 164
Create Drill

Ideal Duration: One to two minutes total.

Grouping/organization: Partners and a ball. Utilize the entire gym.

Frequency of Usage: Daily during pre-season and once a week during the regular season.

This drill teaches:

1) Offensive creativity.
2) Use of all types of fakes.
3) The concept of covering distance with one or two dribbles, "going somewhere with your dribble!"
4) Moving to get open.
5) Moving to meet the pass, "shortening the pass!"

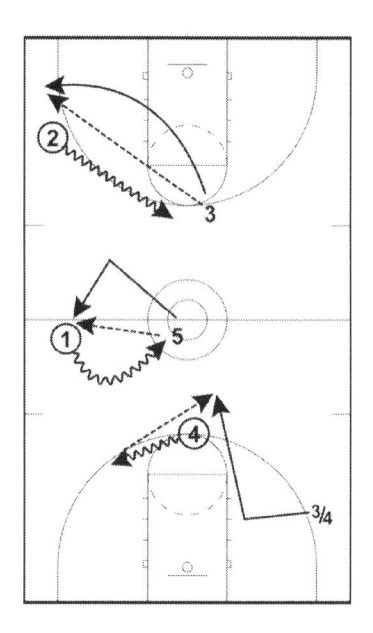

Diagram A

Diagram A depicts the just a few of the nearly infinite number of possibilities of how players may move offensively when working together. It also shows the utilization of the entire court for the drill.

Both players must move a minimum of 15 feet. The ball handler is limited to two dribbles. The cutter must either use a loop, follow cut or v-cut to get open, also moving a minimum of 15 feet. The ball handler must use a minimum of two fakes and pass away from the imaginary defense, both on the ball and away from the denial defender.

Number 165
4/4/4 Drill

Ideal Duration: One minute is ideal with a two minute maximum.

Grouping/organization: Partner and a ball.

Frequency of Usage: Ideal for daily usage all season long.

This drill teaches:

1) Defensive INTENSITY!
2) Handling the ball under extreme defensive pressure.
3) Recognizing how to handle the "five second rule" when under pressure.
4) Crowding the offensive player's pivot foot when the dribble is picked up.
5) Tracing the ball without fouling when on defense.
6) Stepping through pressure when closely guarded.
7) Handling the ball under pressure.
8) Covering maximum distance when dribbling while under pressure.
9) Maintaining low body position while being strong with the ball while under pressure.

The pairs of players spread out all over the gym, ignoring court lines. The drill begins with the coach starting the count. The defense immediately applies maximum pressure on the offensive player without fouling. While the coach counts from one to four the offensive player cannot use the dribble and must maintain good wide, low body balance while being strong with the ball. The four count is used three times to teach players the fact the ball can be held for four seconds, dribbled for four seconds and then held for an additional four seconds before a five second violation takes place, giving the player a total of 12 seconds with the ball.

At the start of the second four count, the offensive player must now dribble the ball while closely guarded for the entire duration of the four count. The third and final four count requires the offensive player to pick up the dribble and handle the extreme defensive pressure.

At the end of the third four count the players switch role. The coach immediately starts another count. This drill is high intensity and to maintain the desired level of intensity ideally should not last for more than one minute. However, the drill can be used more than once during practice.

Number 166
Wolf Drill

Ideal Duration: Two minutes total with players rotating after each repetition.

Grouping: Groups of three with one ball.

Frequency of Usage: One or two times a week.

This drill teaches:

1) both offense and defense.
2) players to hustle back and play defense after committing a turnover. The emphasis is on not fouling (This compounds the mistake)!

3) how to "wolf" the ball without fouling and generate a turnover for the opponent.

4) communication on both offense and defense as the bench for the offense must call "wolf" during a game to warn of a wolf attempt by the opponent.

The "Wolf Drill" teaches players to hustle back and play defense after committing a turnover. In this instance, the defense attempts to steal the ball back without committing a foul. The Wolf Drill starts with the defense one step behind the offensive player and on the opposite side of the hand the offensive player will be dribbling with (**Diagram A**).

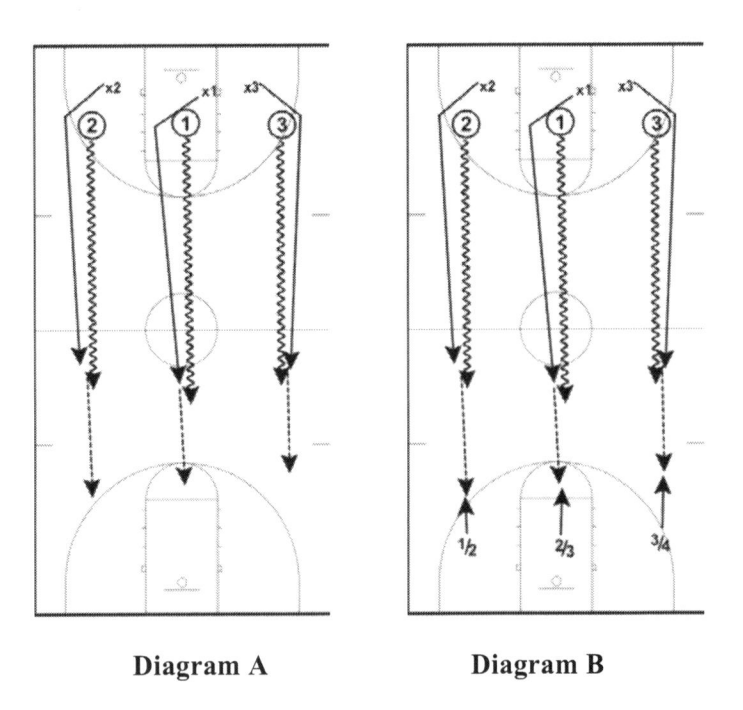

Diagram A   Diagram B

The defensive player must not only sprint to catch up with the offense, but must change sides of the court so the defensive player is on the same side as the hand the offensive player is dribbling with. If the offensive player is dribbling with the right hand, the defensive player must be on the right hand side of the offensive player.

The defensive player reaches with his or her left hand, if on the right side, and tips the ball forward, if possible to a teammate down the court (**Diagram B**). This technique prevents obvious fouls but the defense must be certain to tip the ball and not make contact with the offensive player.

The drill can be made continuous by having the offensive player sprint past the teammate the ball was tipped to, touch the baseline and pursue the new offensive player who begins dribbling after the old offensive player touches the baseline and turns around. The old defensive player becomes the player waiting for a back tip.

CHAPTER TWENTY

Fast Break Drills

Number 167
Modified Cycles Drill*

Ideal Duration: 8-10 minutes
Grouping/organization: Groups of five with a ball. Can be run against the clock.
Frequency of usage: Daily
This drill teaches:

1) the habits necessary to run a fast break attack at maximum speed.
2) all the major concepts in a numbered fast break.
3) timing and filling lanes correctly.
4) options of the numbered fast break.
5) the 5 to 1 inbounds cut and pass.
6) serves as a fantastic conditioning drill.
7) passing on the run.
8) catching on the run.
9) preparing to shoot off the pass received on the run.
10) pushing the ball at maximum speed.
11) making decisions at maximum speed.

201 DRILLS FOR COACHING YOUTH BASKETBALL| 352

- This approach to running the Cycles drill is suited to teach the break as run by the Lady Tigers of Olivet Nazarene or a team that uses Dribble Drive Motion, requiring an open ball side post during the fast break, secondary break and initial phase of offense.

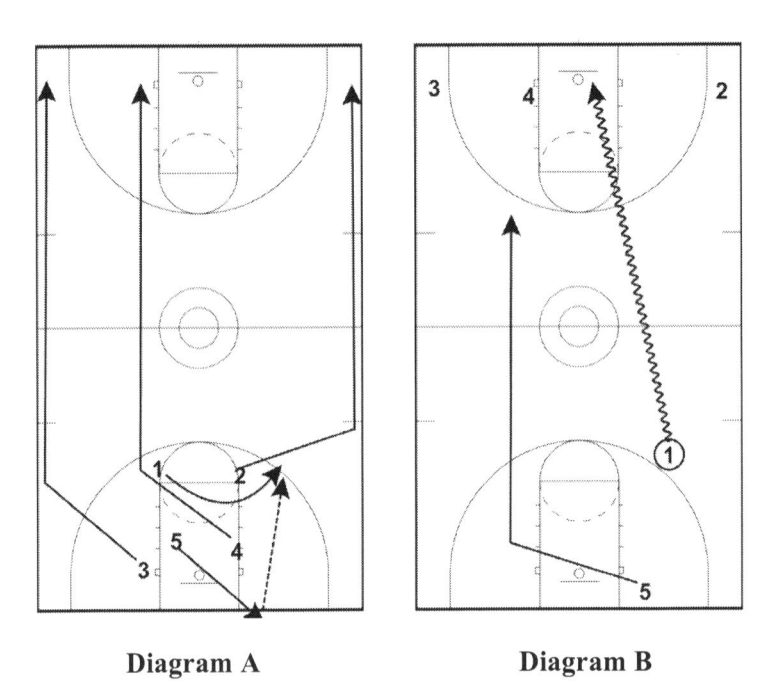

Diagram A **Diagram B**

SIVILS| 353

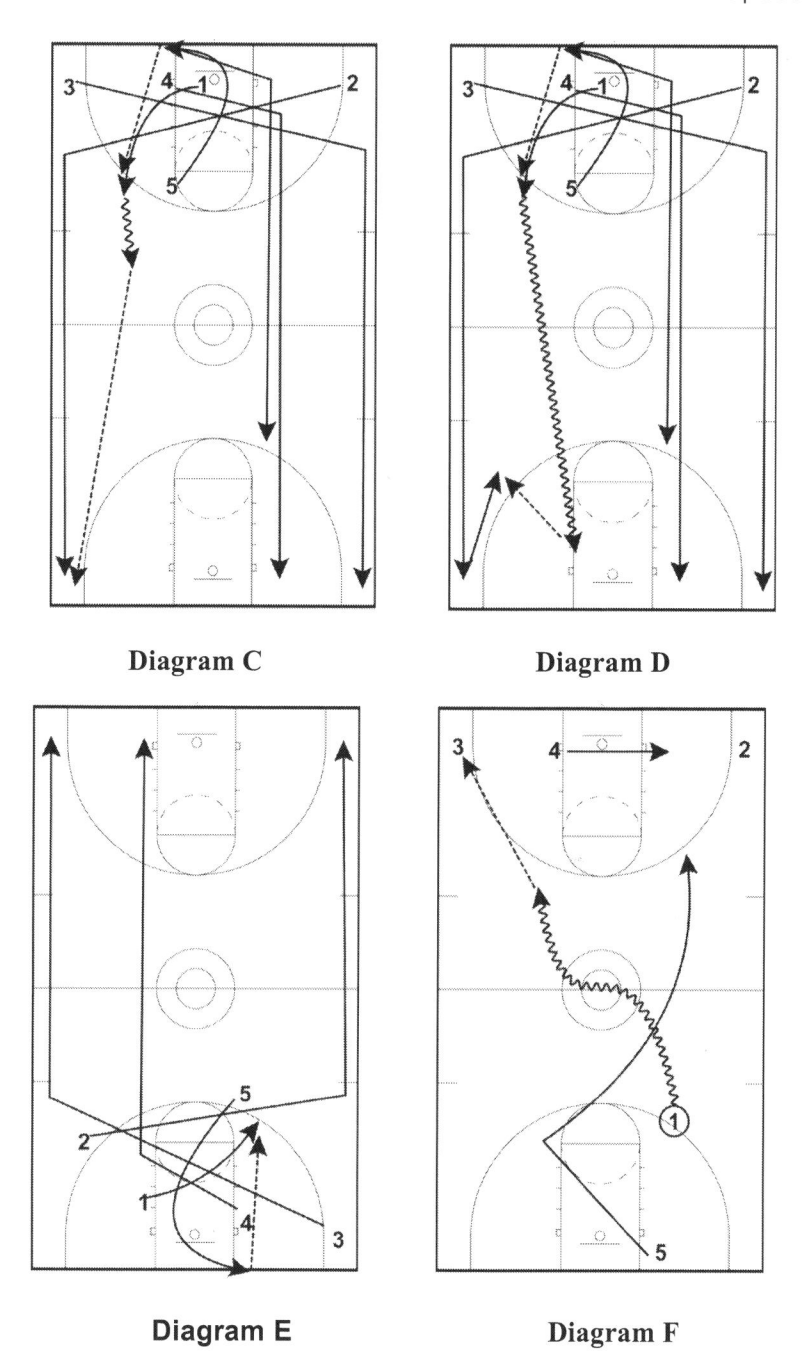

Diagram C

Diagram D

Diagram E

Diagram F

201 DRILLS FOR COACHING YOUTH BASKETBALL| 354

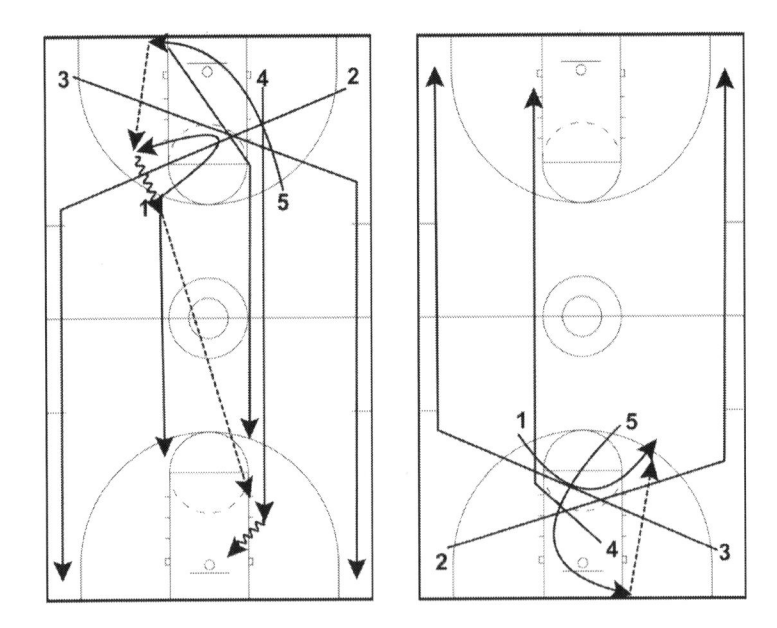

Diagram G Diagram H

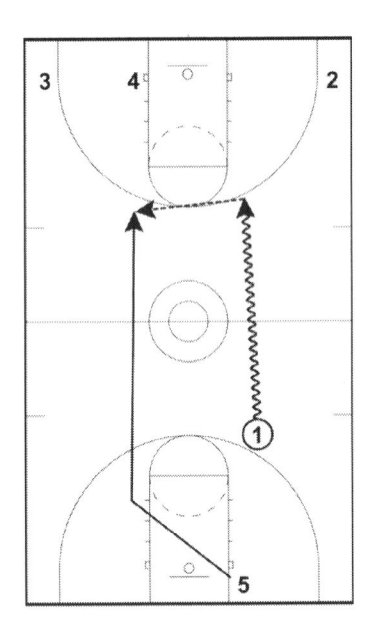

Diagram I

Number 168
5 on 2 on 5 on 3 Drill

Ideal Duration: 2-5 minutes
Grouping/organization: Groups of three players and a ball.
Frequency of usage: Daily or as needed.
This drill teaches:

1) Reading the defense and recognizing scoring opportunities within the system.
2) filling fast break lanes wide.
3) attacking the basket to score.
4) shooting lay-ups at maximum speed.
5) making full court passes.
6) using one-dribble to make a pitch-a-head pass.
7) making the 5 to 1 inbounds pass on a made basket.
8) making the point guard cut on a made basket for the inbounds pass.
9) offensive rebounding off the fast break.

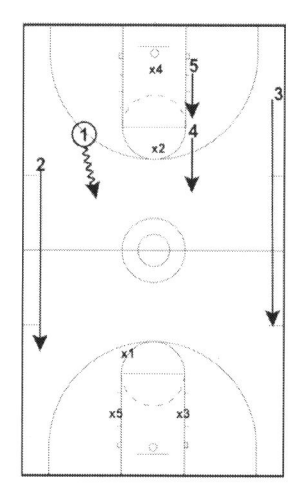

Diagram A

The offense makes a total of four offensive trips, attacking each end of the court twice. The possession changes on a made basket, turnover or defensive rebound.

Should the defense obtain possession of the ball, the offensive unit makes transition and with the defense making the outlet pass. Players must run assigned lanes and look for options within the system. On an offensive rebound the offense looks to score the rebound.

This can be made into a competitive drill by counting the number of trips the offense scores versus the number of stops the defensive unit is able to generate.

Number 169
5 on 4 on 5 on 0 Drill

Ideal Duration: 2-5 minutes
Grouping/organization: Groups of three players and a ball.
Frequency of usage: Daily or as needed.
This drill teaches:

1) using system options to attack a zone defense.
2) offensive rebounding against a zone in transition.
3) filling fast break lanes wide.
4) attacking the basket to score.
5) shooting lay-ups at maximum speed.
6) making full court passes.
7) using one-dribble to make a pitch-a-head pass.
8) making the 5 to 1 inbounds pass on a made basket.
9) making the point guard cut on a made basket for the inbounds pass.

The Primary Fast Break and Drills

Regardless of the style of offensive play utilized, every team needs to be able to convert turnovers into point quickly. Running teams will utilize a full court, up-tempo offense that starts with possession of the ball. Deliberate tempo teams will walk the ball up the floor and initiate their half court offense from a set play or organized offensive entry.

Turnovers are an opportunity to score quickly and with relative ease. Every team needs to have this ability, particularly when trailing in a game. All too often teams are not able to convert these opportunities, called primary fast breaks, into the easy scoring opportunities they are.

The first component of generating points successfully on a primary fast break each and every time is mental. Players, particularly with deliberate teams, often lack the mental sureness, or confidence to convert every time. To eliminate this challenge and create an environment of assertiveness and confidence, utilize the "back rules." The back rules apply for 1-on, 2-on and 3-on situations unless time and score dictates possession of the ball is more important than scoring. The "back rules" are:

- If no defender is "back" attack the basket and score.
- If one defender is "back" attack the basket and score. If you fail to score, the failure is on you the player. If you commit a charging foul, the blame lies on the coach as the coach made the decision to always attack. You have the "green light" to score!
- If two defenders are "back" and the numbers are even, flow into offense.
- If two defenders are "back" and the offense has the numbers, attack and score. See above for who is to blame if the result is not a score.

- Turn all 3-on-1 and 3-on-2 situations into a 2-on-1.
- Be assertive and confident. Success will go to the attacker!
- Be opportunistic and look for primary break opportunities with every possession.

The keys to scoring on primary breaks are the "back rules," the Concept of Best and the ability to turn every break into a 2-on-1. Look-a-heads are also critical because these result in uncontested lay-up opportunities.

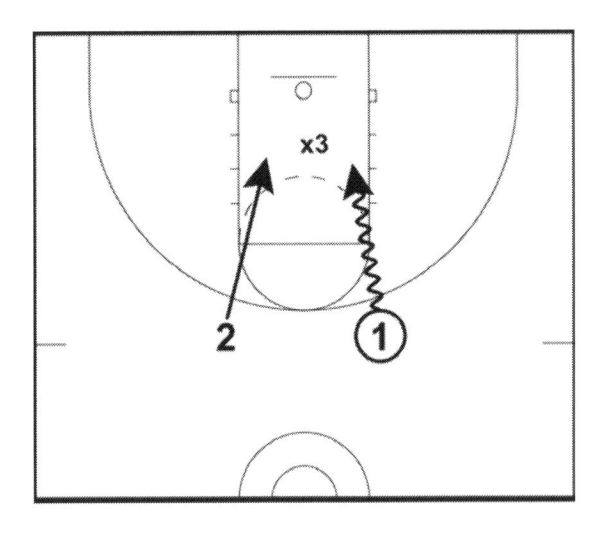

Diagram A

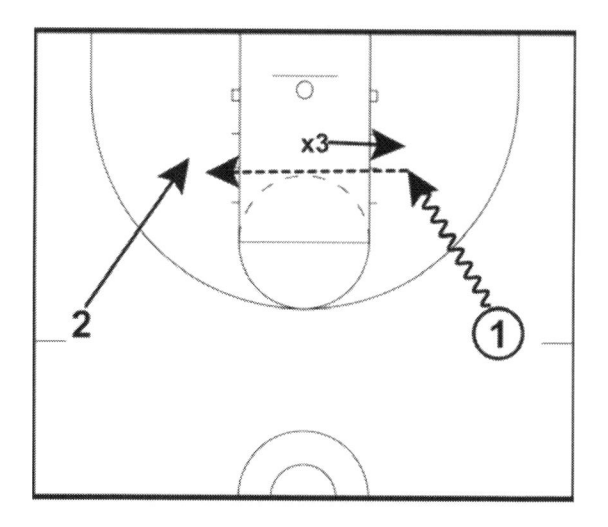

Diagram B

The key to every 2+-on primary break is converting the 2-on-1 every opportunity. **Diagram A** depicts the most common way players attack in a 2-on-1 situation and the reason they fail. The players are too close together, allowing the defender to impede the path of the ball handler and play the pass to the cutter at the same time. The result is often a turnover.

Diagram B depicts a proper 2-on-1 with the attackers wide and attacking at a 45-degree angle, forcing the defender to make a choice, play the ball or play the cutter. Either choice will result in a lay-up for the attackers.

The lone problem with the attack depicted in Diagram B depends on the hand the ball handler is dribbling with. In this example, the ball handler will be attacking with the ball in the right hand. This will require the ball handler to pick the ball up and bring it across his/her body, tipping the defender off when the pass will take place and a shot attempt will not be made.

The solution to this is for the ball handler to always make the attack approach with the ball in the inside hand, in this case the left hand. This allows for the ball to be picked up and passed to the attacking cutter or shot and the defender will not have any indication of what the ball handler is going to do.

Converting 3-on-1s and 3-on-2s

The 2-on-1 is the key and the primary break that must be perfected. Once it has been mastered, every 3-on-1 and 3-on-2 must be converted into a 2-on-1. This approach increases the number of primary breaks that will be successfully converted into points.

Converting the 3-on-1

It is bad enough when a team does not convert a 2-on-1. Failure to convert a 3-on-1 is maddening! The reason teams do not convert 3-on-1s are generally two-fold. First, the players lack confidence and are indecisive. Second, the players are usually too close together, allowing a single assertive and intelligent defender to disrupt the fast break. **Diagram A** depicts the proper approach to converting a 3-on-1 fast break into a 2-on-1.

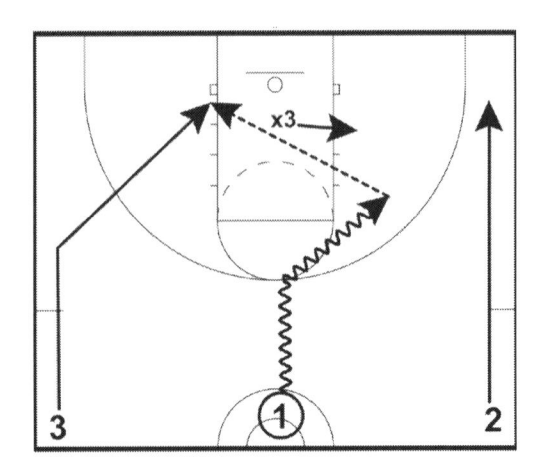

Diagram A

Applying the concept of best rules, the ball handler recognizes the best slasher has filled the left attack lane. To convert the 3-on-1 into a 2-on-1, the ball handler veers away from the best slasher/finisher, moving the defender away from the desired cutter. The other cutter sprints and spots up for a 3-point attempt, also encouraging the defender to shift to that side of the court.

The ball handler must move the ball to the inside hand to create space for the pass away from the defender, allowing for an easy pass for a lay-up. In a perfect game, the right and cutter in this example would be a three-point shooter. If the defender did not shift to stop the ball or anticipate the pass to the shooter, an easy shot will be the result.

Converting a 3-on-2 into a 2-on-1

Once a team has mastered the art of converting a 2-on-1 every opportunity and converting a 3-on-1 into a 2-on-1, scoring on every 3-on-2 fast break will be easy. **Diagram B** depicts the action.

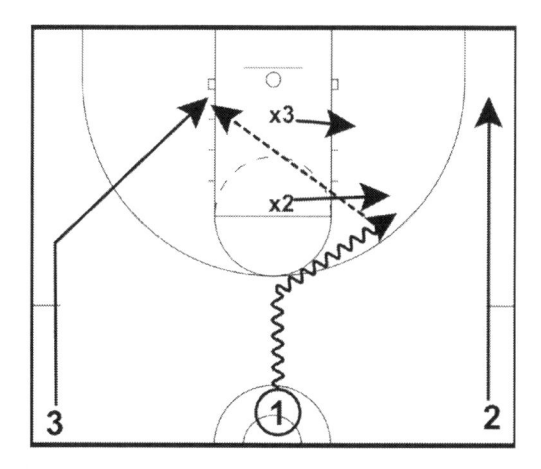

Diagram B

The exact same approach is used in converting a 3-on-1. The defense has been taught for one player to defend the rim and cover the first pass. The other defender is assigned the responsibility of stopping the ball.

The veering action will shift the on-the-ball defender AND the second defender. For some reason, the natural tendency of the second defender is to move in the direction of the ball handler, anticipating the pass to the right hand cutter. This creates the space needed for the left hand attacker to receive a pass away from the defense and an open lay-up.

Number 170
2-on-1 Trap and Fast Break Drill

Ideal Duration: Two or three minutes total.

Grouping/organization: Groups of three or four with players rotating after each repetition.

Frequency of Usage: One or two times per week.

This drill teaches:
1) trapping skills.
2) quick transition from defense to offense.
3) an attacking mindset.
4) how to execute a 2-on-1 fast break and score each time.
5) how to defend a 2-on-1 fast break.

This drill teaches players how to trap and transition from the trap into a fast break quickly and effectively while a player who has committed a turnover learns to defend against a two-on-one fast break attack. **Diagram A** shows the initial alignment and how multiple groups can go at the same time.

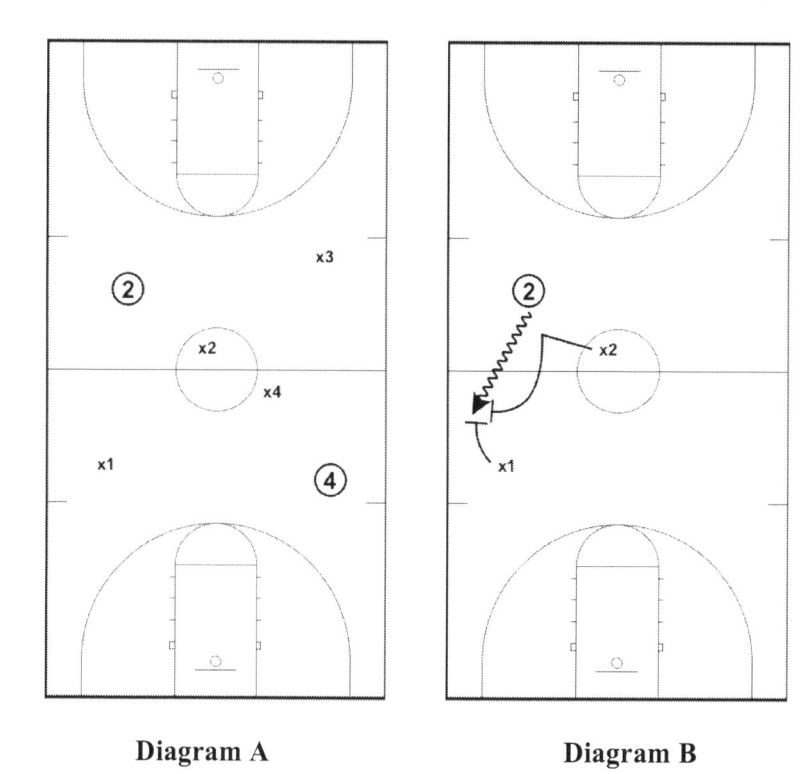

Diagram A

Diagram B

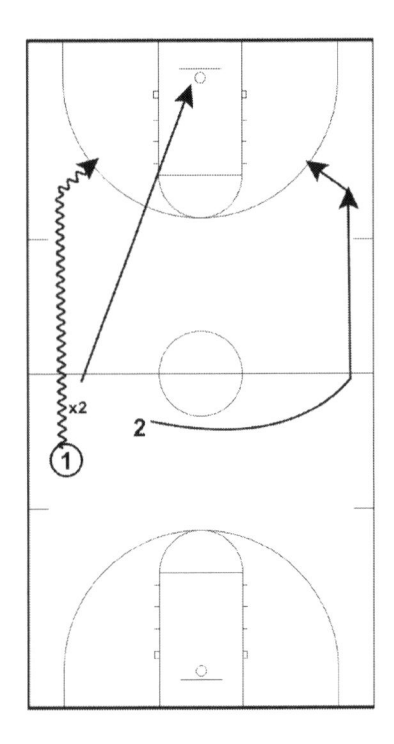

Diagram C

In **Diagram B** #2 dribbles into the trap. X1 and X2 properly execute a trap and exercise hand discipline and pressure the ball. #2 deliberately turns the ball over. X1 and X2 transition into a fast break while #2 sprints back to defend the rim and defend a two-on-one fast break. X2 and X1 get wide first and attack at proper fast break angles, forcing #2 to choose which attacker to defend (**Diagram C**).

Number 171
Continuous 2-on-1 With Defense

Ideal Duration: Three to five minutes total for the entire drill.
Grouping/organization: See **Diagram A**.

Frequency of Usage: For daily usage, particularly if your team is a fast break team.
This drill teaches:

1) The concept of getting wide first for proper spacing for a 2-on-1 fast break.
2) Decision making for a 2-on-1 fast break.
3) The skills and tactics necessary for a successful 2-on-1 fast break.
4) Defending a 2-on-1 fast break with one defender.
5) Defending a 2-on-1 fast break with a pursuing defender.
6) Finishing a 2-on-1 fast break against defense.
7) Defensive tenacity in the face of bad odds.
8) The best ball handler pushes the ball.
9) Competition!

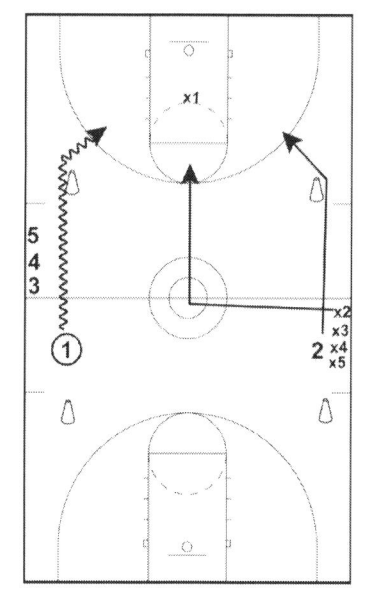

Diagram A 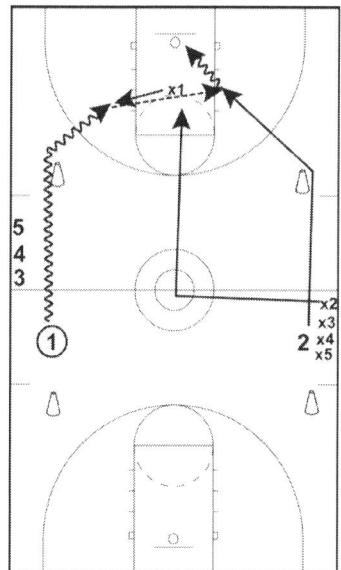   **Diagram B**

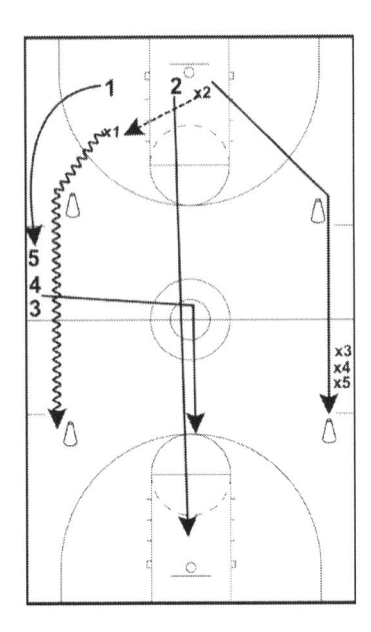

Diagram C

Create two teams for the purpose of this drill and set up as depicted in **Diagram A**. The first pair of offensive players attack following the rules of a 2-on-1 fast break. Once the ball crosses half court the second defender sprints to the jump circle and then pursues. The two groups play until a change of possession takes place, either by a score, turnover or defensive rebound. The offensive player who shot the ball, regardless of a miss or make, or turns the ball over, sprints back to play defense. The two defenders change over to offense, getting wide before passing the first set of cones. The drill continues for the time allotted. Score can be kept, making this drill a team favorite.

Number 172
Continuous 3-on-2-on-1

Ideal Duration: Five to eight minutes total for the entire drill.
Grouping/organization: See **Diagrams A-C**

Frequency of Usage: For daily usage, particularly if your team is a fast break team.

This drill teaches:

1) The concept of getting wide first for proper spacing for a 2-on-1 fast break.

2) Decision making for primary fast break.

3) The skills and tactics necessary converting all 3-on breaks into a 2-on-1 break.

4) Defending primary fast breaks.

5) Assertiveness on the fast break.

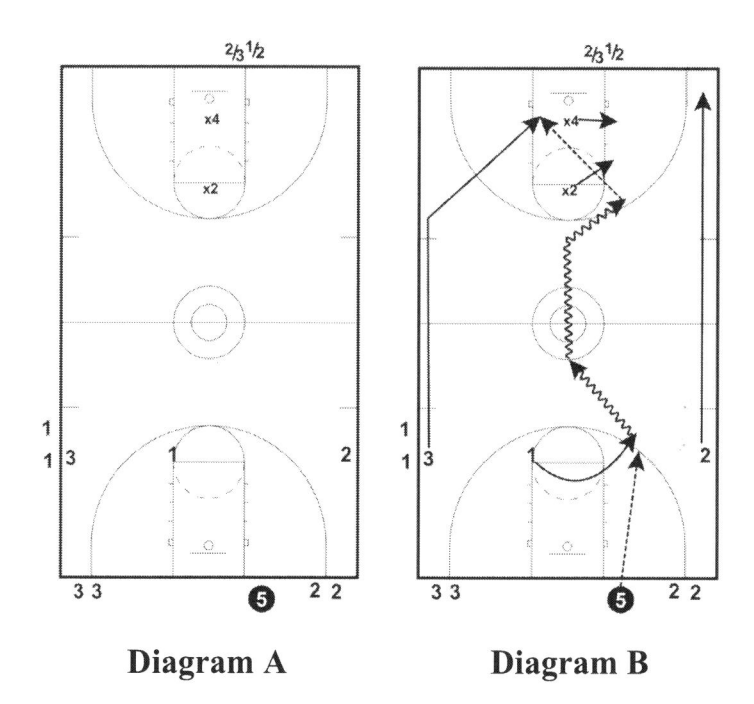

Diagram A   **Diagram B**

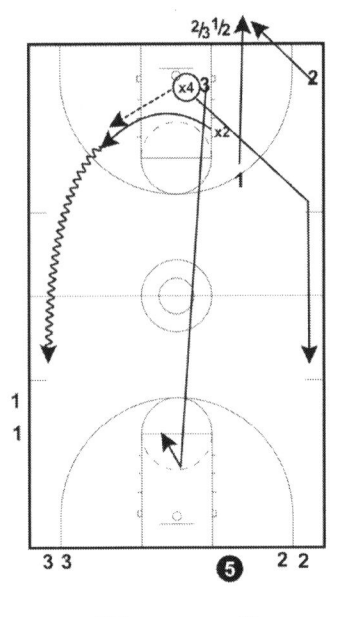

Diagram C

The drill is organized as depicted in **Diagram A**. The drill starts with an inbounds outlet from a made basket by a coach or student assistant coach and a 3-on-2 break is executed (**Diagram B**). The offensive player who shoots, scores, or turns the ball over becomes the lone defender and makes a defensive transition sprint back. The two defenders go over to offense and execute a 2-on-1 fast break (**Diagram C**).

The two players waiting on the defensive end become the next two defenders while the two offensive players on the initial 3-man rush wait for their turn to play defense. After the 2-on-1 break is finished another 3-man rush starts off a made basket.

This drill is a lot of fun for the players and can be used to create an almost endless set of game scenarios to teach the players.

Full Court Partner Fast Break Drills

So much of the game of basketball is about taking advantage of the opportunities that arise during the flow of play during the game. The number of "chances" to score in offensive transition are remarkable for the number of missed opportunities. Players simply do not recognize, or now how to take advantage of, the many opportunities that take place during the transition phase of the game.

Full court partner fast break drills are designed to teach recognition, build habits to reduce thinking during a game, master needed fundamental skills and to make shots at game speed.

Daily usage of these drills early in the season and then as needed build excellent fast break habits and by teaching recognition create aggressive, attacking fast break players.

One of the keys to creating a successful, attacking fast breaking team is to combine recognition with execution, building habits of execution that are so ingrained the players simply execute without thinking, allowing the players to play in the moment. The "less" the players think, the "more" success they will have.

Number 173
Rebound and Outlet for Lay-up

Ideal Duration: 2 minutes
Grouping/organization: See **Diagram A**
Frequency of usage: Daily early in the season and as needed later in the season.
This drill teaches:
1) cutting for the ball handler to get open.

2) fill the fast break lane wide.
3) pushing the ball quickly with as few dribbles as possible.
4) finishing the lay-up at game speed.

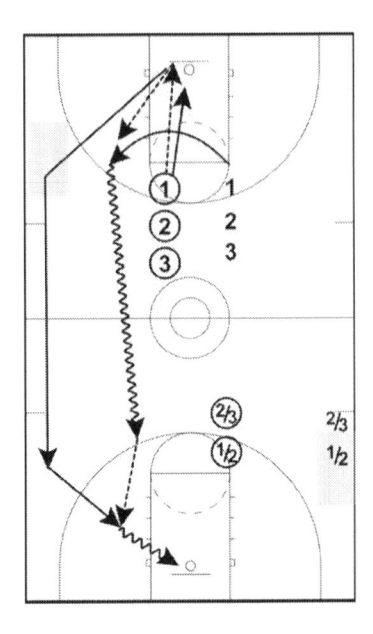

Diagram A

The drill begins with the cutter tossing the ball off the backboard and correctly obtain the rebound. The ball handler executes the curve cut to get open and receives an outlet pass to the outside shoulder. The ball handler pushes the ball up the court as quickly as possible with as few dribbles as possible.

The rebounder gets wide first and fills the fast break lane at maximum speed. The cutter makes a v-cut at a 45-degree angle and receives the pass from the ball handler roughly one dribble outside the lane and finishes the break with a lay-up at game speed. The players move to the end of opposite lines.

The players positioned in the bottom right hand side of **Diagram A** execute the same skills.

After one minute the players should change direction so both strong and weak hand skills are practiced.

Number 174
Rebound and Outlet for Mid-Range Jump Shot

Ideal Duration: 2 minutes
Grouping/organization: See **Diagram A**
Frequency of usage: Daily early in the season and as needed later in the season.
This drill teaches:
1) cutting for the ball handler to get open.
2) fill the fast break lane wide.
3) pushing the ball quickly with as few dribbles as possible.
4) pulling up and making a bank shot at game speed.

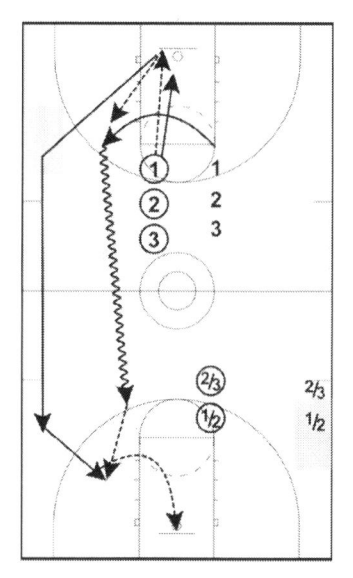

Diagram A

The drill begins with the cutter tossing the ball off the backboard and correctly obtain the rebound. The ball handler executes the curve cut to get open and receives an outlet pass to the outside shoulder. The ball handler pushes the ball up the court as quickly as possible with as few dribbles as possible.

The rebounder gets wide first and fills the fast break lane at maximum speed. The cutter makes a v-cut at a 45-degree angle and receives the pass from the ball handler roughly 12-15 feet outside the lane and finishes the break with a jump shot using the glass at game speed. The players move to the end of opposite lines. The players positioned in the bottom right hand side of **Diagram A** execute the same skills.

After one minute the players should change direction so both strong and weak hand skills are practiced.

Number 175
Rebound and Outlet for Pull-up 3-Point Shot

Ideal Duration: 2 minutes
Grouping/organization: See **Diagram A**
Frequency of usage: Daily early in the season and as needed later in the season.
This drill teaches:
1) cutting for the ball handler to get open.
2) fill the fast break lane wide.
3) pushing the ball quickly with as few dribbles as possible.
4) making a 3-point shot at game speed.

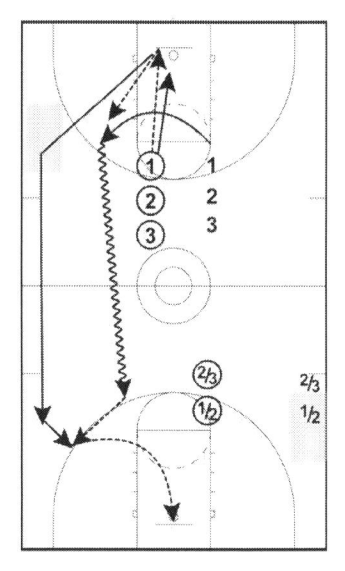

Diagram A

The drill begins with the cutter tossing the ball off the backboard and correctly obtain the rebound. The ball handler executes the curve cut to get open and receives an outlet pass to the outside shoulder. The ball handler pushes the ball up the court as quickly as possible with as few dribbles as possible.

The rebounder gets wide first and fills the fast break lane at maximum speed. The cutter makes a v-cut at a 45-degree angle and receives the pass from the ball handler beyond the 3-point line and finishes the break with a 3-point shot. The players move to the end of opposite lines. The players positioned in the bottom right hand side of Diagram A execute the same skills.

After one minute the players should change direction so both strong and weak hand skills are practiced.

Number 176
Rebound and Outlet and Wolf for Lay-up

Ideal Duration: 2 minutes

Grouping/organization: See **Diagram A**

Frequency of usage: Daily early in the season and as needed later in the season.

This drill teaches:

1) cutting for the ball handler to get open.
2) fill the fast break lane wide.
3) pushing the ball quickly with as few dribbles as possible.
4) chasing the ball handler to execute a defensive "Wolf" (back tip from the side of the ball handler the ball is being dribbled on).
5) finishing under defensive pressure at game speed.
6) executing an offensive "Wolf dribble" if necessary

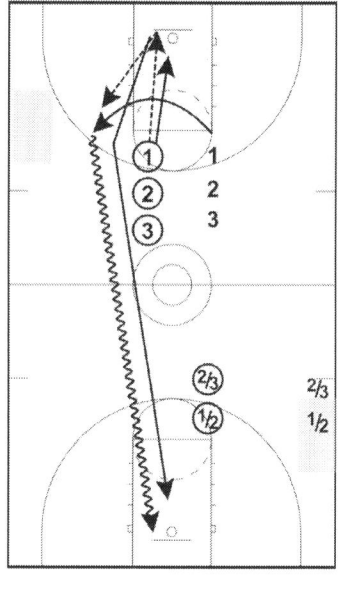

Diagram A

The drill is executed as depicted. Note however, if the ball handler is dribbling with the right hand, the Wolf should approach from behind on the right hand side and execute the back tip with the left hand. The opposite is true if the ball handler is dribbling with the left hand. This is necessary to prevent fouls.

A student assistant should randomly call Wolf (in a game the players resting on the bench are responsible to call "wolf"), and the ball handler will execute a "Wolf Dribble." This entails the ball handler suddenly slowing down, changing the hand the ball is being dribbled with while lowering the height of the dribble and taking a step laterally in the direction of the hand previously being used to dribble with. For example, if dribbling with the right hand, the ball is switched to the left hand while the ball handler steps to the right. This tactic will cause the Wolf Defender to run into the ball handler, drawing a foul, or preventing the loss of the ball through a back tip.

Number 177
Rebound and Outlet Point Guard Pull-up for a 3-Point Shot

Ideal Duration: 2 minutes

Grouping/organization: See **Diagram A**

Frequency of usage: Daily early in the season and as needed later in the season.

This drill teaches:
1) cutting for the ball handler to get open.
2) fill the fast break lane wide.
3) pushing the ball quickly with as few dribbles as possible.
4) making a 3-point shot at game speed.
5) the footwork necessary to stop for a pull-up 3-point shot at game speed.

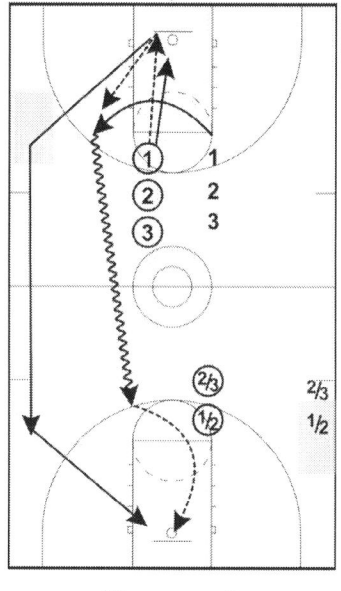

Diagram A

This drill is executed as depicted in Diagram A. The point guard can dribble attack and shoot the 3-point shot as shown or pitch-a-head and receive a pass back from the cutter. Either way, the point guard must correctly execute the footwork required to slow down and be under control to shoot a pull-up 3-point shot. This footwork will vary depending on the shooting system the player has been taught.

Number 178
Dribble Post Up

Ideal Duration: 2 minutes

Grouping/organization: See **Diagram A**

Frequency of usage: Daily early in the season and as needed later in the season.

This drill teaches:
1) cutting for the ball handler to get open.
2) fill the fast break lane wide.
3) pushing the ball quickly with as few dribbles as possible.
4) reading the defense and recognizing a post-up is available.
5) for a wing or post cutter to fill the ball side post.
6) executing a dribble down to feed a low post.

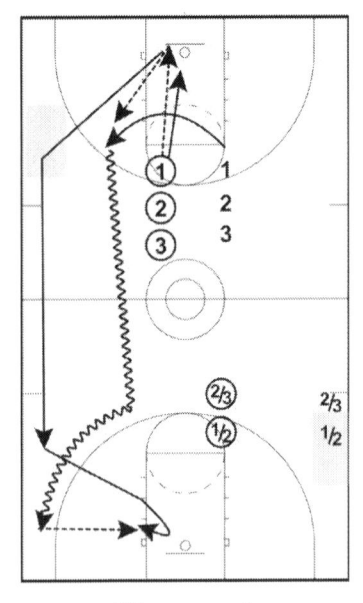

Diagram A

The drill starts as depicted. When learning the skills and the pattern of the drill, no defenders should be introduced. Once the concepts have been learned, two defenders should be added, with the post defender, ideally a student assistant coach, equipped with an air dummy in order to be physical with the offensive post player.

The drill is continuous with players working on both sides of the court. After half of the allotted time for the drill has been used the players should be instructed to attack in the other direction so both sides of the court are utilized, building the habits needed to attack on both the left and right hand sides of the court.

Number 179
Point Guard Post Up

Ideal Duration: 2 minutes

Grouping/organization: See **Diagram A**

Frequency of usage: Daily early in the season and as needed later in the season.

This drill teaches:
1) cutting for the ball handler to get open.
2) fill the fast break lane wide.
3) pushing the ball quickly with as few dribbles as possible.
4) pitching the ball ahead and then cutting to fill the ball side low post.

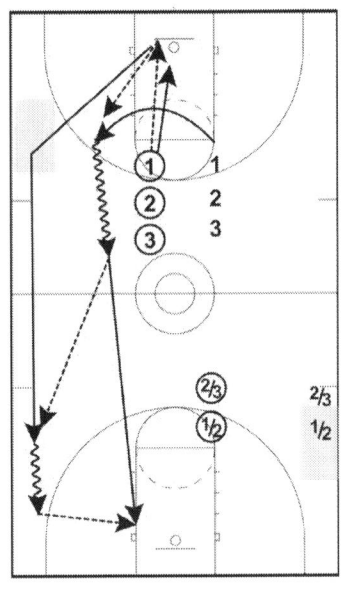

Diagram A

The drill is executed as depicted in Diagram A. The point guard pitches ahead to the cutter and cuts at game speed to the ball side low post for either a give and go type lay-up or a post-up opportunity on the ball side low post.

The drill should be executed in both directions, or sides, of the court.

Number 180
Trap the Rebounder

Ideal Duration: 2 minutes

Grouping/organization: See **Diagram A**
Frequency of usage: Daily early in the season and as needed later in the season.

This drill teaches:

1) cutting for the ball handler to get open.
2) fill the fast break lane wide.
3) pushing the ball quickly with as few dribbles as possible.
4) the tactic of trapping the rebounder to slow the outlet pass and fast break.
5) how to defeat the tactic of trapping the rebounder with a dribble bust out.

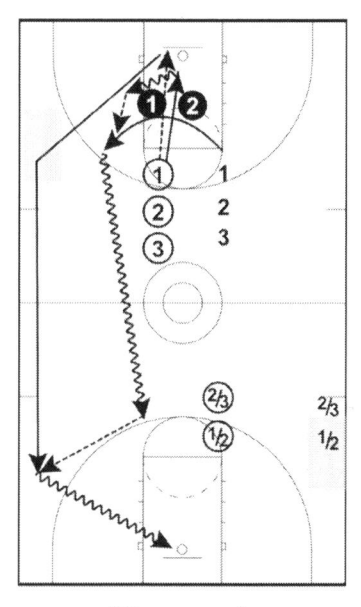

Diagram A

The drill is executed at depicted with the rebounder being trapped and then either splitting the trap or executing a dribble bust out. The rebounder fills the fast break lane and finishes with a lay-up off the pass on the other end.

This drill can be adapted by adding a third line for fast break lane cutters, allowing the rebounder to fill a post lane. As always, execute the drill in both directions.

Fast Break Shooting Drills

Shooting off the dead run or in any fast break situation is different from shooting in a half court offense setting. Like everything else in the game of basketball, the more specific the conditions in practice can be made to simulate the conditions in a game, the better the result will be.

Invest time in practicing shooting off the fast break. In fact, if time is an issue in practice, use fast break shooting drills as conditioning as well. To insure maximum effort simply modify the drills to include a time element and perhaps a specific number of shots to be made as well. Your players will thank you for this approach to conditioning in practice. Shooting the ball and running the fast break are fun. Running for the sake of running to condition is not.

Number 181
Look-a-Head Drill

Ideal Duration: Two minutes total for the entire drill.

Grouping/organization: Partners with a ball working together for the duration of the drill.

Frequency of Usage: Daily usage. This drill will generate 4-5 lay-ups a game!

This drill teaches:

1) filling lanes by getting wide first.
2) always looking to make a pass ahead for a score.
3) assertiveness when obtaining possession of the ball, particularly on a turnover or long rebound.
4) attacking and scoring with confidence.

Regardless of the desired tempo a team may desire to play, even slow tempo teams will want to take advantage of the easy scoring opportunities the fast break presents. Simple drills can be used for a few minutes a day to create positive habits in players to look for the quick fast break scoring opportunity when it presents itself in a game.

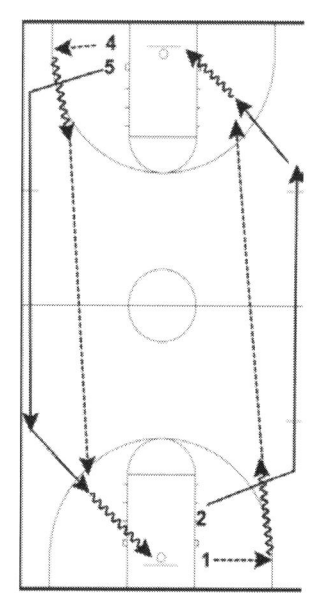

Diagram A

Five uncontested lay-ups a game will make the difference between victory or defeat. Teams must look for these easy scoring opportunities. **Diagram A** depicts the basic structure of this drill. Players work in pairs with a ball. One player rolls the ball towards the corner as if it was a loose ball.

The other player "recognizes" the opportunity for an easy score, gets wide first and funs the fast break lane. The first player turns and aggressively faces-up, takes one or two hard dribbles and passes ahead for the lay-up.

The key habit to build in this drill is for the players to recognize a potential scoring opportunity. The player in possession of the ball must "look-a-head" and recognize the scoring opportunity as must the other player who is filling the lane.

The rebounding version of this drill has one player toss the ball of the backboard, secure the rebound, aggressively face-up, take one or to two hard dribbles and passes ahead for the lay-up. The other player executes filling the lane in the same manner.

Number 182
The Concept of "Best" in Fast Break Shooting Drills

Ideal Duration: Five minutes total for the entire drill with no more than one minute per concept. If more time is desired each of the concepts can be run for two-minute periods spread throughout the entire practice session.

Grouping/organization: Groups of three players working together for the duration of the drill.

Frequency of Usage: Daily early in the season and one or two times per week for the duration of the season, more if your team is focused primarily on fast break offense.

This drill teaches:

1) the concept of "best" on the fast break.
2) running fast break lanes by getting wide first.
3) how to turn all 3-on-2 fast breaks into a 2-on-1 fast break.
4) working together to get the "best" shot possible given the fast break skills available to that group of players.

I learned this great concept working at Don Meyer's Bison Basketball Camp at Lipscomb University many summer ago.

The purpose of this series of drills is to clarify the decision-making process for your ball handler and his/her teammates on the fast break concerning the concept of "best." Some examples of what the concept of "best" means on the fast break:

- The "best" ball handler pushes the ball up on the break. If the best ball handler is not the "best" passer then consider having the "best" decision maker/passer bring the ball up on the break if that player is the 2nd best ball handler.
- The best finisher gets the lay-up - even if that finisher is the ball handler.
- The best "3" takes the 3-pointer on the break - even if that finisher is the ball handler.
- If there is not going to be an easy shot on one pass, the ball handler calls for the "best post" and dribbles to a side. Any perimeter on that side must clear out and the best post player posts up on that side. This is a super quick way to enter the ball into the low post.

Players know who the "best" is even if they don't readily want to admit it. Simply ask players to name who the best is at any category you are concerned with. The team as an entire group will get it right every time and if their idea of who is "best" differs from yours, you might want to rethink who you think is the "best" at that position or skill.

The order of decision making/shot selection is:

- Best lay-up
- Best 3-pointer
- Best post up

The concept of "best" truly helps in the decision making process! Eliminating doubt increases efficiency and confidence, making your fast break attack even more lethal!

The primary job of the coach is to create scenarios that combine a variety of combinations of players in practice and allow the players to learn how to get the ball to the "best" players in the correct locations on the floor as efficiently as possible.

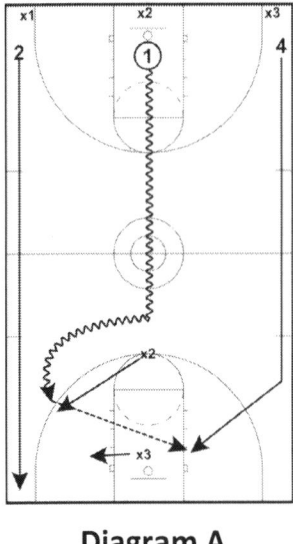

Diagram A 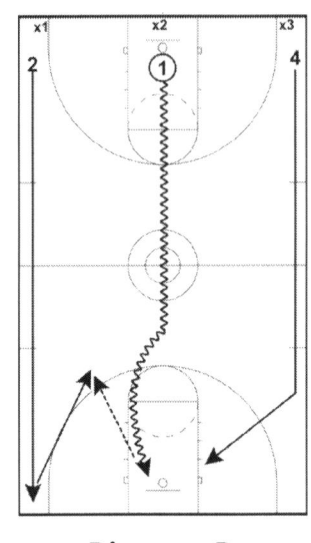   **Diagram B**

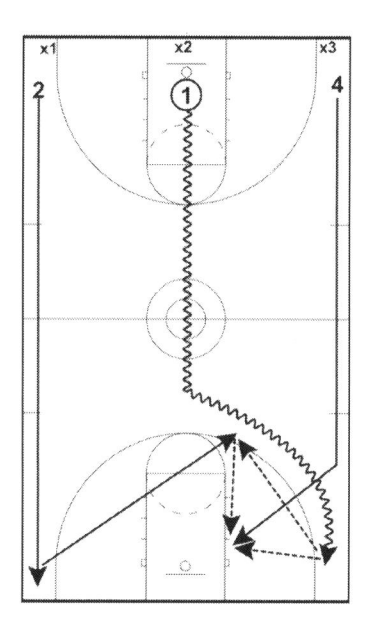

Diagram C

The first example depicts how to convert a 3-on-2 into a 2-on-1 (the most efficient form of attacking with a primary break) and the "best" finisher (**Diagram A**). In this example the post player #4 is the best finisher. The ball handler converts the 3-on-2 into a 2-on-1 in order to get the ball to the best finisher.

This is accomplished by veering away from the intended offensive target, drawing both defenders to the opposite side of the court as depicted in **Diagram A**. This tactic works due to how most teams are taught to defend against a 3-on fast break attack when two defenders are available. The first defender, X2, is responsible to stop the ball. The second defender, X3, defends the rim until the first pass is made and then X3 defends the offensive player who received the first pass.

By veering away from the best finisher both defenders are shifted to the side of the court opposite #4. In order to successfully make the pass to #4 the ball must be passed away from the two defenders using the inside hand to make the pass. The easiest way to accomplish this is for the ball handler to transfer the ball to his/her inside hand to the inside hand on the last dribble before passing.

Diagram B depicts the concept of "best" three. The ball handler penetrates to draw the defender of #2 who moves behind the ball handler to create an open passing lane (please note, this is the tactic I teach in this situation. Adapt to how you teach your players to obtain a 3-point shot on the fast break).

Diagram C depicts the concept of "best" post. The ball handler executes a dribble down on the side of the court of the best post player (note sometimes the best post can be a guard or the ball handler). The other attacker flashes into the ball side high post. The ball can be entered directly into the low post or passed to the attacker who filled the high post area for a high low pass. Note, after feeding the post the perimeter players can cut to receive a pass back in a feed the post and move tactic.

Number 183
Five-Ball Weave

Ideal Duration: 5 minutes. Run this drill against the clock.

Grouping/organization: Utilizes the full court and every player. Requires five balls.

Frequency of usage: Daily. This is a FUN drill that works on many skills!

This drill teaches:

1) conditions.
2) cutting.
3) passing.
4) communication.
5) organization.
6) 3-point shooting.
7) lay-ups.
8) mid-range jump shots.
9) use of the shot fake.
10) one dribble from the 3-point line for a lay-up/attacking the goal.
11) passing and catching on the run without traveling.

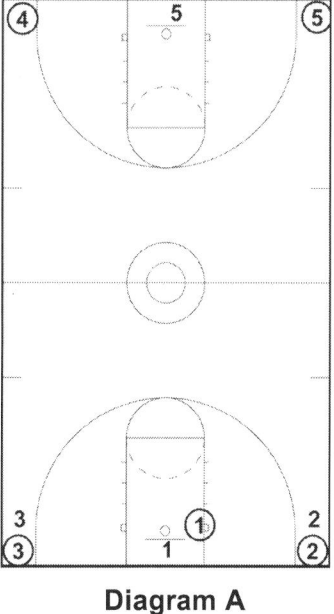

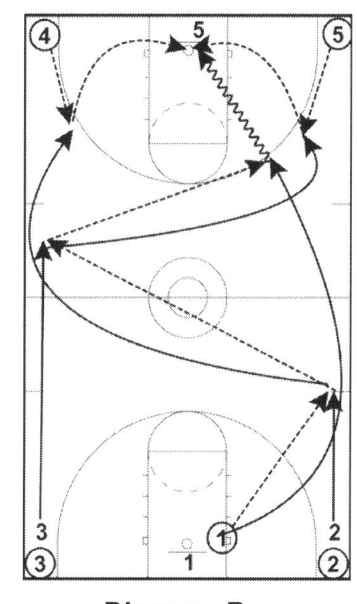

Diagram A   **Diagram B**

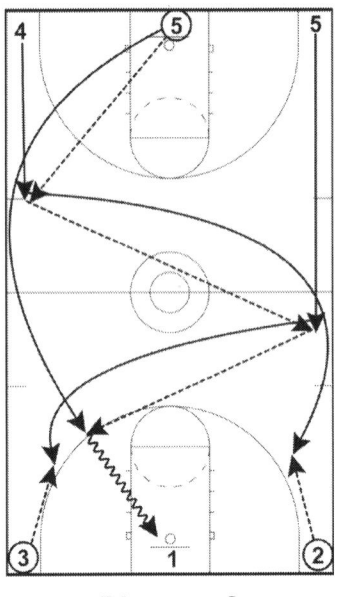

Diagram C

Run five ball weave against the clock. Keep track of the total number of field goals made or the actual number of points scored. Require the players to reach a specific number each day. Keep records and post them for the players to see. This is a FUN drill that is challenging and players will love.

Diagram A depicts the initial alignment with five balls, three at the end with three lines of players and two balls at the end with just three players. Diagram B shows the traditional weave action.

Players may not dribble until attacking the goal for a lay-up. As depicted, only the initial passer, #1 in the first group, shoots a lay-up. The other two cutters shoot 3-point shots. **Note:** depending on what is desired, all three players may shoot lay-ups, 3-point shots, or shot fake, one dribble and pull-up for the mid-range jump shot. Only three passes total are allowed. The other two cutters pull-up as depicted for 3-point shots and obtain their own rebound. The three players in this group assume the positions of the three players who were waiting with a ball in each corner.

The second group returns following the same rules as the first group, no dribbling until the attack lay-up, three pass limit and no traveling (**Diagram C**). It is important to emphasize that the sideline fast break lanes be run WIDE!

Number 184
Four Line Rush (or Four Ball Rush)

Ideal Duration: 3-7 Minutes

Grouping/organization: 4 lines on the baseline with two balls in the middle two lines. Two coaches, or student assistant coaches, with ball are positioned as shown in **Diagram A.**

Frequency of usage: Daily or in rotation with other full court ball handling/fast break drills that include shooting.

This drill teaches:
1) Passing accurately while on the run.
2) Catching the ball without traveling while on the run.
3) Running fast break lanes wide.
4) Cutting hard to meet the pass.
5) Shooting 3-point shots off the dead run.
6) Attacking the goal for a lay-up on the fast break.
7) Eliminating traveling.

201 DRILLS FOR COACHING YOUTH BASKETBALL| 392

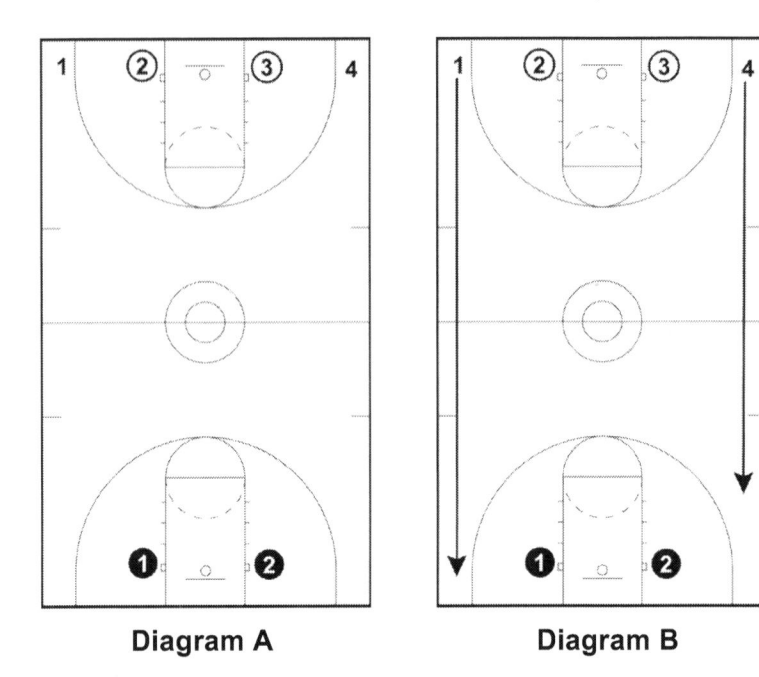

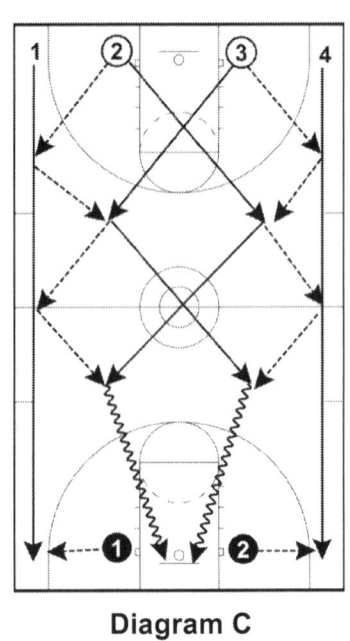

Diagram A

Diagram B

Diagram C

Diagram A depicts the alignment the drill starts with. **Diagram B** depicts two possible fast break lanes the outside cutters can run. Depending on where your fast break system has the wings pull-up, the cutters can run to the baseline/corner or the wing/free throw line extended. The rush starts with the two wing cutters starting.

The interior passers/cutters hit the wings at the free throw line extended and cut hard opposite of their pass for a return pass from the opposite wing/cutter (**Diagram C**). The interior cutter passes the ball back to the wing/cutter and again cuts opposite the pass. When entering the approach to the attack zone the interior cutters upon receiving a pass drive to the goal and finish. The cutters in the fast break lanes pull up for 3-point shots after receiving passes from the coaches/student assistants. Upon finishing the "rush" the players rebound their own shots, return the balls to the coaches, rotate to the right and wait for all of the other groups of four to finish before returning with another rush.

Number 185
2-Man Pitch-a-Heads and Skips

Ideal Duration: 2-4 minutes total. This drill must be done at maximum effort and speed.

Grouping/organization: Can be organized in three lines on the baseline and executed full court, three lines at half court or in groups of 3 to 6 at a goal if the court is large enough to spread out to this extent.

Frequency of usage: Daily early in the season when building fast break tempo and habits.

This drill teaches:

1) filling lanes wide.
2) making the pitch-a-head pass.
3) catching a pitch-a-head pass.
4) shooting the 3-point shot off a pitch-a-head pass.
5) making a skip pass for the 3-point shot.
6) recognizing the skip pass is available for a 3-point shot.
7) preparing to shoot off the skip pass.
8) second shot 3-point attempts.
9) floor balancing.

Players are organized into groups at half court based on their fast break position. A three-player rush moves up the court. In this instance the pass is pitched-a-head from half court and the 2-man shoots a 3-point shot. This drill must be done at game speed with the next group going as soon as a shot is taken (**Diagram A**).

Two variations of this drill can be easily added. The first is for the 3-man to obtain the offensive rebound of the initial shot, regardless of whether or not the shot was made or missed, and for the 2-man to rotate to the top of the key area for a second 3-point shot attempt.

The second variation is to skip pass the ball from the 2-man to the 3-man for a 3-point shot attempt. This can be a direct skip pass or offensive building blocks such as a penetrate and skip can be used to make the pass (**Diagram B**).

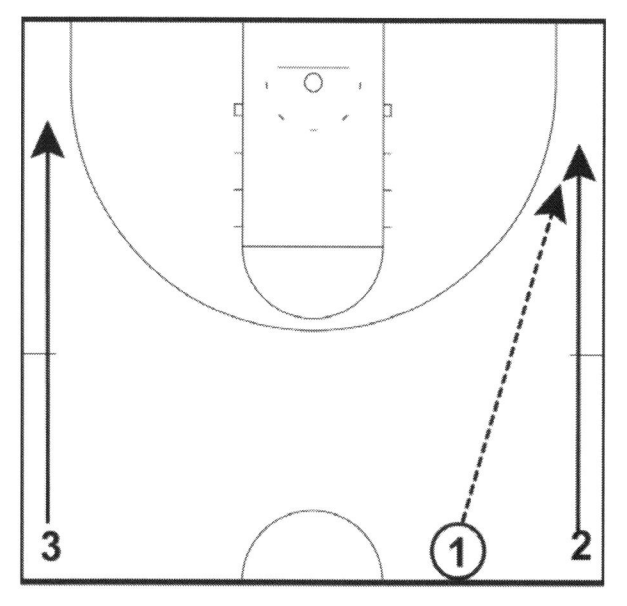

Diagram A

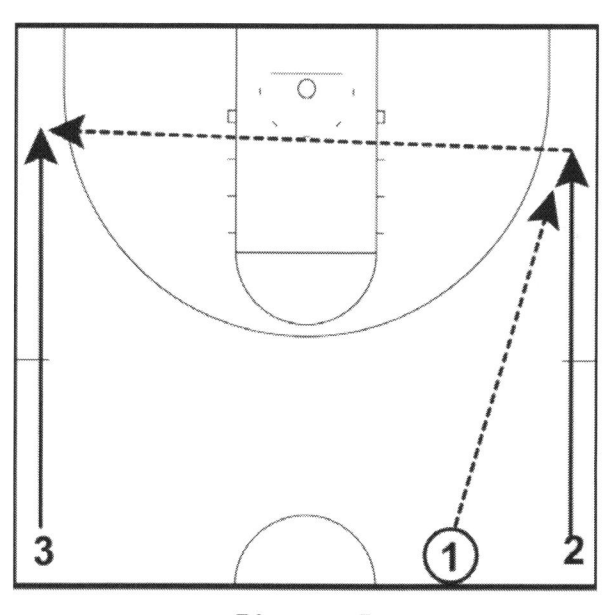

Diagram B

Number 186
3-Man Pitch-a-Heads and Skips

Ideal Duration: 2-4 minutes total. This drill must be done at maximum effort and speed.

Grouping/organization: Can be organized in three lines on the baseline and executed full court, three lines at half court or in groups of 3 to 6 at a goal if the court is large enough to spread out to this extent.

Frequency of usage: Daily early in the season when building fast break tempo and habits.

This drill teaches:

1) filling lanes wide.
2) making the pitch-a-head pass.
3) catching a pitch-a-head pass.
4) shooting the 3-point shot off a pitch-a-head pass.
5) making a skip pass for the 3-point shot.
6) recognizing the skip pass is available for a 3-point shot.
7) preparing to shoot off the skip pass.
8) second shot 3-point attempts.
9) floor balancing.
10) penetration and skip passing.

This drill is similar to the 2-Man Pitch-a-head and Skip. The structure of the drill is the same with a cross-court pitch-a-head pass from the point guard or coach being the main difference (**Diagram A**). In **Diagram B** a penetrate and skip is depicted as the offensive building block used to create the skip pass.

SIVILS| 397

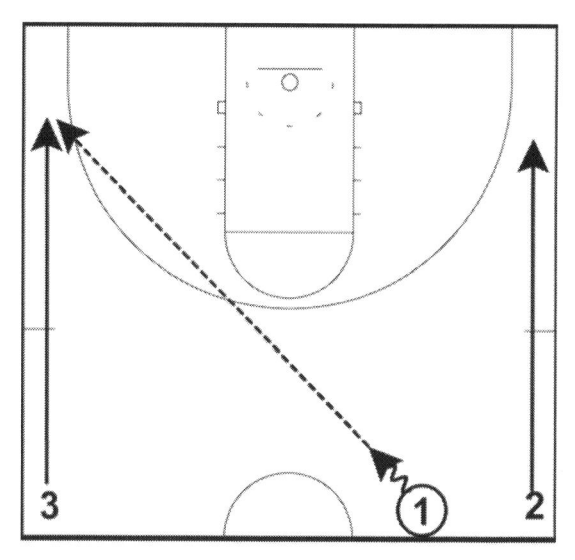

Diagram A

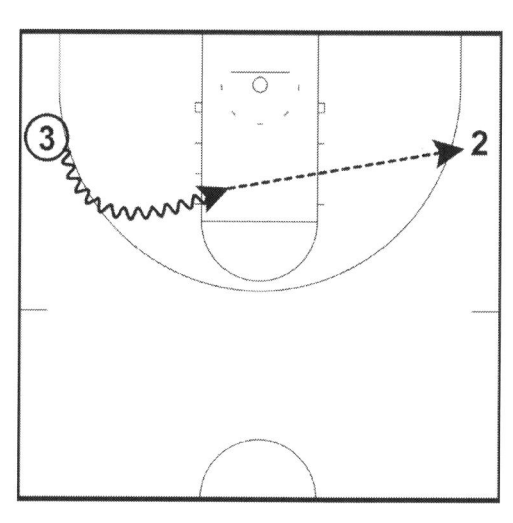

Diagram B

Number 187
4 Dribble Point Guard Lay-ups

Ideal Duration: 2-4 minutes

Grouping/organization: See **Diagrams A** and **B**.

Frequency of usage: Daily early in the season and as needed as the season progresses.

This drill teaches:

1) pushing the ball up the court at break neck speed.
2) using four dribbles to get to the rim (it can be done!).
3) making lay-ups at maximum speed.
4) attacking the rim.
5) making the point guard cut to receive the 5 to 1 inbounds pass.

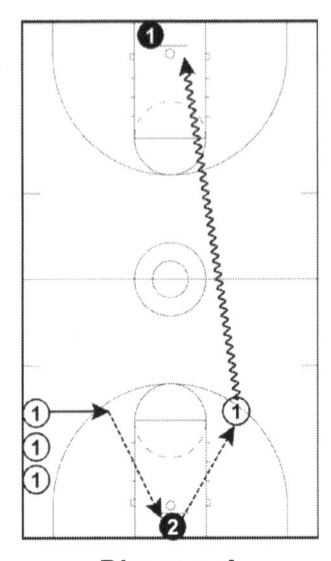

Diagram A

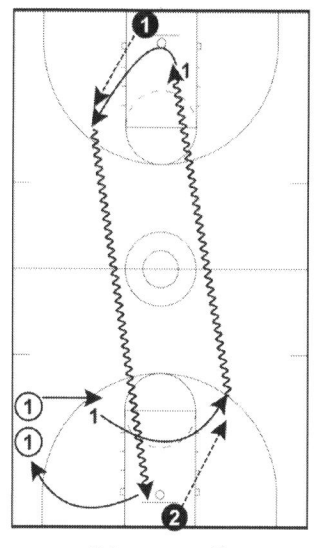

Diagram B

Point guards need to be taught to use as few dribbles as possible. This drill teaches point guards to attack the rim and be as efficient as possible. The drill begins with the first point guard receiving a pass from a student assistant under the rim, turning, facing, looking under the rim, making a decision and attacking.

The point guard works to get to the rim in four dribbles and make a lay-up. The second point guard in line steps out on to the court as depicted and passes the ball to the student assistant under the rim (**Diagram A**).

The first point guard makes the point guard cut to receive an inbounds pass from the other student assistant. The second point guard makes the point guard cut and receives the inbounds pass.

After making the second lay-up the first point guard retrieves the ball and goes to the end of the line (**Diagram B**). The drill continues for the allotted time. To make the drill more game-like or add "pressure" a specific number of lay-ups to be made can be required and have the point guards work against the clock.

Number 188
1-Man Pull-up 3-Point Shot

Ideal Duration: 2 to 4 minutes.

Grouping/organization: See **Diagram A** for organization.

Frequency of usage: Daily early in the season and as needed as the season progresses.

This drill teaches:

1) footwork for a pull-up 3-point shot off the dribble at fast break speed.
2) conditions the point guard.
3) ball handling at fast break speed.
4) the 5 to 1 inbounds cut and pass.

The go to move for a point guard is to penetrate to the goal for a lay-up. This will force the defense to collapse on future penetration allowing the point guard to create scoring opportunities for teammates. The counter move for a point guard is the 3-point shot.

For fast break teams who rely on penetration at the end of their rush up the court, a point guard who can pull up off the dribble and make a 3-point shot will in all likelihood be a devastating penetrator as the defense cannot afford to collapse into the lane to prevent penetration.

The drill is organized as shown in Diagram A. In addition to working on making pull-up 3-point shots, this is an excellent opportunity to work on the inbounds outlet pass to initiate the fast break following a made shot by the opponent.

Like the pitch-a-head drills, a variation of this drill can have the point guard rotating to the top of the key for a second 3-point shot attempt regardless of whether or not the first shot is missed.

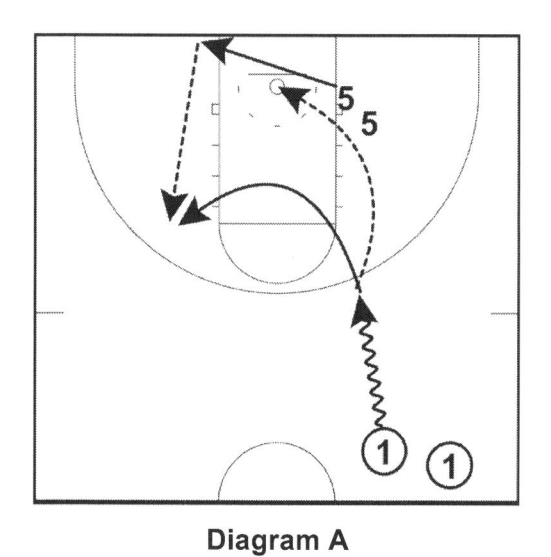

Diagram A

Number 189
5-Man 3-Point Shot

Ideal Duration: 2-4 minutes in duration.

Grouping/organization: Can be organized in groups of three and a ball or two student assistant coaches and all the players who play the 5 position.

Frequency of usage: Daily early in the season and as needed as the season progresses.

This drill teaches:

1) the trailer to shoot the 3-point shot off the fast break.
2) footwork to prepare to catch and receive the ball prior to shooting a 3-point shot.
3) offensive rebounding.
4) the 5 to 1 inbounds pass.

The trailer, the 5-man, is nearly always open on the fast break. If a numbered fast break is used and the designated inbounder/trailer is a post player who can shoot the 3-point shot, this is a devastating weapon, forcing the defense into vulnerable alignments early in the offensive possession.

In addition to working on fast break 3-point shooting, this drill incorporates offensive rebounding as well as working on the all-important inbounds pass following a made basket by the opponent (ideally done in under 1.5 seconds).

Diagram A shows the initial alignment with the rebound/inbounds and outlet pass shown in **Diagram B**. By adding a low post player the fanning of the ball out to the trailer for a 3-point attempt can be practiced as well (**Diagram C**).

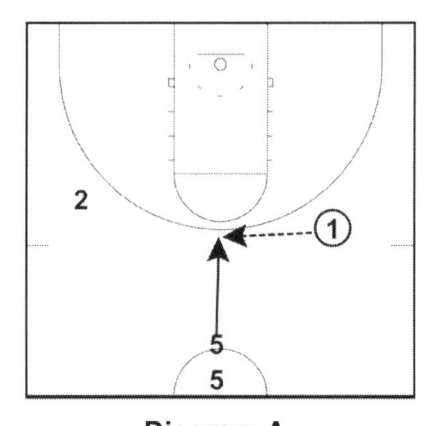

Diagram A

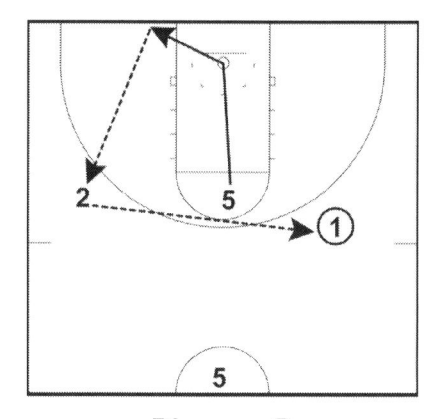

Diagram B

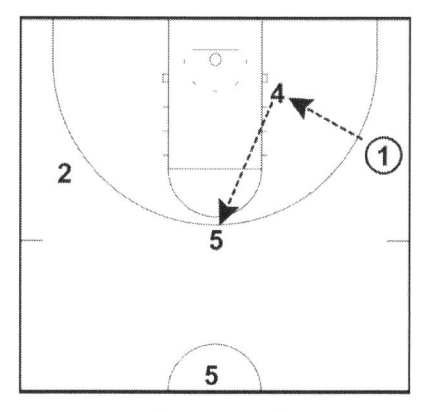

Diagram C

Number 190
Laker Drill

Ideal Duration: 2-5 minutes

Grouping/organization: Pairs of players with a ball. Divide the pairs evenly in number at each end of the court.

Frequency of usage: Daily or as needed.

This drill teaches:

1) filling fast break lanes wide.
2) attacking the basket to score.
3) shooting lay-ups at maximum speed.
4) making full court passes.
5) using one-dribble to make a pitch-a-head pass.
6) making the 5 to 1 inbounds pass on a made basket.
7) making the point guard cut on a made basket for the inbounds pass.

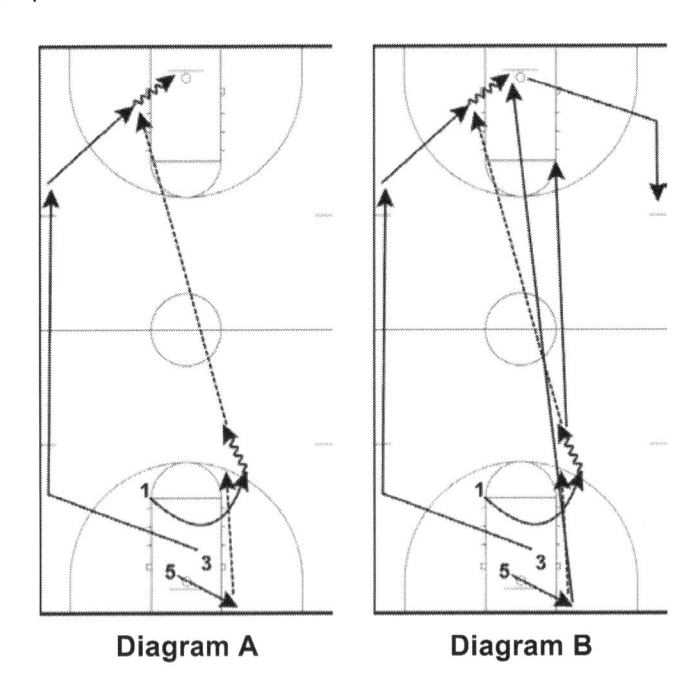

Diagram A   Diagram B

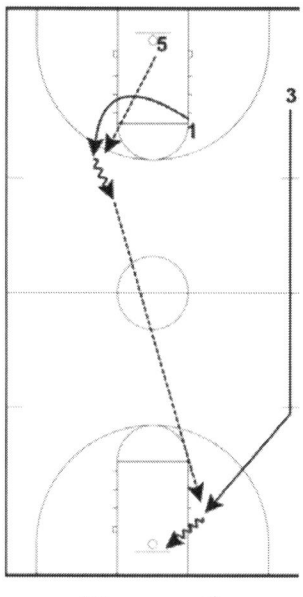

Diagram C

The Laker Drill is an excellent drill to work on filling lanes, rebounding, passing, catching on the run, scoring and conditioning. Players are placed in groups of three for the drill. **Diagram A** depicts the initial stage of the drill.

The drill starts with the coach making a short bank shot. #5 takes the ball out of bounds and makes an inbounds pass to #1 who has made a circle cut. #3 gets wide first and fills the left lane, spring at full speed down the court and breaking at a sharp angle to the goal. #1 takes one dribble and makes a drop pass to #3 who must catch the ball in stride and shoot a lay-up without taking more than a single dribble.

Diagram B depicts the lanes #1 and #5 must take to make transition down the court as quickly as possible. **Diagram C** depicts the process in reverse as #5 and #1 again make the outlet pass and drop pass to #3 who has filled the left lane again.

Players should make two trips up and down the court. Once players have mastered the drill and skills involved the coach can require all four lay-ups be made and no dribbles be taken with a directive that players may not travel. The drill can also be run in the opposite direction and right hand lay-ups are utilized.

Number 191
Three Lane Two Ball Attack Passing

Ideal Duration: 3-5 minutes

Grouping/organization: Three lines as depicted in **Diagram A**. Each player in the two outer lines must have a basketball.

Frequency of usage: Daily early in the season. As needed as the season progresses.

This drill teaches:

1) "valuing" possession of the ball.
2) running without making turnovers by traveling, mishandling a pass or making an errant pass.
3) using vision while running fast break lanes.
4) running lanes with proper spacing and wide.
5) executing skills at game speed.
6) communicating while executing the fast break.
7) attacking the goal to finish.
8) "going somewhere" with the dribble – limit two – preferably one.
9) executing a give and go for a lay-up on the fast break.
10) making fast break lay-ups at game speed.

Diagram A

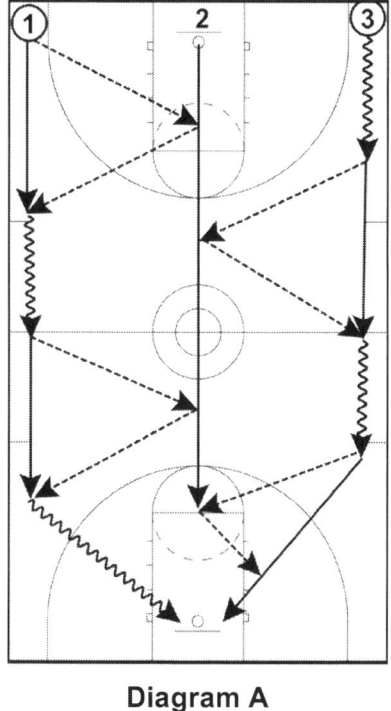

The drill starts with a pass from an outside lane to the middle cutter who without traveling makes a crisp pass back to the passer in the outside lane. The other outside lane cutter dribbles twice and then makes a crisp pass to the middle cutter who without traveling again passes back to the outside cutter. All three players sprint in straight lines, maintain their spacing and occupying the wide fast break lanes and the center break lane.

The drill ends with one fast break lane cutter attacking on the dribble to finish and the other cutter catching the ball in stride for a finish without dribbling.

Rebound and Outlet Drills

Fast breaks start with a change of possession of the ball and with there being only four ways a change of possession of possession can take place. These four ways are:

- a made goal by the opponent.
- a turnover by the opponent.
- an inbounds play in a dead ball situation.
- a defensive rebound.

Obtaining the defensive rebound is a difficult enough task. Quickly making the outlet pass to the ball handler to begin pushing the ball up the court either by a pass across half court or by dribbling is one of the essential skills to master for a team whose offense is based on attacking with a fast break attack.

The speed of the outlet from the rebounder to the ball handler must be quick, sure and accurate. Ideally this pass will be completed in 1.5 seconds or less. It is not enough to obtain possession of the ball via the defensive rebound, the outlet pass must be successfully executed every time as well.

The drills in this chapter are intended to provide a combination of rebounding repetitions combined with the outlet cut and outlet pass, enabling players to build all the necessary habits to create a team that will successfully rebound and outlet the ball in the desired 1.5 seconds or less every possession.

Number 192
Rebound and Outlet

Ideal Duration: 2 Minutes

Grouping/organization: Groups of four are ideal. See **Diagram A** for organization.

Frequency of usage: Daily or as needed.

This drill teaches:

1) rebounding and passing techniques needed to successfully start a fast break off a defensive rebound.
2) ball handlers to turn, look, observe, decide and act.

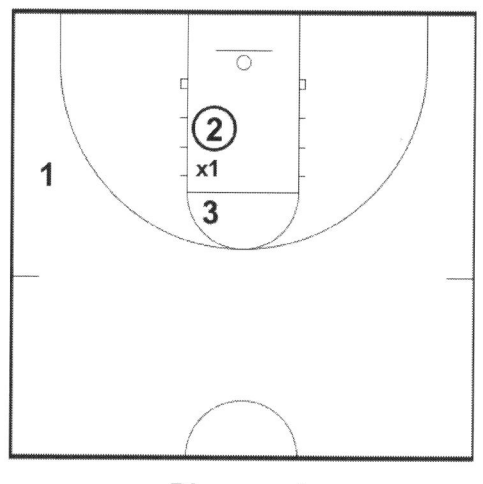

Diagram A

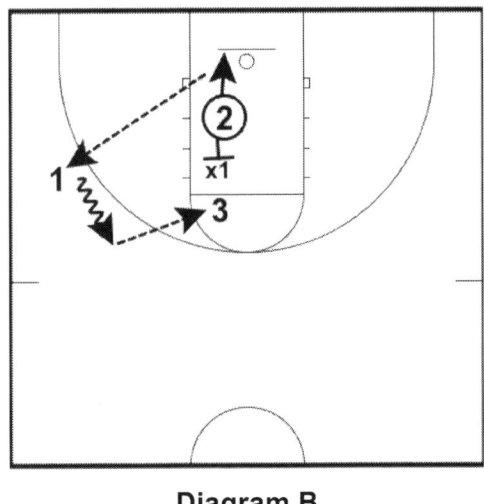

Diagram B

    Diagram A shows the basic alignment for the drill. Four players per group is ideal. **Diagram B** shows how the drill works. X1 shoots the ball off the backboard. #2 blocks out X1 and then rebounds the hand using proper technique and two hands. #2 then pivots and makes a two hand overhead outlet pass to #1 on the wing.

    #1 turns aggressively and takes a hard dribble towards the goal. #1 then passes to #3 and the process repeats itself. The player rotation for the drill is as follows: #2 becomes the outlet receiver on the wing, #1 rotates to the end of the line, #3 becomes the shooter and X1 is the next rebounder.

Number 193
Numbered Outlet Passing

Ideal Duration: 2 Minutes

Grouping/organization: Groups of four are ideal. See **Diagram A** for organization.

Frequency of usage: Daily or as needed.

This drill teaches:

1) rebounding and passing techniques needed to successfully start a fast break off a defensive rebound.
2) ball handlers to turn, look, observe, decide and act.
3) pursuing the ball on a missed shot.
4) identifying an open receiver for an outlet pass.

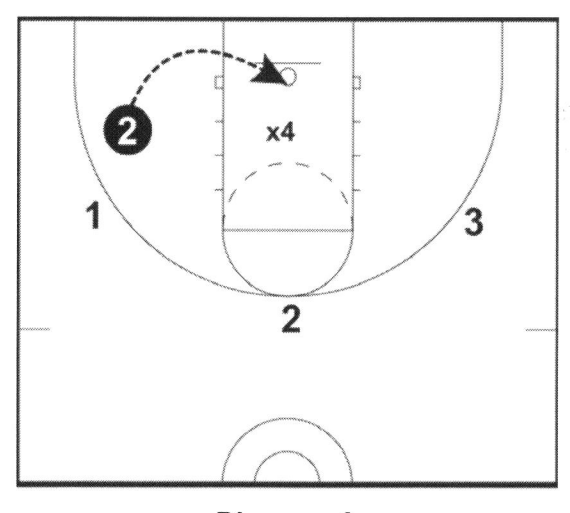

Diagram A

Well coached teams will often disrupt running teams by slowing or actually preventing the outlet pass. For running teams who run highly structured fast breaks, this simple strategy can be highly disruptive.

Smart running teams will have a multiple outlet option built into their fast break system. In order to insure a smooth start to the fast break with a quick and successful outlet pass of the rebound or the made basket, the ability to recognize the defensive tactic being used to disrupt the outlet pass is essential. This allows the passer to make the correct decision in selecting the receiver of the outlet pass.

In this example, the outlet receivers have been positioned according to where they would be located in the fast break system I teach. The drill begins with the coach or a student assistant shooting a shot. The defender obtains possession of the ball. It does not matter if the shot is made or missed.

The instant the rebounder has obtained possession of the ball the coach calls a number that correlates to an outlet receiver. The rebounder must outlet the ball without hesitation crisply and accurately to the correct intended receiver. For example, if the rebounder obtains possession and the coach call the number three, the outlet pass must be made to the player in the number three outlet position.

The goal should be to obtain the rebound and successfully outlet the ball, on a make or a miss, in under 1.5 seconds.

Number 194
Superman Outlet and Cut

Ideal Duration: 2 Minutes

Grouping/organization: Groups of four are ideal. See **Diagram A** for organization.

Frequency of usage: Daily or as needed.

This drill teaches:

1) rebounding and passing techniques needed to successfully start a fast break off a defensive rebound.
2) ball handlers to turn, look, observe, decide and act.
3) aggressive pursuit of all rebounds, even if on the other side of the lane.
4) the Superman rebounding technique.
5) the ball handler cut to get open for an outlet pass.

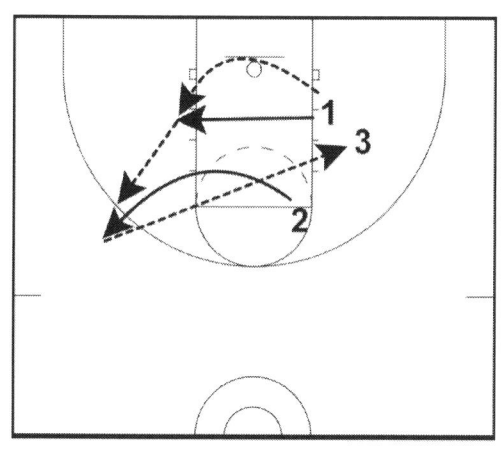

Diagram A

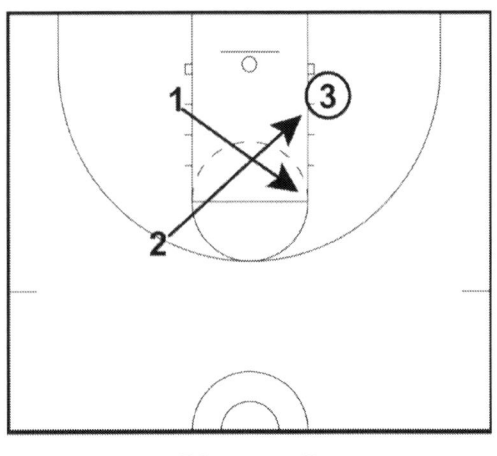

Diagram B

This drill is meant to be a combination of mobile rebounding, outlet pass and the coordination between the point guard and the rebounder making the outlet pass.

Players are divided into groups of three at a goal as shown in **Diagram A**. The drill starts with #3 shooting the ball off the backboard at an angle and #1 executing a Superman rebound jump, landing outside the lane on the opposite side of the lane. #2 times a curl cut to get open for the outlet pass.

After catching the outlet pass #2 aggressively turns, faces up, looks under the net, decides and acts. The point guard turns and makes a quick pass to #3 and follows the pass to the end of the line. #1 fills #2's spot when the drill started. The drill continues without stopping.

Please note, the cut to get open for the outlet pass is based on the fast break system I teach. If your fast break system is different, adjust the drill accordingly.

Number 195
Bust Out Outlet and Go

Ideal Duration: 2 Minutes

Grouping/organization: Groups of four are ideal. See **Diagram A** for organization.

Frequency of usage: Daily or as needed.

This drill teaches:

1) rebounding and passing techniques needed to successfully start a fast break off a defensive rebound.
2) ball handlers to turn, look, observe, decide and act.
3) defeating the defensive tactic of trapping the defensive rebounder to slow the outlet pass and quick initiation of the fast break.
4) filling a lane quickly after making an outlet pass.

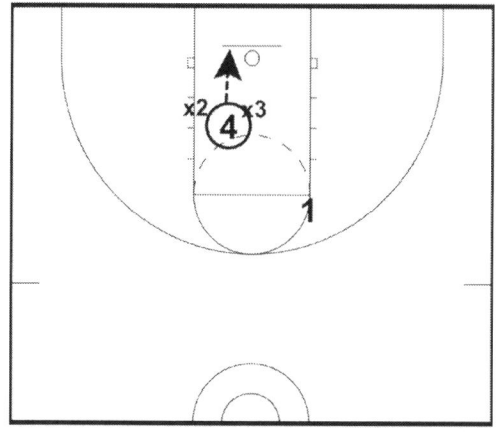

Diagram A

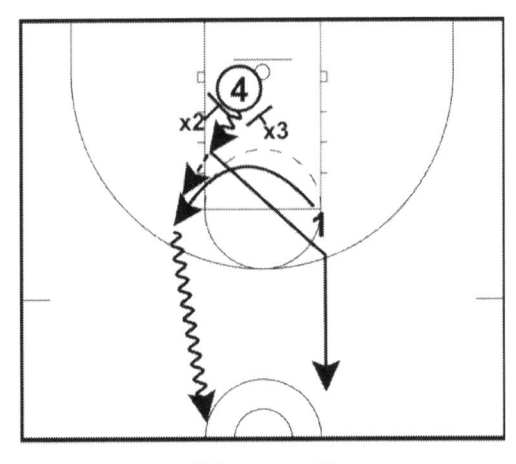

Diagram B

One way to stop fast breaking teams is to slow down or prevent a quick outlet pass. This tactic can be effective against half court teams who are not used to being pressured following a defensive rebound.

The drill starts as depicted in **Diagram A**. The rebounder #4 tosses the ball off the backboard and secures possession of the ball. The two defensive players X2 and X3 trap the rebounder.

#4 must assertively step through with the ball chinned and make a crisp, accurate outlet pass to #1 who is making the cut to get open for the outlet pass.

After passing the rebounder cuts opposite and behind. #1 pushes the ball at breakneck speed to either half court or full court with #4 filling the trailer lane.

This drill can be combined with Fast Break Trailer Combo drill.

Number 196
Fast Break Trailer Combo Drill

Ideal Duration: 2 Minutes

Grouping/organization: Groups of four are ideal. See **Diagram A** for organization.

Frequency of usage: Daily or as needed.

This drill teaches:

1) rebounding and passing techniques needed to successfully start a fast break off a defensive rebound.
2) ball handlers to turn, look, observe, decide and act.
3) finishing a fast break regardless of how the offense executes.
4) offensive rebounding on a fast break.
5) defensive rebounding against an attacking fast break.

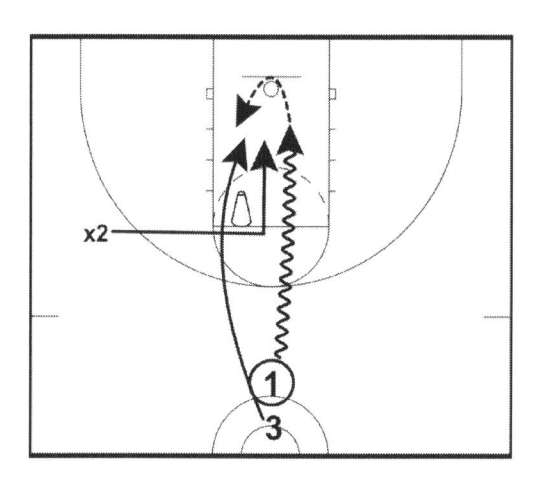

Diagram A

Players are lined up as shown. The ball handler attacks the rim at maximum speed. The trailer follows just behind and to the opposite side of the lane.

As the ball handler and trailer cross the lane line, or pass the cone as shown, the defender can enter the drill.

The ball handler misses the shot on purpose so the trailer can rebound and score.

The defender competes to obtain the rebound and prevent the score.

This is a great 2-3 minute drill to be used every other day to reinforce the key habit of trailers following to clean up any missed lay-ups. It also encourages defenders to get back and compete.

Number 197
Run on Makes Outlet and Go Fast Break Drill

Ideal Duration: 2 to 5 Minutes

Grouping/organization: Groups of four are ideal. See **Diagram A** for organization.

Frequency of usage: Daily or as needed.

This drill teaches:

1) rebounding and passing techniques needed to successfully start a fast break off a defensive rebound.
2) ball handlers to turn, look, observe, decide and act.
3) the inbounds pass and cut on a made basket.
4) filling lanes on the fast break.
5) executing options to score on the fast break.

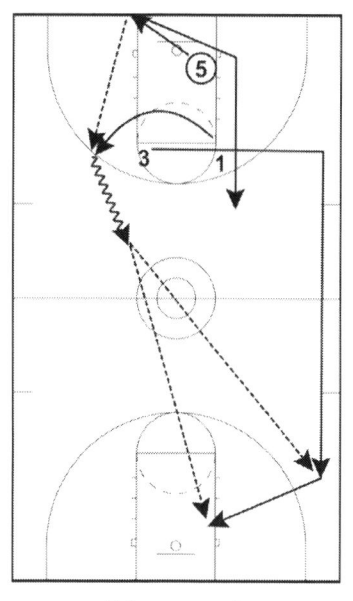

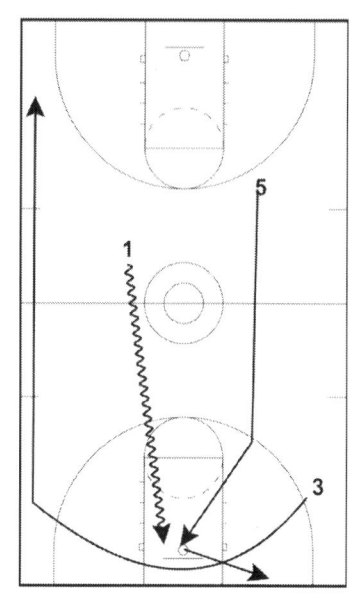

Diagram A

Diagram B

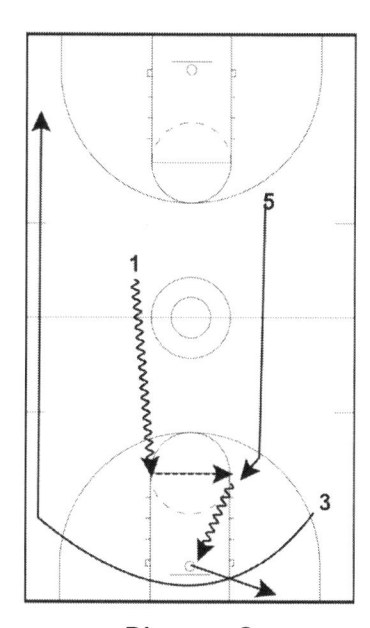

Diagram C

This drill focuses on running off made baskets. The key skill is the 5 to 1 inbounds pass. The sequence of the drill with its various options are shown in **Diagrams A** through **C**.

Change Drills

Players love fast break drills and why not? They get to run, cut, dribble, pass, catch, make decisions and shoot the ball! That's basketball! The three "change drills" in this chapter will be player favorites. These drills are intense, fast paced and incorporate all of the elements of the fast break.

Simple modifications can make these drills more challenging and more fun for the players. Even better, these three drills are fantastic conditioning drills and can be used to take the place of the dreaded, time killing and spirit killing sprints.

Change drills can accommodate large numbers of players by utilizing both ends of the court at the same time. Players must execute the various elements of the drill with both perfection and intensity all the while waiting to hear the command "change," indicating it is time to fast break to the other end of the court.

Modifications can include adding as few as one or as many as four defensive players permanently stationed on the court, working against the clock, requiring a specific number of repetitions of a predetermined skill during each groups turn on the court or a predetermined number of made baskets if the drill allows players to shoot.

Communication, quick decision-making by all players on the court and court awareness are essential for these drills to work and for collisions to be avoided. Players have to pay attention and communicate with each other!

Regardless of the version of change drill, each drill begins with two groups on the court, one at each end. In order for the drill to work there must be one group waiting off the court on one end, waiting for their turn to participate in the drill. The drill starts when the coach yells "change" and the two groups fast break to the other end of the court. After a pre-set number of trips up and down the court, one group steps off on the command to change and the waiting group fast breaks to the other end of the court.

Initially, all change drills should be run without any defense. This allows the groups to have success, learn the concepts and skills being taught and to perfect timing. Once the players have mastered the skills and concepts, defenders can be introduced to increase the level of difficulty and to keep the drills challenging.

Number 198
3-on-0 Change Drill

Ideal Duration: 3-7 minutes

Grouping/organization: Groups of three and a ball with a minimum of nine players and a maximum of 15 players. The ideal number of players is nine to twelve. Defensive players may be added at one or both ends to make the drill more challenging once the concepts have been learned.

Frequency of usage: Daily early in the season and as needed as the season progresses.

This drill teaches:

1) primary fast break skills.
2) primary fast break attack.
3) primary fast break decision making.

4) conditioning.
5) ball handling skills.
6) getting open to receive and making the outlet pass.
7) getting wide first then filling lanes.
8) use of the dribble – as few as possible.
9) court awareness (avoid collisions!) and spacing.

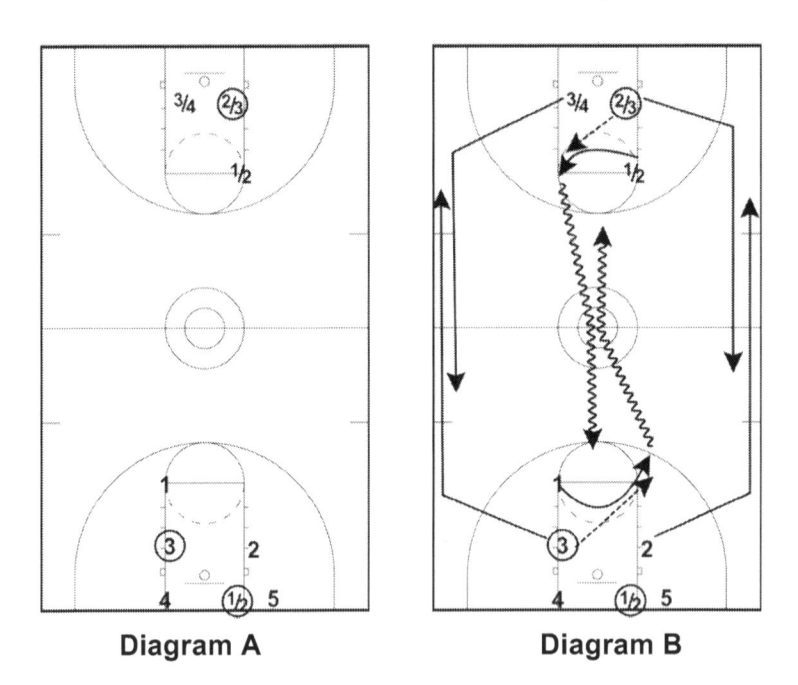

Diagram A   **Diagram B**

3-on-0 Change is fantastic for teaching primary break skills and concepts. Diagram A depicts the drill being set up for the minimum number of players, nine. Diagram B depicts the start of the drill and how the two groups transition past each other.

With an odd number of players, such as shown in this example, the group waiting for their first turn would rotate off after the group on their end has gone down and back. The group who started on the far end will have to make three trips in order to rotate off initially.

If an even number of players is available, 12 or 15, then groups can make two or four trips before rotating off and two groups wait out-of-bounds, one group on each end of the court.

Every possible primary break scenario involving three players can be practiced as well as flowing into half court offense without the post players. What can be practiced in this drill is limited only by the imaginations of the coach and the players.

Number 199
4-on-0 Change Drill

Ideal Duration: 3-5 minutes

Grouping/organization: Groups of four ranging from a minimum of two groups to a maximum of four groups.

Frequency of usage: Daily or as needed.

This drill teaches:
1) rapid transition from one end of the court to the other.
2) quick organization of the fast break.
3) filling fast break lanes and running entries into half court offense.
4) half court offense.
5) conditioning and timing.

Diagram A **Diagram B**

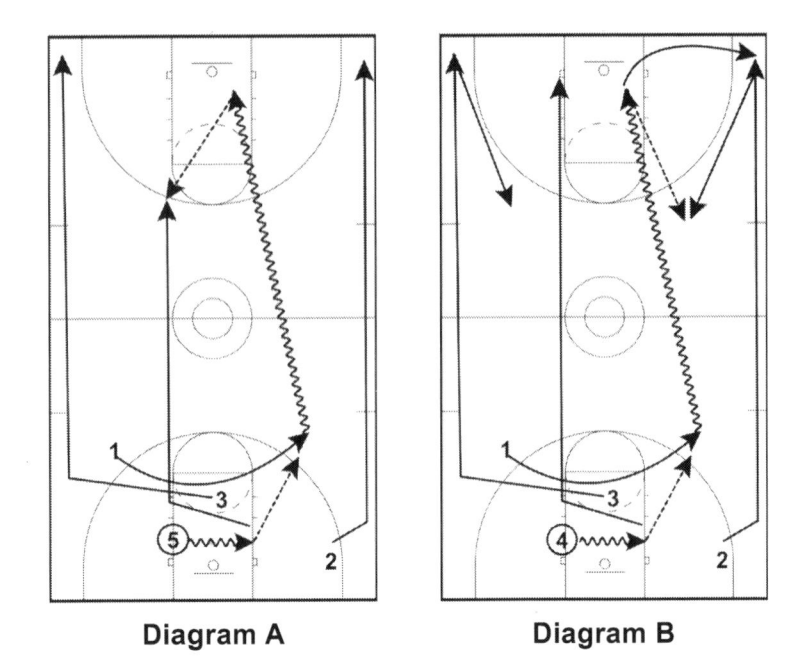

The focus of 4-on-0 Change is on post play and integrating post play successfully with the perimeters during the fast break phase of transition. It is also an excellent way to work on post play and the integration with perimeter players in half court offense.

You will note in **Diagram A** the post player, #5, will focus on playing in the high post area in transition and half court offense. In **Diagram B** the post player, #4, will focus on the low post area during transition and half court offense.

Number 200
5-on-0 Change Drill

Ideal Duration: 3-5 minutes

Grouping/organization: Groups of five ranging from a minimum of two groups to a maximum of four groups.

Frequency of usage: Daily or as needed.

This drill teaches:

1) rapid transition from one end of the court to the other.
2) quick organization of the fast break.
3) filling fast break lanes and running entries into half court offense.
4) half court offense.
5) conditioning and timing.

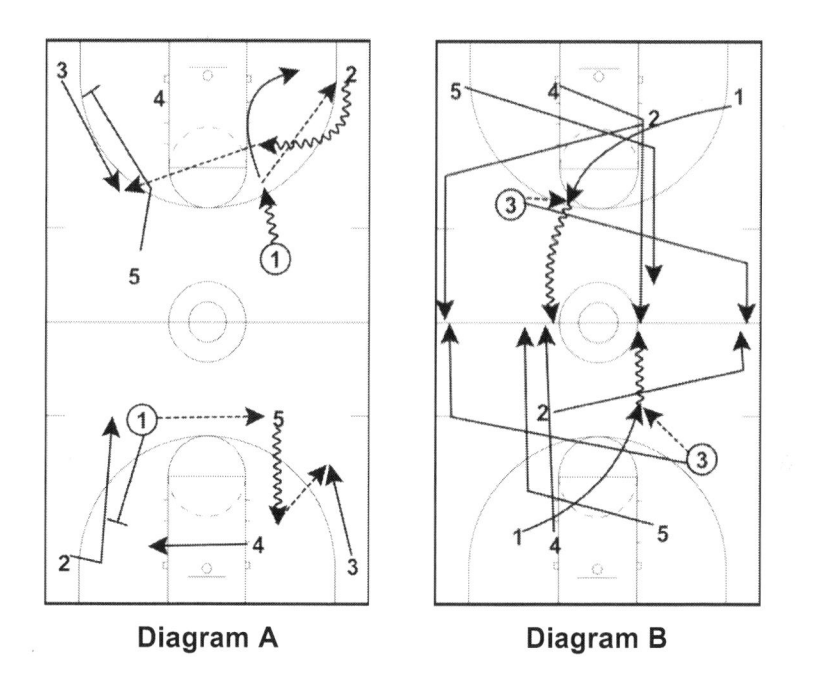

Diagram A **Diagram B**

This drill offers opportunities to work on transitioning smoothly into half court offense. On the command change the five offensive players fill their fast break lanes and transition to the other end of the court. NOTE: players must be instructed repeatedly to exercise great caution to avoid collisions.

This format offers realistic scenarios that are constantly changing without the pressure of facing a defense while practicing all the various fast break options available and then transitioning into half court offense smoothly.

5-on-0 Change offers opportunities for game-like conditioning and a chance to work on both half court offense and the fast break at the same time. A third group can be waiting on one end to transition in for one of the groups on the court, allowing players to maintain maximum effort for the duration of the drill.

Pointers for Making the Break Work

This chapter consists of a summary of the "little things" that will make the fast break work. Take the time to study these details carefully.

- Fundamentals are essential and players must be able to execute them perfectly at game speed.
- Make the easy pass, not the "assist pass."
- Never deviate from the pattern
- Always run it at warp speed
- The first key pass is the 1-5 pass – it must be in 1.5 seconds or less.
- The second key pass is the pass across half court. It must be as quick as possible.
- Pass for a score.
- Dribble as little as possible.
- Less is more
- Run lanes to perfection.
- 2 & 3 must run their lanes as wide as possible.
- Players must play so hard their feet and lungs burn.
- Conditioning is paramount.

- A fast break team must be more disciplined with the ball than a deliberate team – teach the players that a turnover means they did not get to shoot!
- Once a player has been green-lighted to shoot, never criticize a shot they take during a game.
- Teach shot selection!
- Defense is what speeds the game up, not offense.
- Players must be able to read the defense and make sound decisions.

Primary Break Pointers

The following are a collection of "little things" that will make the primary fast break work.

- Must have 5-6 look-a-heads every game – this is how you win!
- Must be able to score every time in a 2-on-1 situation.
- Get wide first –then attack!
- Concept of best – players know who is "best" – the best handler handles – the best finisher finishes.
- Turn all 3-on-1 and 3-on-2 situations into a 2-on-1 situation
- Veer away from the best scorer to shift the defense over and create space – this is how you create a 2-on-1.
- Put the ball in the hand opposite the direction you will veer in, i.e. if you veer to your right, dribble with your left hand.
- Give the cutter the ball where he or she can do something with it.
- Cutters and penetrators must be able to finish at the rim – teach power lay-ups!

- The ball handler should never penetrate after passing – should step to the ball side "T" for a return pass.
- If the cutter cannot score, he or she should quick stop and "Euro" the ball back to the passer.
- If you cannot score then post up the post and fill the perimeter spots and swing the ball.

CHAPTER TWENTY-ONE

Pressure Inbounds Game Situations

Pressure inbounds situations can be problematic for the pros. They are often even more so for youth teams. This drill teaches several tactics to inbounds the ball in pressure situations. These tactics can all be adapted to special plays used to break a press, score or simply inbounds the ball. By making this a competitive daily drill players will enjoy these situations as they master the skills and tactics involved. The confidence built in these daily two or three minute competitive situations will pay huge benefits in the final minutes of a close game.

Number 201
Pressure Inbounds Situations

Ideal Duration: Two minutes total for the entire drill.
Grouping/organization: Groups of three or four players with a ball working together for the duration of the drill. Some coaches may only want to use this drill with designated inbounders and point guards, allowing other players to work on other skills.

Frequency of Usage: Daily usage early in the season. As needed for the remainder of the season.

This drill teaches:

1) inbounding the ball against extreme defensive pressure.
2) recognition of various types of defensive pressure against the inbounds pass.
3) special situation tactics and strategies to inbound the ball.

Before describing the drill, it is necessary to provide some background information on what is being practiced. The two tactics described are used against intense defensive pressure designed to prevent an inbounds pass from being made or an interception of the inbounds pass.

The following material is excerpted from *Fine Tuning Your Team's Position Play*.

Post Up on the Baseline

Well-coached defensive teams will often try to prevent the point guard from making him or herself available to the ball, particularly after a made basket. Posting up on the baseline is an excellent tactic to defeat this defensive approach. Usually it can only be used after a made basket as the inbounder almost always must be able to change location in order to make the inbounds pass. Rules permit this following a made basket if the inbounder is on the baseline. It is not permitted in any other inbounds situation.

If the defense is denying the point guard in a normal ¾ denial stance, the point guard cuts hard to the baseline and with the baseline side foot six inches from the out-of-bounds line, posts up at a right angle to the baseline as shown in **Photograph A.**

Photograph A

Photograph B shows the inbounder has relocated and is now able to make a bounce pass "back" to the point guard. The point guard holds this position until the ball is over halfway to the point guard.

201 DRILLS FOR COACHING YOUTH BASKETBALL| 432

Photograph B

Photograph C

Photograph D

Photographs C and **D** show the point guard after receiving the ball. The point guard has turned, is looking under the net, will make a decision and then act.

Set Up for the Lob

If the defense attempts to completely deny the point guard as shown in **Photograph A**, the point guard should set up for a lob pass in order to become available to the ball.

Photograph A

Photograph B

The point guard simply walks the defender to the baseline and sets up to receive a lob pass as shown in **Photograph B**.

Photograph C

The inbounder lobs the ball to the point guard after looking to make certain there are no defender's capable of intercepting the lob pass. The point guard holds position until the ball is directly overhead and then releases to catch the ball (**Photograph C** and **D**).

Photograph D

Photograph E

After receiving the ball, the point guard must turn, look under the net, make a decision and then act (**Photograph E**).
(This material was excerpted from the book *Fine Tuning Your Team's Position Play*)

The drill starts with groups of three spread out on the baseline or sideline. It is important to note that the inbounder can move ONLY on the baseline AFTER a made basketball by the opponent. If any of these tactics are to be used in any other situation, the point guard must set up in such a way that the inbounder does not have to move in order to make the pass.

The defense plays live and tries to prevent the inbounds pass or to intercept the pass. If there are only enough players to work in groups of three, the defender must guard the point guard. If there are enough players to work in groups of four the group should consist of two designated inbounders and two point guards.

In a group of four the drill can be made competitive. One inbounder and one point guard compete against the other pair in the group. Each group is allowed 30 seconds before letting the other group go on offense.

The objective of the group on offense is to successfully inbounds the ball as many times as possible in 30 seconds. Each successful attempt is worth 1 point. The objective of the defense is to prevent the ball from being inbounded in five seconds, intercept the inbounds pass or otherwise create a turnover. Success in any of these three objectives is worth 1 point.

After each inbound attempt, regardless of success or not, the point guard must start from the foul line. The defense can pressure the inbounder or play in front of the point guard with one defender and behind with the second defender. At the end of the two-minute period the pair with the highest point total wins and receives a reward. The losers should suffer a mild consequence such as five push-ups.

CHAPTER TWENT-TWO

About the Author

A 25 year veteran of the coaching profession, with twenty-two of those years spent as a varsity head coach, Coach Kevin Sivils amassed 479 wins and his TEAMs earned berths in the state play-offs 19 out of 22 seasons with his TEAMs advancing to the state semi-finals three times. An eight time Coach of the Year Award winner, Coach Sivils has traveled as far as the Central African Republic to conduct coaching clinics. Coach Sivils first coaching stint was as an assistant coach for his college alma mater, Greenville College, located in Greenville, Illinois.

Coach Sivils holds a BA with a major in physical education and a minor in social studies from Greenville College and a MS in Kinesiology with a specialization in Sport Psychology from Louisiana State University. He also holds a Sport Management certification from the United States Sports Academy.

In addition to being a basketball coach, Coach Sivils is a classroom instructor and has taught U.S. Government, U.S. History, the History of WW II, and Physical Education and has won awards for excellence in teaching and Teacher of the Year. He has served as an Athletic Director and Assistant Athletic Director and has also been involved in numerous professional athletic organizations.

Sivils is married to the former Lisa Green of Jackson, Michigan, and the happy couple are the proud parents of three children, Danny, Katie, and Emily. Rounding out the Sivils family are three dogs, Angel, Berkeley, and Alec. A native of Louisiana, Coach Sivils currently resides in the Great State of Texas.

CHAPTER TWENY-THREE

To Contact the Author

If you have any questions about the content of **Coaching Basketball's Fast Break Attack: 50+ Drills to Teach the Up Tempo Game** or any of my other books, please feel free to contact me! I can be contacted by e-mail at:

mailto:kcsbasketabll@comcast.net

To sign-up for my FREE e-Newsletter, **The Roundball Report**, please visit my website CoachSivils.com and register for the newsletter.

Website

To visit my website please go to kcsbasketball.com

eBook/PDF Store

Many of my books are available as downloadable pdf ebooks from the eBook/PDF Store on my website.

CHAPTER 24

Drill Index

Defensive Drills

On (the) Ball Defense Drills

Number 1 Mass Defense 33

Number 2 Zig-Zag Drill.. 34

Number 3 Steer Drill 36

Number4 4/4/4 Drill... 37

Number 5 Mirror Drill.. 38

Number 6 Continuous 1-on-1.. 39

Closeout Drills

Number 7 3-on-0 Mass Closeouts 41

Number 8 Full Court Closeouts..................................... 42

Number 9 1-on-1 Closeouts.. 43

Number 10 2-on-2 Closeouts.. 45

Number 11 3-on-3 Closeouts 46

Contesting the Shot

Number 12 Mass Contesting the Shot...........................48

Drills for Defending Cutters

Number 13 2-on-1 Flash Cutter..50

Number 14 2-on-1 Ball Side Cutting................................51

Drills for Defending Screens

Number 15 2-on-2 Ball Screens 53

Number 16 3-on-3 Ball Screens 54

Number 17 3-on-2 Screening Series 56

Number 18 5-on-4 Screening Series 59

Drills for Defending the Post

Number 19 Post Denial 60

Number 20 Low Post Denial (Dead Front) 61

Number 21 3-on-3 Low Post Cover Down......................63

Number 22 High Post Cover Down 66

Number 23 3-on-4 Low Post Defense With Help Side 67

Drills for Denial Defense

Number 24 3-on-0 Mass Denial.......................................68

Number 25 1-on-1 Denial 70

Number 26 L-Cut Denial 71

Number 27 3-on-2 Denial.. 72

Number 28 3-on-2 Eliminate Ball Reversal..................... 74

Number 29 Double Denial.. 77

Number 30 5-on-1 Denial... 81

Drills for Early Help Defense

Number 31 2-on-2 Early Help 82

Number 32 3-on-3 Early Help 84

Number 33 4-on-4 Early Help 86

Number 34 5-on-5 Low Post With Early Help Rotation ... 88

Odds and Ends

Number 35 2-on-1 Cutter/Closeout//Help Side 89

Number 36 Continuous 2-on-2....................................... 90

Number 37 1-on-1 Charge Drill...................................... 91

Number 38 2-on-1 Charge Drill...................................... 92

Number 39 Loose Ball Drill 94

Number 40 Save the Ball Drill.. 95

Number 41 2-on-1 Trap and Fast Break Drill 96

Number 42 Wolf Drill.. 97

Drills for Defensive Rebounding

Number 43 Finish Every Drill With BOPCRO 99

Number 44 NBA Drill 99

Number 45 Circle Block Out 100

Number 46 3-on-0 Mass Block Out 102

Number 47 1-on-0 Block Out and Outlet 103

Number 48 1-on-1 Rebound and Outlet 104

Number 49 Competitive Rebounding 105

Drills for TEAM Defense

Number 50 2-on-2 On a Side 107

Number 51 3-on-3 On a Side 108

Number 52 Shell Drill 110

Number 53 Defensive Cutthroat 113

Number 54 5-on-4 Disadvantage Drill 114

Transition Defense

Number 55 Transition Sprints 116

Number 56 1-on-1 Full Court "Stop Ball" Drill 117

Number 57 2-on-2 Full Court "Stop Ball" Drill 118

Number 58 3-on-3 Conversion 119

Number 59 4-on-4-on-4 Transition Defense 121

Number 60 5-on-5 Head Start Transition Drill............... 123

Competitive Rebounding Drills

Number 61 1-on-1 Competitive Offensive Rebounding Back Roll or Swim Drill.. 125

Number 62 1-on-3 Competitive Closeout and Contest Rebounding.. 126

Number 63 1 versus 5 Competitive Block Out Drill...... 127

Number 64 2 versus 5 Competitive Block Out Drill....... 128

Number 65 2-on-2 Competitive Reaction Block Out.... 129

Number 66 3-on-3 Competitive Block Out Drill............. 130

Number 67 Competitive Cross Block Out Drill.............. 131

Number 68 Competitive Rebounding........................... 132

Movement, Passing, Footwork & Essential Fundamentals

Number 69 Fundamental Lines: Easy Running............ 138

Number 70 Fundamental Lines – Live Ball................... 140

Number 71 Fundamental Lines – Pullback Crossover. 142

Number 72 Fundamental Lines – Pullback and Go...... 144

Number 73 Fundamental Lines – Flick Passing........... 146

Number 74 Fundamental Lines - Post Entry Pass........ 149

UCLA Basic Movement Drills

Number 75 Change of Pace 151

Number 76 V-Cuts 152

Number 77 Starts/Stops/Turns 155

Number 78 Step Lunges 157

Number 79 Backdoor Cuts 158

Number 80 Circle-up Drill 160

Basic Ball Handling Drills for Point Guards and Perimeter Players

Number 81 Mass Ball Handling 163

Number 82 Two Ball Passing 165

Number 83 Two Ball Dribbling 166

Number 84 Back to Passer 167

Number 85 Live Ball Dribble Move Shooting 167

Number 86 Dribble Tag 169

Number 87 3-to-1 170

Shooting Practice

Warming Up The Shot: The Shooting Progression

Number 88 Shadow Shooting 177

Number 89 Shadow Shooting With a Ball 180

Number 90 Straight Line Shooting 181

Number 91 Green Light Shooting 182

Number 92 Grooving the Shot 184

Lay-Up Drills

Number 93 One Bounce Lay-ups 187

Number 94 One Bounce Power Lay-ups 191

Number 95 X-Outs 192

Number 96 X-Crosses 195

Number 97 Partner Lay-ups... 198

Number 98 Backdoor Lay-ups 200

Number 99 Two Line Lay-ups... 203

Free Throws

Number 100 Plus Four – Minus Two 207

Number 101 Free Throw Swish 208

Number 102 Team Free Throw Bonus Competition 209

Number 103 80% Free Throw Shooting 210

Number 104 Daily Shooting for 75%.............................. 211

Number 105 Situational Free Throws 212

Number 106 Free Throw Challenge............................... 213

Number 107 Free Throw League................................... 214

Number 108 Shoot Two (or One or Three).................... 216

Number 109 Scrimmage Free Throws........................... 217

Number 110 Make Three in a Row – Score 65 217

Developmental Shooting Drills

Number 111 Line Shooting 219

Number 112 Mass Shooting (Shadow) 221

Number 113 Dribble Pick-Ups 222

Number 114 Triple Threat Off the Pass 223

Number 115 One Hand Shooting (Groove Your Shot) .. 224

Number 116 One Pass Shooting (Head On) 225

Number 117 One Pass Shooting With ¼ Face-up 226

Number 118 One Pass Baseline Shooting With Face-up 227

Number 119 One Bounce Shooting Head On 229

Number 120 One Bounce Shooting With ¼ Face-up 230

Number 121 One Bounce Baseline Shooting With Face-up 231

Number 122 Bank Shot Range Shooting 233

Number 123 Footwork Jump Shooting 235

Number 124 Shot Fake Shooting 236

Number 125 Count the Steps – Triple Attack 237

Number 126 Count the Steps – Baseline Dribble Off or Baseline Cut 239

Number 127 Screening Progression 241

General Shooting Drills

Number 128 Rapid Fire Shooting 245

Number 129 Machine Gun Shooting 247

Number 130 Four Corner Shooting 249

Number 131 Three Man Motion Perimeter Shooting 251

Number 132 Three Man Motion Blocker/Mover Shooting 253

Number 133 32-Point Drill 255

Number 134 Modified 32-Point Drill 258

Number 135 Fan the Ball – Two Perimeters and a Post 261

Number 136 Beat the All Star 263

Number 137 Two Minute Shooting 263

Number 138 Three Pass Partner Shooting 265

Number 139 Three Pass Shooting With Screening 268

Number 140 Three Cut Shooting 270

Number 141 Second Cutter Shooting 272

Competitive Shooting Drills

Number 142 Partner Competitive Shooting 276

Number 143 4-Up 280

Number 144 Beat the Game Competitive Shooting 282

Number 145 Team Competitive 284

Number 146 Two Minute Shooting 285

Three-Point Shooting Drills

Number 147 3-Point Shoot-out 289

Number 148 Partner Threes 290

Number 149 Closeout 3's 295

Number 150 Five by Twenty Spot Shooting 297

Number 151 Four Line 3-Point Shooting 299

Number 152 Two-Ball Threes 303

Shooting Drills for Post Play

Number 153 Duck Cut Shooting 305

Number 154 Point Blank Shooting & Point Blank Offensive Rebound Shooting 309

Number 155 Feeding the Post Skill Progression 313

Number 156 Power Put Backs 322

Number 157 10/2 Shooting – Put Backs Count 324

Fun Shooting Drills

Number 158 Knock-Out 327

Number 159 Team Spot Shooting 329

Number 160 Timed Team Range Shooting 330

Number 161 Make 25 Don't Miss 2 In a Row 332

Two-Minute Intensity Drills

Number 162 Loose Ball Drill 340

Number 163 Save the Ball Drill 342

Number 164 Create Drill 344

Number 165 4/4/4 Drill 346

Number 166 Wolf Drill 347

Fast Break Drills

Number 167 Modified Cycles Drill* 351

Number 168 5 on 2 on 5 on 3 Drill 355

Number 169 5 on 4 on 5 on 0 Drill 356

Number 170 2-on-1 Trap and Fast Break Drill 362

Number 171 Continuous 2-on-1 With Defense 364

Number 172 Continuous 3-on-2-on-1 366

Full Court Partner Fast Break Drills

Number 173 Rebound and Outlet for Lay-up 369

Number 174 Rebound and Outlet for Mid-Range Jump Shot.. 371

Number 175 Rebound and Outlet for Pull-up 3-Point Shot 372

Number 176 Rebound and Outlet and Wolf for Lay-up 374

Number 177 Rebound and Outlet Point Guard Pull-up for a 3-Point Shot 376

Number 178 Dribble Post Up 377

Number 179 Point Guard Post Up 379

Number 180 Trap the Rebounder 380

Number 181 Look-a-Head Drill 382

Number 182 The Concept of "Best" 384

Number 183 Five-Ball Weave 388

Number 184 Four Line Rush (or Four Ball Rush) 391

Number 185 2-Man Pitch-a-Heads and Skips 393

Number 186 3-Man Pitch-a-Heads and Skips 396

Number 187 4 Dribble Point Guard Lay-ups 398

Number 188 1-Man Pull-up 3-Point Shot 400

Number 189 5-Man 3-Point Shot 401

Number 190 Laker Drill 403

Number 191 Three Lane Two Ball Attack Passing 406

Rebound and Outlet Drills

Number 192 Rebound and Outlet 409

Number 193 Numbered Outlet Passing 411

Number 194 Superman Outlet and Cut 413

Number 195 Bust Out Outlet and Go 415

Number 196 Fast Break Trailer Combo Drill 416

Number 197 Run on Makes Outlet and Go Fast Break Drill 418

Change Drills

Number 198 3-on-0 Change Drill 421

Number 199 4-on-0 Change Drill 423

Number 200 5-on-0 Change Drill 424

Pressure Inbounds Game Situations

Number 201 Pressure Inbounds Situations 429

Want more information on how bench coaching, strategy and tactics?

Available in paperback and ebook editions from online book retailers.

Other Coaching Books by Coach Kevin Sivils:

Fine Tuning Your Team's Position Play

Fine Tuning Your Three-Point Attack

Fine Tuning Your Fast Break

Fine Tuning Your Zone Attack Offense

Fine Tuning Your Man-to-Man Defense

Game Strategy and Tactics for Basketball: Bench Coaching for Success

The Game of Basketball

The Fine Art of Cutting and Screening: The Game of Basketball's Most Effective Offensive Tactic

Want more information on how to plan effective practices for your team?

Designing Effective Practices for Team Sports

KEVIN SIVILS

Available in paperback and ebook editions from online book retailers.

Printed in Great Britain
by Amazon